Henry Box Brown

Henry Box Brown

From Slavery to Show Business

Kathleen Chater

McFarland & Company, Inc., Publishers

Jefferson, North Carolina

This book has undergone peer review.

LIBRARY OF CONGRESS CATALOGUING-IN-PUBLICATION DATA

Names: Chater, Kathleen, author.
Title: Henry Box Brown : from slavery to show business / Kathleen Chater.
Other titles: From slavery to show business
Description: Jefferson, North Carolina : McFarland & Company, Inc.,
    Publishers, 2020 | Includes bibliographical references and index.
Identifiers: LCCN 2020030103 | ISBN 9781476679228 (paperback) |
    ISBN 9781476639437 (ebook) ∞
Subjects: LCSH: Brown, Henry Box, 1815 or 1816– | Fugitive slaves—Great
    Britain—Biography. | African Americans—Great Britain—Biography. |
    African American abolitionists—Great Britain—Biography. | Fugitive
    slaves—United States—Biography. | African American entertainers—
    Great Britain—Biography.
Classification: LCC E450 .C44 2020 | DDC 306.3/62092 [B]—dc23
LC record available at https://lccn.loc.gov/2020030103

BRITISH LIBRARY CATALOGUING DATA ARE AVAILABLE

ISBN (print) 978-1-4766-7922-8
ISBN (ebook) 978-1-4766-3943-7

On the cover: The unboxing at Philadelphia of Henry Brown, who
escaped from Richmond, Virginia, in a box three feet long, two and
a half feet deep and two feet wide, ca. 1850 (Library of Congress)

Printed in the United States of America

McFarland & Company, Inc., Publishers
  Box 611, Jefferson, North Carolina 28640
    www.mcfarlandpub.com

Acknowledgments

Thanks are due primarily to the unknown, unsung people who digitize and upload all the books, documents, and other primary and secondary sources that have transformed researchers' lives. Individuals who have been helpful and supportive are Rory Rennick, who alerted me to a number of sources; Jeffrey Green, whose website is a constant supply of interest and surprise; Bernth Lindfors, whose biographies of Ira Aldridge and Samuel Morgan Smith reveal unexpected aspects of Victorian theater and performances; and Martha J. Cutter, who has generously shared her research on Henry's life after 1875. I disagree with some of her interpretations, but I can't fault her excellent, pioneering research.

As always, the expertise of archivists has been essential: thanks to Terry Wright and the other staff of the Magic Circle's library; to Susan Snell of the Library and Museum of Freemasonry in London; to Peter Nixon, curator of the Ancient Order of Foresters Friendly Society; to Anna Bagniani, then at the Société Jersiaise in Jersey; and to Sarah Ferbrache at the Prilaux Library in Guernsey. Harriet Lund, Head of Events at the Old Shire Hall in Warwick, gave information about the courtrooms in the 19th century there.

Fortuitously, two exhibitions about magic appeared in London while I was researching this book: *Staging Magic* from the Harry Price collection in the library of University College London opened on January 21, 2019, in Senate House, and from April 11, 2019, the Wellcome Collection showed *Smoke and Mirrors: The Psychology of Magic*. I also benefited from the library of University College London. Thanks too to everyone at the Institute of Historical Research in Senate House, who maintain such an extensive collection of primary sources and provide such a civilized place in which to work.

I have also used the work of the many nonprofessional scholars and enthusiasts who upload their researches on Wikipedia. Although there are some problems of verification with this site, the entries here, if used with caution as all sources should be, seem to me no more unreliable than many other sources.

A Note on the Name

Born plain Henry Brown, Henry Box Brown acquired his distinctive middle name to commemorate his method of escape from enslavement. At first it was a sobriquet, sometimes put in quotation marks, but he then adopted it as his official name.

Contents

Preface

Some years ago, while I was working on my doctorate about "average" black people in England during the long 18th century, I reviewed a reissue of the second (1851) edition of Henry Box Brown's autobiography. Later I wrote a short article about him for a family history magazine, and in the course of doing this research I found evidence of his establishment of a second family in England. I thought his life was fascinating but at that time the focus of my work was the 18th century, although I also wrote an entry for the *Oxford Dictionary of National Biography*.[1]

A few years ago Rory Rennick, an American magician and entertainer who does an act based on Henry Box Brown, contacted me to enquire about some of the information included in the brief biography that I had also posted on Jeffrey Green's website.[2] He commissioned me to do further research. I had for some time meant to do more, and Mr. Rennick's interest, enthusiasm, and correspondence spurred me on to investigate Henry Box Brown's life in greater depth. I realized little had been done about his time in Britain, even though it was a substantial period of his adult life, and his experiences illuminate lesser known aspects of Victorian history and culture in Britain.

Henry's life intersects a number of academic fields: abolitionism, culture, performance. Paul Gilroy's work *The Black Atlantic: Modernity and Double Consciousness* (1992) explores cultural exchanges across the Atlantic between Africa, the New World, and Britain to create a distinctive political and cultural fusion. He focuses on post-modernist theories, but it is people who transport cultural practices and ideas. With the current increasing emphasis on bottom-up history, microhistory, and individual biographies, rather than grand, top-down abstractions, Henry Box Brown might also be located in this Atlantic sphere. He traveled through and experienced many cultures on both sides: from the American Southern states to the Northern; from industrial to rural Britain; back to the United States and finally to Canada; from a republic to a monarchy, then back to a republic, and finally to an imperial colony.

Unfortunately, we have no record of how his outlook on life and his perceptions changed, what he took from and brought to each environment. He became moderately famous in Britain, sometimes the first person mentioned in the context of popular entertainment, but he himself remains largely an enigma because almost nothing in his own voice survives. His first autobiography was ghost-written by a man on a religious and antislavery mission. Although the second was more personal, both editions finish before his arrival in England. Nothing is recorded of his thoughts about his life thereafter; there are only official documents and references in newspapers to his professional work, which include little of what he said and in any case are mediated through reporters.

While researching this book, I have been interested to see how this blankness is filled by the preoccupations of those studying him: to Marcus Wood he is a rebel against the conventions of his day; to Audrey A. Fisch, an example of the British public's "negrophilism," an object of their worship of the exotic; to Britt Rusert, a performance artist using popular science; to Suzette A. Spencer, a political commentator who critiqued "global modes of industrialization and colonial expansion"; and to Daphne A. Brooks, he is a popular scientist who made "significant contributions to nineteenth century transatlantic culture."[3]

Nor am I exempt from this tendency. I refer to Henry Box Brown as "Henry" throughout. This is mainly because there are other fugitives also called Brown, but it also seems more in keeping with his stage persona: approachable, affable, and informal, the kind of person I often worked with during my time in the media. Initially, Henry was defined by enslavement, but in 25 years in Britain he transformed himself into a popular entertainer, one among hundreds or possibly thousands on the Victorian stage. I have focused on this aspect of Henry's life and how he adapted himself to changing trends in entertainment, partly because it is now possible to examine this in detail and partly because it reflects my own experience. I have always worked in the mass media: initially in television production and training at the BBC, then in media training and consultancy, and latterly in writing for and speaking to the history and genealogy market.[4] Like Henry, I have been self-employed for more than 25 years, not in an academic environment but presenting material to the general public, and have had to adapt to what the people and changing fashions in my fields are looking for. I cannot claim to identify in any other way with a 19th-century male, fugitive American slave's life, but I do understand and experience the demands of his professional life.

In researching this book, I followed the journalistic way of working that I learned at the BBC: gather facts first, then consider opinions and interpretations and weigh them against the facts, but be aware that facts are established only until evidence against them becomes overwhelming. It was hammered into those working on factual productions that every word that went out should stand up in a court of law or before the Broadcasting Complaints Commission, which adjudicated factual, moral, and ethical matters, and that there is always at least one alternative point of view. I have tried to follow these standards.

Jeffrey Ruggles's admirable biography *The Unboxing of Henry Brown* also concentrated on his work and remains, in my opinion, the best introduction to his early life, but apart from references in his book, there has been no full account of his career in Britain.[5] This is partly because intellectual life in the second half of the 20th century was heavily influenced by Marxism. With the emphasis not on individuals but on mass movements, any man who was not politically active was regarded as of little or no value, except as a victim of capitalism, colonialism, or imperialism. After his escape, Henry went his own way and was no one's victim so could not be recruited for this cause. Now personal identity is the mode, and this shift has made Henry of more interest as he transforms himself from abolitionist lecturer, who later spoke on other topical subjects, to his career in pure entertainment, first as a mesmerist, then as a magician.

The second reason for now being able to produce a detailed biography of Henry's period in Britain is practical. Many sources were not until recently readily available. The works of the literate middle and upper classes, like the campaigners both for and against abolition, have always been easy to find in libraries, especially their published works, and the private papers of such people were also valued and carefully preserved. The lives of those lower down the social scale could in the past only be recovered in fragments from scattered and difficult-to-access sources that were time-consuming to investigate. At the time Ruggles was writing, not even the name of Henry's English wife was known. This discovery was made possible through an early phase of indexing of British census returns, and it was Dave Annal at The National Archives in Kew who in 2005 suggested to me her surname was Floyd, which allowed a whole new and extremely important aspect of Henry's life to be opened up.[6] His partnership with Jane (and it was a true partnership, both professional and personal) was fundamental to his life in Britain and continued after they returned to America in 1875, but she has barely been mentioned in previous works. As a 1970s-era feminist, I found Jane's role in the development of his career of interest, especially as it contradicts the stereotypical picture of Victorian womanhood.

At the time of the publication of Ruggles's work, research on non-elite individuals comprised a laborious process of making appointments by telephone (a fixed landline for most people, though some had brick-sized cell phones with limited access to a network) or letter, traveling many miles to record offices, sifting through piles of documents, squinting at microfiches and miles of microfilm for hours to find or fail to find a solitary reference. This did have some benefits. The researcher got a strong sense of the world in which the subject lived and what was happening to other people in the same time, place, and circumstances, whereas today, with so much available through a narrow keyword search, individuals become isolated. Experiences appear specific to that person instead of being shared by contemporaries. While taking full advantage of the speed and convenience of modern technology, I have examined the wider British society in which Henry lived and worked.

It is not just the increasing interest in individuals that makes Henry's life worth reconstructing. He shows that it was possible for a black man in Britain to make a good living over a number of years. Marcus Wood, writing before 2000, said, "This world had, after all, ordained certain roles for blacks in London: if they were lucky, servants, pugilists, nigger minstrels; if not, crossing sweepers, beggars and other avenues for survival open to the destitute." This is not in any way to dismiss Wood's work, because this was how black people appeared in the published works available to him at that time, but the digitization of British newspapers from 2011 onward and other sources, like transcripts of the trials at the Old Bailey between 1674 and 1913, have revealed that black people occupied many other roles and social classes both in and outside London over many centuries. Jeffrey Green's recent publication *Black Americans in Victorian Britain* draws on previously hard-to-access records to indicate how many black Americans there were in decent, respectable occupations that allowed them to live quiet, everyday lives, just like their white neighbors. As well as Americans, there were many other black people from British colonies living in the mother country without attracting much official interest, like Fanny Eaton, a charwoman, who came from Jamaica to London. Her husband delivered goods, and she would be unknown to history had her looks not been so attractive to the pre–Raphaelite painters, who depicted her in a number of works.[7] These and other non-elite lives are as valuable as those of the politically active, who have previously been showcased, in gaining a rounded and more nuanced picture of black British history and the history of the Black Atlantic.

A further reason for detailing Henry's life is his career in entertainment. Because records have been hard to access, there is as yet little academic work on the astonishing richness and variety of the entertainment industry in Victorian England that catered to working-class people. During his time in Britain Henry was a star in the provinces, and he illuminates what is still a relatively unexplored field as he passed from lecturing to mesmerism and magic. With the digitization of British newspapers and the increasing availability of other periodicals and publications on the Internet it has been possible to detail his career throughout his 25-year stay, although I cannot claim that every place he visited, every performance he gave, has been found yet. The digitization of newspapers in the United States and Canada has also made it possible to trace more of his life in those countries, but much remains to be discovered here too.

Terminology

The whole issue of how to describe people of color, any color, is problematic. It is now generally agreed (although questioned) that race is a social construct and the preferred term is ethnicity, since this incorporates both geographical origins and culture, but that still leaves the issue of how to describe people who have obvious nonwhite ancestry, who are a minority in Western societies. In *Imagining Black America*, a study of black identity throughout the history of America, Michael Wayne summarizes the arguments against regarding race as a natural or permanent division among peoples and provides the terminology he uses to describe peoples with African ancestry in America. Others, like Vincent Sarich and Frank Miele in *Race: The Reality of Human Differences* and Kenan Malik in (my favorite title) *Strange Fruit: Why Both Sides Are Wrong in the Race Debate*, suggest that the irrelevance of race is less clear-cut.[8]

Britain, however, never needed to develop the careful classification of people with any percentage of African descent (mulatto, quadroon, sambo, etc.) because there has never been legal discrimination on this basis. The acceptable words since the 20th century have been Negro, colored, black/Black, Afro-American/Caribbean, and currently African American/Caribbean, of color, and so on. For those with parents from different ethnicities the terms have been half-caste, colored, black/Black, and mixed race/heritage or biracial. Although the preferred term employed by officials and the media in the United States is African American, which is adopted elsewhere, this is not a term everyone is happy to use. Some black Americans consider it implies that people of a minority ethnic background are not fully American.

For the sake of simplicity I prefer to use black. Although over the centuries the word Negro has been the most frequently used official word in Britain, the everyday word since Tudor times has been black, and Black British is the current umbrella term for those with some kind of African ancestry, either directly from Africa or through the Caribbean. The legacy of the British Empire also brought migrants from the Indian subcontinent, and in the 1970s both communities were called "black" because they were presumed to suffer the same kind of racial discrimination. However, their cultures are so different that since the 1991 census (the first to introduce a question on ethnicity) they have been separated in official forms.

A Note on British Money

The pound sterling (£, sometimes written as *l* = libra) was divided into 20 shillings. Each shilling consisted of 12 pence (singular = penny, represented by d). Other terms were the guinea (£1 1s, i.e., 21 shillings), the crown (5s), the half-crown (2s 6d), the ha'penny (½ d), and the farthing (¼ d).

There are various ways to compare the value of money in the past to the present. I use the Measuring Worth website, www.measuringworth.com, because it provides a range of equivalents. However, the relative costs of, for example, housing and the price of commodities are different now from what they were in the past, so it is not easy to determine exact equivalents. It is notoriously difficult to give equivalent values in modern currency, not least because the proportionate price of items has changed over the centuries.[9] For example, in the 19th century eating chicken was a rare and expensive treat for British people but today this is one of the cheapest meats. I find it more helpful to estimate how long a person would need to work to pay for something. In the mid–19th century a factory hand in Manchester would earn about 15s per week; his wife and children probably also worked, for a much lower rate, to contribute to the household budget. A farm laborer in the West Country (where there was less industry to offer competitive wages) earned about 12s per week but in the North was able to get more. In both regions they might have subsidized housing and be able to grow vegetables and/or rear pigs and chickens. At the top end of the working class, a skilled artisan could earn up to £5 5s per week. A quick, but rough, figure to use is that the average man earned about £1 per week. *Round About a Pound a Week*, Maud Pember Reeves's study of poverty in a deprived area of London, was published in 1913 but does give a good picture of the way in which many of the poor survived in the Victorian era. By the early 20th century, however, sanitation and other health measures had improved living conditions.

Websites and Abbreviations

Unless otherwise stated, all newspaper reports come from the British Newspaper Archive on www.britishnewspaperarchive.co.uk or *The Times* index. I have preserved British English spelling in the quotations from the British sources. I used The Genealogist website on www.thegenealogist.co.uk to access British census returns, to supplement and check FreeBMD records, and to access other miscellaneous sources.

AAS = American Antiquarian Society, Historical Periodicals Collection, Series 3 (1838–1852), Series 4 (1853–1865), and Series 5 (1866–1877) hosted on www.ebsco.com.

Ancestry on www.ancestry.co.uk is owned and run by the Church of Jesus Christ of Latter-Day Saints.

BL = British Library.

Family Search on www.familysearch.org is owned and run by Ancestry and is free to access.

FMP = Find My Past on www.findmypast.co.uk is a British website, owned by the Scottish publisher D.C. Thomson.

FreeBMD on www.freebmd.org.uk has the registrations of births, marriages, and deaths in England and Wales from the establishment of general registration in 1837. As it is a volunteer project, not all records from local register offices have yet been entered, but it is more reliable than the General Register Office's indices, which were compiled from documents copied and recopied from the originals.

GRO = General Register Office, which has maintained a national register of birth, marriages, and deaths since 1837 and issues certificates as proof of these events.

JSTOR on www.jstor.org is a digital library of academic journals, books, and primary sources.

LMA = London Metropolitan Archives.

NA = Newspaper Archive on www.newspaperarchive.com.

PM = Project Muse on https://muse.jhu.edu is a digital library of books and journals in the humanities and social sciences.

PQ = ProQuest on www.proquest.com is an online source of newspapers, journals and e-books.

TNA = The National Archives.

Prologue

Unless otherwise indicated, the information about Henry's early life is taken from the *Narrative of the Life of Henry Box Brown Written by Himself*, the second edition published in Manchester, UK, in 1851.

Henry Brown stated that he was born in 1815 in Virginia, some 45 miles northwest of Richmond, on a plantation called The Hermitage owned by John Barret. He probably did not know that he was then one of some one and a half million slaves in the United States. John Barret was a veteran of the American War of Independence (1775–83) and owned one of the larger estates in Louisa County, which had been formed from Hanover County in 1742. He was the grandson of Charles Barret, born in England, who seems to have settled on this land around 1710 when it was still part of Hanover County. John's father, also Charles Barret, had served as a member of the House of Burgesses of Louisa County, and John Barret served as Mayor of Richmond for a time.[1] The Barrets were thus a long-established and influential family.

In 1820, when Henry was about five, the census shows he was one of the 10 male and 12 female slaves under the age of 14 years at The Hermitage. There were also seven male and seven female slaves between the ages of 14 and 26; two female slaves of ages 26–45; and one male slave and one female slave over the age of 45.[2] This comparatively small total number (41) meant it was possible for Barret to know each individual, although there may have been others loaned out or working away from The Hermitage. Unusually, Henry grew up with both his parents and seven siblings, and his master seemed to the boy "uncommonly kind." On Barret's death on June 9, 1830, at age 82, the family was divided among Barret's four sons. Again and again, slave owners claimed that it was regarded as dishonorable to split up families, as Anthony Trollope, the English writer, was told on his visit to America in 1862.[3] But as always, when profit was at stake, the practice was very different. Henry's parents remained on the plantation but the rest of the family went elsewhere. Henry and one of his sisters, Jane, became the property of John

The Hermitage Plantation in Louisa County, Virginia, where Henry Brown was born. Louisa County Historical Society, "Henry 'Box' Brown," *Piedmont Virginia Digital History: The Land Between the Rivers,* **at piedmontvahistory. org/archives14/index.php/items/show/249.**

Barret's son William. Another sister, Martha, became the "keep Miss" of William. It is not clear what this phrase means; it does not seem to appear anywhere else. Did it mean she was a housekeeper, or was she a kept woman in a sexual relationship? The rest of the siblings, brothers Edward, Lewis, and John and sisters Mary (who had children of her own) and Robinnet, went elsewhere.

William Barret took Henry to Richmond, where he had a tobacco business, and put him to work in a factory under a succession of overseers, mostly cruel but one or two kind and honorable. Barret made it clear that Henry should not be physically punished, and in Richmond Henry was more autonomous than he would have been as a field hand on the Barret plantation. As Frederick Douglass observed, in towns the enslaved had relative freedom. It was here, however, that Henry first encountered the gap between the Christianity professed by the owners and overseers of slaves and their behavior toward the poor whom they oppressed, despite Biblical injunctions. They had separate churches: the whites a splendid new building, and the blacks took the whites' rundown old meetinghouse, for which they were initially asked $3,000 but never managed to own outright, as more sums of money were continually demanded every time the question of ownership was raised.

The preacher at the colored church was the Rev. Robert Ryland, a white Baptist from the Virginia Seminary whose congregation had to pay him $700 a year, even though they had no say in his appointment. His sermons, Henry observed, were largely on the theme of obedience to masters. Ryland seems to have had a particular interest in people of African origin. In 1835 he addressed a group of Baptist missionaries planning to go to Africa and was the author of the *Scripture Catechism, for Colored People*, published in Richmond in 1848, as well as a number of sermons. His account of a murder in Richmond in 1852, after taking the confession of those condemned, suggests he was also a prison chaplain, which Henry seems not to have known. His prison work may have kept him busy. Despite his salary, he only came to preach at the church about 40 times a year, "when he was not otherwise engaged."[4]

As well as becoming aware of the hypocrisy of many who professed themselves pious, Henry developed a keen understanding of the economics of slavery and the profits that masters could accrue by the work of people like him. In his *Narrative* he often details prices and sums of money paid both for slaves and for their work, and what was taken from them for doing work that did not directly benefit their owners, as agricultural labor did. Out of his earnings, Henry paid $25 per month to Barret. Despite this taxation on his earnings, his wages brought him enough to live on and to consider marriage when he was about 20.

Marriage and Separation

Henry met Nancy, another slave whose master Mr. Leigh was a bank clerk, although at that time she was working for a minister, Mr. Reevs (probably Reeves or Reaves). He may be the Samuel Reeves who became the Corresponding Secretary of the Bible Society of Virginia in 1848, or one of his relatives. In 1834 or 1835 they were given their respective masters' permission to marry, along with assurances that they would not be sold. However, a year after their marriage, when they already had a child, Nancy was sold to a saddler, Joseph Colquitt. He and his wife treated her cruelly; then she was sold to Philip M. Tabb, Jr., for $450. The firm of Philip M. Tabb & Son, a slave dealer, managed hiring contracts for slaves. The received picture of slavery in the Southern states is of huge *Gone with the Wind*–type plantations, but slavery was all-pervasive, not just on plantations (and most were comparatively small) but also in towns. Many here were domestic servants; others, like Henry, were factory workers. Plantations owners might hire out some of their workers, either to other plantations or to factories in towns. The Tabbs operated an agency subcontracting such workers and placed advertisements listing their services.[5]

Mrs. Colquitt regretted the sale and Nancy was repurchased, later being sold again to another saddler, Samuel Cottrell. He had only $600 of the $650 asked for Nancy and the child. Reluctantly, Henry made up the sum and the sale went through. Then Cottrell demanded that Henry hire a house for his family and furnish it, or he would sell Nancy. As a slave Henry could not enter into such a financial arrangement, so he asked a black friend, James Cæsar Anthony Smith, a free man, to help him, which he immediately did. Cottrell had not finished with his extortion. He now demanded that Henry pay him a regular sum, $50 a year, not to sell Nancy, and that, as well as waiting on his wife, she do his washing, usually accounted a separate task. Henry had no choice but to agree. From his earnings at the tobacco factory, despite the payments to Barret and Cottrell, he managed to keep his family fed and together until August 1848, when Cottrell told Henry that he needed money. The couple thought he might be intending to sell one of their children, but by the end of the day when he returned from work, Henry found that Nancy and all three of their children had been sold. Henry pleaded with his master to buy them and to help him recover all the possessions in his house, which Cottrell had also seized, but Henry's master refused. While Henry was making frantic efforts to recover his family and his possessions, Barret remarked that he could always get another wife. Henry reminded him of the Christian injunction "whom God hath joined together let no man put asunder," and he was driven out of the house. He saw his children and managed to speak to his wife as she was being marched South with others who had been sold, but at this point recognized that this was the end of their marriage.

Henry had been a leading member of the choir in the Affeviar church in Richmond. This name was given only in his work and is probably a misprint or a mishearing for African. Now, in the light of the way that all these people professing to be Christians had behaved, he stopped attending for a few months but was persuaded back for a concert. In the course of singing an anthem he resolved to free himself. Henry quotes only the first two lines of the work that inspired him.

> Vital spark of heavenly flame,
> Quit, O! quit the mortal frame—

This is not a Biblical passage but a poem by the Englishman Alexander Pope (1688–1744) called "The Dying Christian to His Soul." It was always a popular work and often set to music or adapted as hymns. John Ernest gives two examples, drawn from American hymn books.[6] Henry would have expected that his readers knew the rest, especially the last two lines, now the most often quoted:

> O grave! where is thy victory!
> O death! where is thy sting?

The belief that death is only a transient phase before the soul takes flight and is reborn into heaven is fundamental to the Christian faith, but these verses had particular resonance for Henry at this moment. He would no longer collude in the buying and selling of his body and his soul, nor in the social death of slavery (as Orlando Patterson calls it), nor was death by suicide an option. He would take earthly flight, convinced that freedom for himself and all people was what God wanted, despite what was preached by ministers and masters. Although he was disparaging about the forms of Christianity he saw around him in the slaveholding states, Henry had faith in some higher power that would actively intervene in human affairs and that wanted the best for him.

Indirectly, therefore, it was an Englishman who set Henry on the path which ultimately led to Britain. About five months later he discussed methods of escape with a sympathetic white shopkeeper, Samuel Smith (not named in the *Narrative*: his identity was not revealed until many years later), but none appealed to him. While working he prayed for inspiration, and the idea of being mailed to freedom flashed across his mind. With the aid of this shopkeeper and two other, unrelated, men named Smith, one a minister who was involved with the Underground Railroad and the other his friend James Cæsar Anthony Smith from the church choir, the plan was put into action. He burned his finger with acid to get a few days off work so he would not be immediately missed. On March 23, 1849, he was nailed into a crate three feet, one inch long, two feet wide, and two feet, six inches high (94 cm × 61 cm × 76 cm) and mailed to the Pennsylvania Anti-Slavery Society in Philadelphia, arriving the next day.[7] It was a tight squeeze: Henry was five feet, eight inches tall and weighed about 200 pounds (1.73 m and 90.70 kg). Samuel Smith charged Henry $86 for his help, although in fairness it must be said that Smith did incur expenses.

The 350 miles to Philadelphia took 27 hours. He had only a bladder of water and a few biscuits to sustain him, and a man who had said he would accompany the box did not keep his promise. Although the box had been clearly labeled "This side up, with care," sometimes this instruction was not followed. What had not been anticipated was that the majority of laborers actually moving the box would have been, like Henry himself, illiterate. At one point, upside down, he believed he was going to die. He prayed for assistance and luckily (or by the intervention of divine Providence, as he believed), two men needing a seat righted it. Finally the box reached its destination, the Anti-Slavery Society's office in Philadelphia, where three members of the Society, James Miller McKim, William Still, a free black man, and Lewis Thompson, were anxiously awaiting his arrival. Charles Dexter Cleveland, who ran a girls' school, was also present. When they opened the box Henry was unable to stand and fainted, but when he recovered he launched into a

psalm—even at this stage in his life he was aware of the importance of a theatrical entrance. He must have felt as if he had risen from the dead. As the
anthem that inspired him promised, he had been reborn, if not into heaven,
at least into freedom, and the image illustrating his arrival in Philadelphia
shows him as if he is emerging from a coffin. The psalm, the fortieth, that he
sang reinforced this message:

> I waited patiently for the Lord;
> And he inclined unto me and heard my cry.
> He brought me up also out of an horrible pit, out of the miry clay,
> And set my feet upon a rock, and established my goings.
> And he hath put a new song in my mouth, even praise unto our God.[8]

He might have selected another psalm: a number speak of being saved
from oppression, but the reference to being brought out of the miry clay
evoked entombment in the earth and then resurrection. The box later became
iconic and its symbolism is frequently discussed in academic works, but it
must be emphasized that Henry did not select this means of escape because
of its emblematic value—it was at that time a previously unknown way and
practicable. A day's confinement was about the limit of what could be endured
with a chance of success. It was not a method that a fugitive from a state further south could have contemplated.

Henry was by no means the first or the only slave to escape from bondage. Since the beginning of enslavement in the American colonies there had
been hundreds, probably thousands of runaways, each with their own life
histories and individual reasons to take flight. There were still some 3.2 million slaves recorded in the American 1850 census: Henry made it now one
fewer and joined thousands of fugitives.

Miller took Henry home to give him breakfast and a bath, which after
more than a day in a hot, confined space must have been necessary. Then he
was taken to the home of Lucretia Mott. She and her husband James were
Quakers, and James had been among the founders of the American Anti-
Slavery Society. As a preacher Lucretia often spoke in the abolitionist cause,
and the Motts' home welcomed a number of escaped slaves. She described
Henry as "an exciting fugitive case." Then he stayed for a couple of days with
William Still.[9] During the time he was in Philadelphia, his experiences and
his way of relating them must have impressed his hosts.

Black Campaigners

Both William Lloyd Garrison in America and George Thompson in
Britain, the most prominent men in the abolition movements on either side
of the Atlantic, were white like the majority of other campaigners, but their

THE RESURRECTION OF HENRY BOX BROWN AT PHILADELPHIA.
Who escaped from Richmond Va. in a Box 3 feet long 2½ ft deep and 2 ft wide

"The Resurrection of Henry Box Brown at Philadelphia." Library of Congress. There are a number of representations of this event. This lithograph by Samuel Rowse is the earliest and the one Henry took to Britain and later used in his publicity there.

organizations needed black people to be involved, partly for the authenticity of their firsthand experiences of slavery and partly to prove that they could be as responsible and educated as white people—that they were worthy of freedom, as so many slave owners denied. John Collins wrote a letter to *The Liberator* in 1842. He had been traveling with Frederick Douglass, at that time the most prominent of the fugitives, and described his effective manner of speaking, "so lucid and occasionally so spiced with pleasantry, and sometimes with a little satire." He called for more like him to be recruited: "The public have itching ears to hear a colored man speak and particularly A SLAVE. Multitudes will flock to hear one of this class speak…. It would be good policy to employ a number of colored agents," adding cautiously, "if suitable ones can be found."[10]

The most suitable proved to be Frederick Douglass (1818–95) and William Wells Brown (c. 1814–84), both compelling speakers and talented writers. In addition, they had noticeable white ancestry. It was rumored that Douglass was the son of his mother's master. Wells Brown was the acknowledged son of a white man and his features are plainly European. Henry Bibb, another prominent black abolitionist, also had obviously white ancestry. Sometimes this was noted as a bonus point at a time when the tenets of scientific racism, with Caucasians at the top, were regarded as proven. Like many of those involved in abolitionism, Wells Brown was a strong advocate of temperance, total abstinence from alcohol, and Douglass too supported this movement. Both also opposed the use of tobacco, and these were further factors in their favor. A number of black people involved in abolitionism were ministers of religion, like Nathaniel Paul, Henry Highland Garnet, and James Pennington, which gave further evidence of their probity. Others, like Charles Lenox Remond and his sister Sarah Parker Remond, were born free to respectable, hard-working, middle-class families. These were the stars of the show, but there were a number of others whose varied experiences made them also valuable, like Henry Brown.

The history of abolition movements in both Britain and America is an amalgam of religious convictions, political commitments, and personal agendas. Time smoothes out dissent. The end result is acclaimed and the side issues are minimized, but it needs to be reiterated that there was no single, united abolition movement, neither in America nor in Britain, but a complicated mix of moral, theological, and secular convictions, political expediencies, and interpersonal friendships and enmities. Into this complex swirl in April 1849 stepped Henry Brown. By this point, the American abolitionist movement in the North was well organized and had a string of supporters and sympathizers. Henry, with black ancestry on both sides of his family, uneducated and not a political operator but personable and determined, was among those considered suitable to promote the cause. He must have had a steep learning curve, and there was a lot to discover about public speaking when he joined the circuit.

The Mirror of Slavery Panorama

Early on, Henry came up with another novel idea. He would commission a panorama, which originally referred to a cylindrical room or building in which the spectator was surrounded by a visual representation of some scene. It was later used to describe a method of showing large-scale pictures on a system of rollers and pulleys, which allowed them to be showing in sequence—not unlike a computer presentation system, except today the images change with a click, not the efforts of stagehands winding the images on canvas.

It was a popular form of educational entertainment, often showing geographical locations. In 1847 William Wells Brown had seen a panorama about

The panorama, showing the mechanism used to hang and move the images, from *Scientific American*, 1848.

the Mississippi in which the depiction of slavery seemed to him "very mild." One on Egyptology and the Nile had arrived from England in November 1849 and was also being shown in New York. The proprietor, George Gliddon, was born in England but had been raised in Egypt, where his father was the American consul. He believed the polygenesis theory, that the black and white races were separate species, not sharing the same origins. He argued that Egyptian culture was created by Caucasians and furthermore that both the Bible and Egyptian art showed that Africans were intended for menial, subservient tasks. It would be going too far to say that Henry's panorama was inspired by a need to counteract this kind of presentation, but undoubtedly the time was ripe. Others in Boston saw the need to redress the negative picture of Africans and black Americans. In 1836 Robert Lewis, of Native American and African ancestry, published *Light and Truth*. It was a history of mankind from an African and Native American perspective. He made the opposite case from George Gliddon, saying, for example, that Athens was founded by Egyptians who brought a colony from the Nile to settle in the region and that this "was the first step towards that civilization which rendered Athens the most distinguished city on the earth."[11] Lewis's book, originally published in his native Maine, was reprinted in Boston in 1844 by Benjamin E. Roberts (1815–81), a printer and writer born in that city, a free black man from a family long involved in activism on both the paternal and maternal sides who continued this tradition.

While the panorama was being prepared, Henry moved on from Philadelphia. In April 1849 he spent time in New Bedford, Massachusetts, a whaling town, where he stayed with Joseph Ricketson while his finger healed and apparently worked as a porter. At this point Henry's abilities as a speaker had not yet fully emerged, but already he was making an impression. Ricketson said his guest "appears to be a fine fellow and has found considerable employment." Ricketson thought that he himself might be able to employ Henry if he returned to the oil business, adding that Henry was "the greatest Lion of the age." It seems that, although not yet in print, Henry's method of escape had emerged. A visitor, Charles Morgan, seems to have heard his story and perhaps met him: "I never heard of an instance of greater fortitude and daring and he has well earned the freedom which he will now enjoy." As Kathryn Grover observed, Morgan was one of those who thought slaves had to earn freedom, not that it was a human right for both the deserving and the undeserving.[12]

On April 12, 1849, the *Burlington Courier* newspaper in Vermont described Henry's hitherto unknown and dramatic means of escape, which until then had been carefully concealed, but it could not have been kept secret for much longer since it was so remarkable. Once his method of flight had been revealed, Henry acquired the nickname "Box" Brown, which he adopted for the rest of his life. He was probably not the only fugitive to use this or a similar method of escape. A few months after Henry left, Samuel Smith, the shopkeeper who had helped him in Richmond, was arrested for boxing up two other men (who were captured) and served seven years in prison. James Smith, the free black friend who had assisted the shopkeeper, was unaccountably acquitted and traveled north to join Henry. Later in 1857 the enslaved Lear Green, with the help of her fiancé and his mother, both free black people, traveled in a chest between Baltimore and New York.[13] Most slave narratives were cagey about revealing the people, places, and methods used, not only to protect individuals but also to hide precise information that slave catchers could use. There was some annoyance that Henry revealed a method that might have been employed by others, and Frederick Douglass was among his critics, but *The Liberator*, when reprinting the item from the *Burlington Courier*, widely publicized this method of escape and said it was something that should be circulated by every European journal.[14]

Henry met other fugitives. Wells Brown introduced him at the New England Anti-Slavery Convention, which opened in Boston on May 29, 1849. William and Ellen Craft were present, as well as Frederick Douglass, who also spoke, and there were two others not named.[15] The Crafts' method of escape also made them newsworthy, but their subterfuge was one that very few could employ so there were no reservations about publicizing it. Ellen, the daughter of her master and a slave, could pass as white and disguised herself as a young, male invalid. With her future husband accompanying her as her enslaved valet, they openly traveled from Georgia to Philadelphia. They and Wells Brown often appeared on the same platform in America and later in Britain. Ellen Craft was one of the few enslaved women who did speak publicly.

Slave Narratives

Travel memoirs of people who had visited and been shocked by slavery in America were valuable in raising awareness, especially in Britain, and there were also some novels. The best known is *Uncle Tom's Cabin*, published in 1853, but the first, *The Life and Adventures of Jonathan Jefferson Whitlaw; or Scenes on the Mississippi* (1836), was written by Fanny Trollope (mother of Anthony). Fanny Trollope's earlier travel book, *Domestic Manners of the Americans*, had already caused outrage in the United States when it was published in 1832. The third genre, but perhaps the most important literary form in spreading the message beyond the well-educated, intellectual elite, was the slave narrative. It is, of course, impossible to know the number of slaves who fled to freedom. It is estimated that some 100,000 used the network of safe houses and routes to the northern states, to Mexico and the Caribbean, and later to Canada, which became known as the Underground Railroad. Of the autobiographers, only a few, like Henry Bibb and John Andrew Jackson, mention such an established system. Others found their own way, often helped informally in chance encounters. Firsthand accounts of the experiences of the enslaved were essential to bring home to ordinary people what slavery meant beyond abstract, academic arguments about theology, morality, and economics. Between 65 and 70 so-called slave narratives published between 1760 and the end of the American Civil War in 1865 have been identified.[16]

The first edition of Henry's autobiography, *The Narrative of Henry Box Brown, Who Escaped from Slavery, Enclosed in a Box 3 Feet Long and 2 Wide. Written from a Statement of Facts Made by Himself. With Remarks Upon the Remedy for Slavery. By Charles Stearns*, was rushed through the press to appear in early September 1849. It was probably printed by Benjamin Roberts. As James Olney observes, these accounts followed a template.[17] Although Henry's *Narrative* did not include all the parts Olney identified, it largely followed the standard format: an account of childhood; the cruelties and injustices of enslavement; reflections on the hypocrisy of Christian masters and ministers; the decision to escape; the perils encountered on the journey; and finally freedom. Like the other narratives, Henry's account included testimonials from prominent persons to his veracity because these stories, often seen as exaggerated, needed to be vouched for by white people in positions of authority. As the slaves themselves were illiterate (and their histories often mention masters' attempt to keep them so), the majority were ghost-written by people with a political and very often also a religious agenda. They were published in order to highlight the iniquities of the system the abolitionists wanted to change, hence the rigid format and the tight control of the kind of information given.

Carl Ostrowski perceives a link between slave narratives and fictional exposés of urban life by popular authors, and he details specific links between Henry's escape and the novels *City Crimes*, in which a prisoner in Sing Sing escapes through being shipped out in a crate, and *The Empire City; or, New York by Night*, which features escaped slaves.[18] In light of Henry's later appeal to working-class audiences who read these lurid crime stories, this is important, but I would argue that the strongest parallel is between the slave narrative and the religious conversion narrative, a major genre in the 17th and 18th centuries among nonconformists, but still significant in the 19th century, especially in America, where there were organized religious revivals. It detailed an individual's spiritual awakening or conversion to another Christian church. Very often the person's previous state was likened to imprisonment or enslavement, to being in thrall to sin and moral darkness. The fourth verse of Charles Wesley's popular 1738 hymn "And Can It Be?" is a succinct example:

> Long my imprisoned spirit lay,
> Fast bound in sin and nature's night;
> Thine eye diffused a quickening ray—
> I woke, the dungeon flamed with light;
> My chains fell off, my heart was free,
> I rose, went forth, and followed Thee.

To a society in which religion played a major role in public life, this was a familiar template. By freeing themselves from the chains of slavery, the enslaved could know and follow Christ, something their masters often denied them. The slave narratives also drew other associations between sin and slavery. By keeping them in ignorance, cutting off their slaves from literacy, denying them the opportunity to read the Bible, and by curtailing the free exercise of their consciences and free will, by breaking up the sacred bonds of family, the masters became the major sinners.

Charles Stearns, a long-time campaigner against slavery, actually wrote Henry's biography and his name appears as the author. Despite the claim that it was written from Henry's testimony, very little of Henry's actual voice seems to come through so it cannot really be called an autobiography. However, Stearns also published the *Christian Reformer and Workingmen's Advocate*, which he advertised in Henry's *Narrative*. He said the aim of this journal was twofold:

First, to expose the rotten systems of error, which usurp the place upon which should stand the beautiful temple of "pure and undefiled religion." Secondly, to erect on the spot now occupied by these temples of sin, or adjacent thereto, a broad and stately tabernacle of perfect love to God and man, into which all the human race may crowd, and find a heaven for their souls, by developing and perfecting their mental, moral, and physical faculties. The object of this paper is to redeem man from all bondage to his fellow men, and from all slavery to wrong doing, and to present him a "perfect man in Christ Jesus."

This is an accurate summary of his agenda, but Stearns must be commended for his desire to give Henry equal credit: the title page announced that it was published by Brown & Stearns.

The opening is a good example of the work's overblown literary style, laden with adjectives and comparisons that an illiterate slave would never have encountered or used:

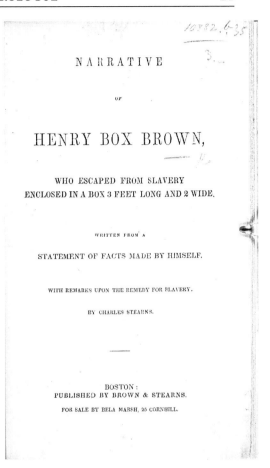

The title page of the *Narrative of Henry Box Brown*, 1849 edition, published in Boston. British Library, London, UK. © British Library Board. All rights reserved/ Bridgeman Images.

I am not about to harrow the feelings of my readers by a terrific representation of the untold horrors of that fearful system of oppression, which for thirty-three long years entwined its snaky folds about my soul, as the serpent of South America coils itself around the form of its unfortunate victim. It is not my purpose to descend deeply into the dark and noisome caverns of the hell of slavery, and drag from their frightful abode those lost spirits who haunt the souls of the poor slaves, daily and nightly with their frightful presence, and with the fearful sound of their terrific instruments of torture; for other pens far abler than mine have effectually performed that portion of the labor of an exposer of the enormities of slavery.

Occasionally there are echoes of what must have been genuine thoughts, albeit expressed in the language of the Boston middle class: "Tell me not of kind masters under slavery's hateful rule.... There is no such thing as a person of that description." Even before Henry's supposed account begins, Stearns's preface expressed his own opinions, and at the end of this edition, he inserted his own essay, "Remarks Upon the Remedy for Slavery." Henry is reported to have said that this essay "may not be as interesting as the account of my sufferings," but he encouraged people with "pure intentions" of helping his enslaved brethren to hear what Stearns had to say.[19]

Soon after the publication he and Stearns went on a punishing book tour, appearing in towns across Massachusetts almost every day for two months. The book, a 92-page pamphlet, cost 25 cents, around $8.50 (£6.25) in today's purchasing power, the price of a paperback novella or pamphlet. It must be presumed that Stearns took a leading role in the presentations, with Henry used as an illustration of his ideas, but whatever his true thoughts, Henry had little option but to assent. In Stearns's agenda it was not enough to free slaves; they must become perfect Christians. Later Henry would rebel against this, but for the moment he chose to fit into the mold. Slaves had long experience of doing this. To escape punishment they needed to please, so had to study the characters and personalities of those who wielded power over them, whether masters or overseers, whether white or black, in order to adjust how to behave or to do the work required of them in a particular way. In their first months or even years of freedom the fugitives were dependent for shelter, food, drink, clothing, and other forms of assistance on the abolitionists who were directing their lives, much as their masters in enslavement had done. If they refused to perform as required, they risked being excluded and left destitute, or they might have a lingering fear that, whatever the high-minded sentiments expressed by white abolitionists, they could be returned to slavery if they failed to conform to expectations. Although Henry was accustomed to supporting himself and his wife and family by doing a skilled job, this was not the time to strike out for independence. His knowledge and experience of work with tobacco availed him little in the North. Besides, he was discovering another skill. Respected as a singer in his church, he was now learning how to hold an audience by what he said. Initially he was described as an "artless" speaker who gave a "brief, simple" account of his escape, but only a few weeks after the start of the book tour, Stearns (who genuinely seems to have accepted that black people had equal abilities) trusted him to speak alone. At the Methodist Church in Milford, Worcester County, Massachusetts, on October 28 he spoke for an hour and finished with a song, which was applauded.[20] At this stage he probably recounted only the iniquities he and his wife had suffered and how he had escaped; humor and satire would come later.

The Panorama

While he was on his initial speaking tour, his panorama was being prepared in Boston by Josiah Walcott, a sign painter and a supporter of abolition, assisted by two other artists, Samuel Rowse (who had produced the lithograph of his unboxing) and David Johnston. No doubt Henry had some input into the content, but it was, in compliance with the fashion of the times, more literary than someone of his background would have been able to suggest and he would have known nothing of the accuracy or otherwise of the representations of most of the scenes. As Ruggles, who identified this source, considers, the decision to use *The Nubian Slave* as the basis is most likely due to Walcott and Charles Stearns, both of whom would have been familiar with this illustrated antislavery poem, published in Boston in 1845. It was advertised as "A series of seven Designs drawn on stone [i.e., lithographs], with intermediate pages being occupied by a Poem, which by uniting the scenes preserves the unity of history." The author, Charles C. Green, was probably known to both men.[21] His representation of African life was as inaccurate as that of the racists, but at least it portrayed a positive, albeit idealized, picture. Historically, Nubia had been an independent region between Egypt and the Sudan on the northeast side of the vast continent, but in 1820 it was invaded and taken over by Egypt. In East Africa the slave trade was actually in the hands of Arabs, although the poem says that Christian robbers enslaved this nuclear family of father, mother and son. One of the plates shows the father, with a quiver of arrows on his back, doing the child care while the mother spins with a spindle and distaff. This looks like an early American settler family, drawing parallels between the readers and their ancestors to portray a common humanity and values. Depicting polygamy, the norm throughout Africa, would have alienated Christian sensibilities, but the aim of the panorama was not historical accuracy: Green was concerned to harness "pictorial art to moral truth."

Touring with the Panorama

On April 11, 1850, Henry showed his panorama for the first time in Boston. At the beginning of May he started to tour with it, going first to Lynn, Massachusetts. When he later spoke in Worcester, *The Liberator* carried a letter signed "Clarkson" that said that Henry had spent 10 days in the town and gave "an entertainment" at the City Hall on Sunday evening. This is a significant term that Henry continued to use for his appearances. His aim was to engage people's interest, to divert them from everyday concerns, as well as gain their moral support. It was an indirect way of persuading   *[cont. p. 27]*

The Mirror of Slavery

Most of the scenes are self-explanatory, but I have added some notes in italics.

Part 1

The African Slave Trade.
The Nubian Family in Freedom.
The Seizure of Slaves.
Religious Sacrifice.
Beautiful Lake and Mountain scenery in Africa.
March to the Coast, View of the Cape of Good Hope.

Why this scene was included in the panorama is unknown. Elementary research among sea captains would have shown this was implausible. Maybe one of the artists just wanted to paint Cape Town with the dramatic backdrop of Table Mountain. The Cape of Good Hope, at the tip of South Africa, was where ships sailing from Europe to Asia, particularly of the British East India Company and the Dutch Vereenigde Oost-Indische Compagnie (United East India Company), stopped off to replenish supplies, repair ships, and so on. In 1652 the Dutch established here a permanent settlement, which developed into Cape Town. Although slaves were brought in to provide labor for the Dutch settlements, the main slave-trading depots were in East Africa in Madagascar and Zanzibar. The trade in Zanzibar was controlled by Arabs, who trafficked African slaves to Persia, Arabia, the Ottoman Empire, India, and Egypt until this trade was suppressed by the British in 1897. Slaves from Nubia would have been taken here for sale, as it was a far shorter distance to be marched. There was very little traffic between Madagascar and the Americas, and it ceased in 1721; the main trade was to India and islands in the Indian Ocean, and largely run by Arabs.[22]

Interior of a Slave Ship.
Chase of a Slaver by an English Steam Frigate.

After 1807 and 1808 the British and then the Americans attempted to prevent the transatlantic slave trade. Given the profits involved and the vastness of the oceans, it could never be entirely successful, but the attempt was made, and the British navy in particular expended a great deal of money and effort.

Spanish Slaver at Havana.

After the abolition of the British and American slave trades, the Cuban slave trade continued until 1867. Slavery itself was not abolished here until 1886.

Landing Slaves.
Interior of a Slave Mart.
Gorgeous Scenery of the West India Islands.
View of Charleston, South Carolina.

The Nubian Family at Auction.
Grand 4th of July Celebrations

This would have given the opportunity to comment satirically on the preamble to the declaration of American independence from Britain, lavishly celebrated since 1776: "We hold these truths to be self-evident, that all men are created equal, that they are endowed by their Creator with certain unalienable Rights, that among these are Life, Liberty and the pursuit of Happiness."

Separation after Sale of Slaves.
Grand Slave Auction.
March of the Chain Gang.
Modes of Confinement and Punishment.
Brand and Scourge.
Interior of the Charleston Workhouse with Treadmill in Full Operation.

The treadmill was introduced in England in 1818. There were 24 steps, 18 inches (c. 45 cm) apart, which turned, compelling the prisoners walking side by side to climb a never-ending staircase. Because the steps were further apart than a real staircase, the users needed a handrail to hold. It was a hard, painful, tedious, and pointless effort and one of the most dreaded punishments.

Part II

Sunday among the Slave Population.
Monday Morning with Sugar Plantation and Mill.
Women at Work.
Cotton Plantation.
View of the Lake of the Dismal Swamp.

This is another literary reference that the audiences would know. The Great Dismal Swamp once spread across a huge area of southeastern Virginia and northeastern North Carolina. Up to 2,000 black men, some free, others technically owned by a master but largely autonomous, lived here like the maroons in the highlands of Jamaica. Henry Wadsworth Longfellow's poem of 1842 "The Slave in the Dismal Swamp" opens

> *In dark fens of the Dismal Swamp*
> *The hunted Negro lay;*
> *He saw the fire of the midnight camp,*
> *And heard at times a horse's tramp*
> *And a bloodhound's distant bay.*

Later the Dismal Swamp would become a crucial element in one of Henry's legal challenges in Britain.

Nubians Escaping by Night.
Ellen Crafts Escaping.

Whipping Post and Gallows at Richmond, Va.
Henry Box Brown Escaping.
View of the Natural Bridge and Jefferson's Rock.

The Natural Bridge is a stone arch over a canyon in Virginia, the remains of the cave or underground tunnel through which the Cedar Creek once passed. Thomas Jefferson bought land including it in 1774 and built there a log cabin, which he used as a retreat. He was one of the Founding Fathers who signed the Declaration of Independence and was President of the United States from 1801 to 1809. He was a gradualist who worked to end slavery over the long term, so was regarded as a hero by both black and white. At this time it was probably not widely known that he had a slave mistress and four children by her and that he needed to keep his slaves because of financial problems.

City of Washington, D.C.
Slave Prisons at Washington.
Washington's Tomb at Mount Vernon.
Fairmount Water Works.

Philadelphia, Pennsylvania, was the city to have the second municipal water-works, started in 1812 and completed in 1872. It became a tourist attraction.

Henry Box Brown released at Philadelphia.
Henry Bibb Escaping.

Henry Bibb, born in 1815 in Kentucky, had a white father. He escaped to Canada in 1837 but later was recaptured several times. Finally he succeeded, and his autobiography Narrative of the Life and Adventures of Henry Bibb, an American Slave, Written by Himself *was published in New York in 1849. He died in 1854.*

Nubian Slaves Retaken.
Tarring and Feathering in South Carolina.

Stripping a man and smearing him with hot tar on to which feathers were stuck was a folk punishment in early Europe and survived in America until the 20th century; it was revived in Ireland during The Troubles in the 20th century. It was generally employed on government employees carrying out unpopular tasks, like collecting taxes regarded as unfair, or on those who transgressed the codes of a vigilante group. A Presbyterian Minister, Thomas S. Kendall, had been tarred and feathered in South Carolina in 1840 when he read a letter from the Synod about slavery from his pulpit, and there may have been others. All over the South people (often ministers of religion) who advocated emancipation were threatened and sometimes assaulted, as in the case of Amos Dresser, who was publicly whipped with a cowhide, like a slave, in Nashville, Tennessee, in 1835. He published an account of his ordeal.[23]

The Slaveholder's Dream.
Burning Alive.
Promise of Freedom.
West India Emancipation.
Grand Industrial Palace.
Grand Tableaus Finales.

UNIVERSAL EMANCIPATION.
An idealized utopia in which black and white were shown as equal.

people, rather than haranguing them to make them feel guilty. At this event, Benjamin Roberts, the printer, described the scenes from the panorama and gave a lecture on the "Condition of the Coloured Population of the United States." In 1848, the year before he met Henry, Roberts had brought a lawsuit against the Boston authorities on behalf of his daughter Sarah, then five, who attended a segregated school. Roberts wanted her to be enrolled in one that was nearer their home and had a better standard of education but where the pupils were white. The case went to the Massachusetts Supreme Judicial Court, but Chief Justice Lemuel ruled against him and upheld racial segregation in schools. This demonstrated that despite the Northern states' professed commitment to abolition, their definition of equality had limits, and Roberts probably used these lectures to remind people of the disadvantage he and his daughter suffered. Only Henry's own knowledge and experiences would have been incorporated into the sections set in Virginia, and he also sang spirituals. It was a novelty to have two black men, not led and directed by white men, as Clarkson added: "What makes the enterprise more interesting is that fact that the whole is conducted by colored men." Their next stop was due to be Springfield on April 20.[24]

The Liberator was enthusiastic about the panorama, this "novel mode of advancing the anti-slavery cause," but its welcome was tempered: "*Some* parts of the Panorama are very well executed" (my italics). It was an early warning for Henry that even people who shared his views might be critical. There was another reminder of the drawbacks of depending on the general public's interest: Gliddon's *Egyptian collection and Grand Moving Transparent Panorama of the Nile Egypt and Nubia* opened in Boston on June 21, 1850, and three days later he unwrapped one of the four mummies with which he had been traveling.[25] The unwrapping of a mummy would have been stiff competition for Henry, so he must have been pleased he had managed to display his novelty a few months before it. Many local people must have attended both showings, with their contrasting views on African life.

A couple of years later, Wells Brown presented his own panorama in Britain, so he and Henry Brown were probably working on the same idea simultaneously but independently; the two productions were very different. William Wells Brown's panorama was much less literary, much more factual and focused on iniquities in America, rather than a romanticized Africa. He published *A Description of William Wells Brown's Original Panoramic Views of the Scenes in the Life of an American Slave, From his Birth in Slavery to his Death or his Escape to his first Home of Freedom on British Soil* in London in 1850.[26]

"Old Uncle Ned"

One of the best-known composers of minstrel songs was Stephen C. Foster, a white man born in Pennsylvania in 1826. His family did not support the abolition of slavery but he later came to side with the Union cause and to include in his songs elements showing the true effects of enslavement. In 1848 he wrote "Old Uncle Ned," a song for which the popularity has not endured to the present day, although it was one of the most often performed in his lifetime. It is a good example of the contemporary representation of the speech of black Americans and (verse 3) the sentimental picture of the relationship between master and slave, typical of much American writing from the South's perspective. It became so well known in both America and Britain that Henry took it as his signature tune, singing his own lyric about his escape from slavery and selling song sheets with the new words at his appearances. His audiences would be aware of the contrast. Henry's version, "The Escape of Henry Box Brown," was far less passive, becoming the instrument of his own emancipation, not resigned to growing old and feeble thorough toil with only a little musical entertainment and the promise of a better afterlife. He was taking back his stolen rights in this life and vowing this would not happen again. Nor was it couched in patronizing, minstrelsy language, but in standard English.

The Fugitive Slave Act

Henry also spoke in Maine, New Hampshire, Connecticut, Rhode Island, and Pennsylvania. He was probably going around to small towns where he was advised there were known abolitionists. So far, I have not found notices about his appearances in the press in most of these states, which probably indicates how little public interest in abolitionism there was even in the North outside a small nucleus of committed campaigners. While he and other fugitives were spreading the word about their experiences, congressmen were debating legislation that would curtail their activities. A previous Fugitive

1. Dere was an old Nigga, dey call'd him Uncle Ned
He's dead long ago, long ago!
He had no wool on de top ob his head—
De place whar de wool ought to grow.

CHORUS

Den lay down de shubble and de hoe,
Hang up de fiddle and de bow:
No more hard work for poor Old Ned—
He's gone whar de good Niggas go,
No more hard work for poor Old Ned—
He's gone whar de good Niggas go.

2. His fingers were long like de cane in de brake,
He had no eyes for to see;
He had no teeth for to eat de corn cake,
So he had to let de corn cake be.

CHORUS

3. When Old Ned die Massa take it mighty hard,
De tears run down like de rain;
Old Missus turn pale and she gets berry sad,
Cayse she nebber see Old Ned again.

CHORUS

1. Here you see a man by the name of Henry Brown,
Ran away from the South to the North;
Which he would not have done but they stole all his rights,
But they'll never do the like again.

CHORUS

Brown laid down the shovel and the hoe,
Down in the box he did go;
No more Slave work for Henry Box Brown,
In the box by Express he did go.

2. Then the orders they were given, and the cars did start away;
Roll along—roll along—roll along,
Down to the landing, where the steamboat lay,
To bear the baggage off to the north.
When they packed the baggage on, they turned him on his head,
There poor Brown like to have died;
There were passengers on board who wished to sit down,
And they turned the box down on its side.

CHORUS

3. When they got to the cars they threw the box off,
And down upon his head he did fall,
Then he heard his neck crack, and he thought it was broke,
But they never threw him off any more.

CHORUS

4. When they got to Philadelphia
   they said he was in port,
And Brown then began to feel glad,
He was taken on the wagon to his
   final destination,
And left, "this side up with care."

CHORUS

5. The friends gathered round and
   asked if all was right,
As down on the box they did rap,
Brown answered them, saying: "yes
   all is right!"
He was then set free from his pain.

CHORUS.[27]

Slave Act was passed in 1793, requiring that escaped slaves be returned to their masters, but it had been circumvented in the Northern states. This new legislation introduced punitive fines for officials who failed to report or return a fugitive, and rewards for those who turned them in. Slaves were also denied the right to ask for a jury trial to determine whether a claim was justifiable.

With the passing of the Fugitive Slave Act on September 18, 1850, freedom became an academic question. Now even those who had escaped to the free states had to be returned to their previous masters without any judicial enquiry into the truth of their claims. A few weeks before this legislation was passed, it had ceased to be only a theoretical problem for Henry. On August 30 in Providence, Rhode Island, while he was out walking there was an attempt to force him into a carriage, but he fought off his proposed abductor. Soon after, in the same town on a separate occasion, he was beaten up by Thomas Kelton and others. This was probably also an attempted kidnap, but might not have been: Kelton was drunk and he claimed he did not know who Henry was. The case went to court and Kelton was fined $15 and costs for the assault.[28] This was the first of Henry's many brushes with the law and, auspiciously, he won. But these events made him aware of how fragile his freedom in the North was and, like many others, he resolved to go to Britain in order to remain at liberty.

ACT 1: LIBERTY

Scene 1

A New Land, a New Life

When Henry Box Brown arrived in Britain on November 1, 1850, on the *Constantine* from New York, his story had already crossed the Atlantic. A few newspapers had copied an article from a Boston newspaper or, like the *Bradford Chronicle*, reproduced it from an antislavery news sheet sent out by Anna Richardson, an abolitionist in Newcastle-upon-Tyne. William Wells Brown, who had been in Britain since 1849, had already mentioned the dramatic story of his escape in Chelmsford, Essex, in 1849, but did not, it seems, name Henry, according to the local paper's report of Wells Brown's talk.[1]

Henry landed at the Waterloo Dock in Liverpool with James Smith. A local paper carried news of their arrival, calling him "a fine intelligent looking man about thirty-five years of age" and saying he was accompanied by James "Boxer" Smith. The piece added that funds were needed to get the panorama out of storage, where it was being held until the cost of its passage could be met. This item was copied by other newspapers across the country, and Henry and Smith were soon able to recover their panorama. Less than two weeks after their arrival, they gave their first presentation on November 12 in the Concert Hall on the north side of Lord Nelson Street. It could seat 2,700 people and had been built for the use of socialists, as the commissioner John Finch was a follower of Robert Owen, and was opened in 1840. The people arranging Henry's tour would have been in touch with their counterparts in America and been made aware of his appeal to the working classes rather than the middle and upper classes. In 1851 there was a religious census of England and Wales that revealed a high attendance in dissenting churches, especially in industrial areas, rather than in the Church of England. What also appalled the authorities was how many working-class "unconscious secularists" there were who did not attend any religious service regularly. Although the results were not published until 1854, people on the ground would have been well aware of the state of affairs in their locale.[2] Another reason for the use of this secular site rather than a church was the size of the panorama and its associated equipment. However, clergymen, usually of dissenting denominations, took a prominent part in such presentations.

On the day of the first appearance of Henry with James Smith, there was a long article in the *Liverpool Mercury*. This, combined with the previous article and advertisements in the press, should have attracted a substantial audience, but the attendance was sparse. By their fourth and last appearance on November 15, a group called the Minstrel Fairies, who boasted it had appeared before the Queen, was billed above them, and Henry and Smith were scheduled only to sing songs, not to show their panorama or exhibit the box. The Mayor of Liverpool had become a patron of their concerts and was planning to attend. A piece in the *Liverpool Mail* praised them as "well worth a visit," but this appeared on the day of the last scheduled performance, too late for many people to attend.³ It may be that there were other competing events in the city, including numerous theaters and places of entertainment, classes to help working people improve their skills, and, for the more high-minded, learned societies offering lectures on a range of subjects. Henry was only the latest in a line of ex-slaves recounting their experiences; people may have felt they had heard it all before. Because Liverpool was the major port dealing with the United States, many fugitives began their tours here. Moses Roper, Frederick Douglass, and William Wells Brown were among those who had spoken here, as well as people like the Member of Parliament George Thompson and other white campaigners for the abolitionist cause.

Black People in Britain

Nor were black people, especially Americans, a novelty in Liverpool. Its history as a major British slave-trading port in the 18th century and then its role in global trade had left a substantial legacy of people of African and Asian origin in the town. Even before the Fugitive Slave Act of 1850, it had been the place to which many Americans fled to freedom, especially following the 1772 Mansfield Judgment. This judgment, however, covered legal, not social, matters. All societies discriminate against outsiders, so undoubtedly black people, like other minority groups, faced low-level, day-to-day intolerance and disadvantage, but in general American visitors to Britain were overwhelmed by the lack of obvious prejudice and discrimination they found. It is difficult to find accounts of overt racism. However, there was one blatantly racially motivated assault in Liverpool a few years after Henry's arrival. In 1855 four white men were tried for assaulting George De Morce, the "coloured" keeper of a lodging house in Liverpool, and three of his lodgers, also black, who were walking together in the street. A crowd gathered and "began to hiss and make some unpleasant allusions to 'darkies.'" One of them demanded money from De Morce, who was robbed of his gold watch and chain. The men were assaulted but managed to make their way back to the lodging house, where the crowd smashed windows. Two of the assailants were heavily fined, one was remanded, and the fourth was discharged.[4] The men who were attacked were probably from the East Indies; the extensive East India Company ran lodgings for its seamen. In many port cities there were prejudice and occasional attacks against foreign seamen because they were seen as taking the jobs of locally born men by undercutting wages. This kind of economic competition is still a political issue.

The usual contemporary journalistic terms were "men of colour" or "coloured men," and identifying those of African American origins is a problem because "coloured" was also used for people of mixed race, as well as those from the Indian subcontinent and colonies in the Caribbean. In British ports there were also mariners from West Africa, who seem to have been most often identified as "negro," but this was not consistently done. "Black" was the everyday word usually employed by witnesses and described anyone who was very dark-skinned, whatever their ethnicity or nationality, including native Britons. There are very few "women of colour" mentioned, partly because fewer came to Britain and partly because women were (and are) more law-abiding. Many of the "colored" women are likely to have been of Indian origin because of Britain's colonies in Asia and the employment of ayahs (children's nurses) in families traveling between India and Britain. The official court documents themselves very rarely identify color or ethnic origin, another frustration for the historian.

Assaults in public houses or in the streets were the commonest cases reported, but they were usually the result of a quarrel or an attempt to rob, rather than on racial or nationalistic grounds. Occasionally they involved Americans, like this one at the Thames court in London, which dealt with minor offenses:

National Prejudices.—Charles Mitchell, an American, was charged with assaulting John Gibbs, a man of colour, and native of the United States.—The prisoner, the prosecutor, and several others were conversing together at 65, Prescott-street, Whitechapel [a poor area of East London]. The prisoner accused Gibbs of being a runaway slave, which he denied, and called the prisoner a liar: on which the prisoner took a basin and threw it at Gibbs's head, who was immediately covered with blood. The prisoner was following the attack with spittoon, when the prosecutor, who was suffering from rheumatics at the time, took up another vessel, and struck the prisoner in his own defence.—The prisoner said he always took the prosecutor's part in any national prejudice, but would strike any man that called him a liar.—Gibbs stated that he afterwards extracted a bit of the basin from his head.—Mr. Yardley: The prosecutor may not like to be called a runaway slave, although you may think there is nothing dishonourable in it. You must keep your passion more controlled. This not a very violent assault, and I fine you 10s., or seven days' imprisonment.[5]

It is interesting to note that "slave" was regarded as such an insult among Americans. English people occasionally referred to themselves or to each other as slaves casually and with no rancor. They saw slavery solely in terms of demanding physical work and had no understanding of the psychological burden or the social degradation the word connotated for Americans. The magistrate was dismissive of such a routine case, apparently unaware of any subtext.

Even those who committed more lurid crimes were treated even-handedly. In 1850 the *Era* carried the story of Elijah, otherwise Eliza, Scott, a 20-year-old "man of colour" who "had been in the habit of walking the streets at night, attired like a woman for the basest of purposes." Nothing was made of his color; there was no attempt to stereotype black people as particularly licentious or morally repugnant; it was simply a description. He was accused of assault with sodomitical intent on another man, who initially assumed he was a female prostitute and was willing to become a customer until s/he lifted the veil. Scott was found guilty of common assault and sentenced to 12 months of imprisonment, a standard sentence for this kind of offense. The case was only summarized in the *Proceedings* of the Old Bailey, the official record of trials that was also published and sold to the public. No details of the evidence were given—no doubt they were considered too shocking for the eyes of women and children—and Scott's color was not mentioned.[6]

How many of the court and other cases involving black people in Britain Henry heard about cannot be known, but the more dramatic ones would have been widely discussed, and people must have assumed that he and Smith would be interested to hear about those who were, like him, of color. This would have given Henry a greater understanding of the position of black people in Britain, how they were treated by the authorities and how they were regarded by society generally. He would, especially in Liverpool and its hinterland, have had the opportunity to speak to black people, but it was overwhelmingly a white society, another fresh experience. Although there were quarters where particular ethnic minorities were concentrated, there were no ghettos.

Attitudes

On plantations in the Americas, where black slaves outnumbered their white owners, there was the ever-present threat of assault and rebellion, an uprising that would imperil the lives of the family and the wider society. Rebellions increased restrictions on black people's freedom of movement: They could not travel outside certain limits without written permission and they could not socialize or meet freely. In Britain, however, there was no such danger. Black people here were much fewer in number and they held positions that offered no threat to the general population, like students from the colonies being inculcated with British beliefs and values, mariners and general workers adding to the prosperity of the country, or servants performing useful functions, but crucially none was under any legal coercion or the threat of random, extreme physical punishment, so they had few motives to sabotage the work they were undertaking. Consequently, there had never been any need for legal discrimination against black people, nor was segregation practiced informally. As Frederick Douglass wrote:

> I gaze around in vain for one who will question my equal humanity, claim me as his slave, or offer me an insult. I employ a cab—I am seated beside white people—I reach the hotel—I enter the same door—I am shown into the same parlor—I dine at the same table—and no one is offended…. I find myself regarded and treated at every turn with the kindness and deference paid to white people. When I go to church, I am met by no upturned nose and scornful lip to tell me, *"We don't allow niggers in here!"*[7]

These passages, and others, were aimed at his American readership to promote the cause of abolition by showing that equality was possible, so they need to be treated with some caution, as Fionnghuala Sweeney explores in her study of Douglass's tour of Ireland in 1845. She is, however, among the commentators who recognize that what travel in Britain and mainland Europe enabled these one-time slaves to do was to feel fully masculine and to assert that masculinity with confidence. In his essay on David Dorr's travels in Europe, Lloyd S. Kramer also makes this point.[8]

As William Wells Brown said, "I was recognized as a man, and an equal. The very dogs in the street appeared conscious of my manhood." He also mentioned seeing black students in the streets of Edinburgh and London, and in 1851 he gleefully and frequently visited the Great Exhibition at Crystal Palace in South London, noting visitors from all over the globe and the indiscriminate mixing of the British social classes (which was exceptional at this time). His particular pleasure was in walking, arm in arm, with a white woman under the furious gazes of fellow Americans, whom he teased with criticism that would, in his native land, have earned a beating or worse:

> I was pleased to see such a goodly sprinkling of my own countrymen in the Exhibition—I mean colored men and women—well-dressed, and moving about with their fairer brethren. This, some of our pro-slavery Americans did not seem to relish very well. There was no help for it. As I walked through the American part of the Crystal Palace, some of our Virginian neighbors eyed me closely and with jealous looks, especially as an English lady was leaning on my arm. But their sneering looks did not disturb me in the least. I remained the longer in their department, and criticized the bad appearance of their goods the more.[9]

Black women too were treated equally. In 1854 Wells Brown's daughter Josephine described her and her sister's education in France and England:

> We spent the first year in France in a boarding school, where there were some forty other young ladies, and never once heard our color alluded to in disrespectful terms. We afterwards returned to London where more than two hundred young ladies were being educated [in the Home and Colonial School, a teacher training establishment] and here, too, we were always treated with the greatest kindness and respect…. My sister is mistress of a school in Berden, in Essex, about forty miles from London…. My pupils are some of them sixteen years of age and I am not yet fifteen. I need not say to you, that both my assistant and pupils are all white.[10]

Today in Britain the teenaged headmistress of a school with more than 100 pupils would be headline news, especially if she were black, but in 1854 this passed unremarked in the local press in both Plumstead, Kent, where Josephine was teaching, and in Berden, where Clarissa was employed.

Harriet Jacobs came to Britain from North Carolina in January 1845 as nursemaid to her master's daughter and spent ten months in England. In her autobiography, published in fictionalized form under the pen name Linda Brent, she wrote of her stay in a London hotel immediately after her arrival:

> For the first time in my life I was in a place where I was treated according to my deportment, without reference to my complexion. I felt as if a great millstone had been lifted from my breast. Ensconced in a pleasant room, with my dear little charge, I laid my head on my pillow, for the first time, with the delightful consciousness of pure, unadulterated freedom.[11]

Later in rural Steventon in Berkshire she met the same welcome. Her brother John Jacobs also came to Britain and married an Englishwoman. Jean Fagan Yellin argues that John Jacobs was the writer of *A True Tale of Slavery*, serialized in a family magazine published in London in 1861.[12]

Prejudice in Britain

This is not to say there was no discrimination in Britain. Here, however, it would have been more on the grounds of class and education, which were at this time (and still are) closely linked and also, as previously noted, because of economic competition. David Cannadine has explored this in two works: *The Rise and Fall of Class in Britain* and *Ornamentalism: How the British Saw Their Empire*,[13] which takes issue with some of Edward Said's arguments in *Orientalism* that the West's depictions of the peoples and cultures of the East were patronizing. As Said's work and Cannadine's rebuttal of it deal more with attitudes toward peoples from the East rather than toward those from the West, they are not of immediate relevance to this biography, beyond indicating how class rather than color is enmeshed in British history and culture.

There were some black people from privileged backgrounds, but they are hard to research because color is so rarely mentioned. John Audain, one of the governing council of St. Vincent, a British colony in the Caribbean, and his black wife came to England around 1860. Their five surviving children had careers typical of their class and prosperity. Had it not been for a few newspaper accounts mentioning three of the children, Ida, Cyril, and Claude, there would be nothing to indicate their origins, so there remains an open question of how many others there were who attracted no press interest.[14]

Beyond entrenched racial and class prejudices and Liverpool's familiarity with black people of whatever origins, there is another possible reason why people did not come flocking to Henry and James Smith's panorama: a lingering wariness of association with the slave trade. The local inhabitants may not have wanted to be reminded yet again of their role. An oft-repeated story tells of how George Frederick Cooke (1756–1812), an actor in a Liverpool theater, when booed and heckled for being drunk, riposted, "I have not come here to be insulted by a set of wretches, every brick in whose infernal town is cemented with an African's blood." Here too there were some who were still sympathetic to slave owners. When in 1843 Moses Roper was touring the country speaking of his experiences, the *Liverpool Mail* wrote of his appearance in Wakefield, Yorkshire, "The lecturer, previous to running away, had been sold by public auction no less than fifteen times. (That, we suppose, shows he was not good for much)." Another fugitive slave, James Watkins, was well received in Liverpool when he arrived, but when he tried to get work, many years after the ending of slavery in the British Empire, he found prejudice:

> I applied to some large Liverpool merchants who, after asking me a great many questions, declared that they could not think of employing a "nigger who would steal." Upon my expressing my entire innocence of ever having acted dishonestly towards my master, I was informed that my having escaped from slavery was looked upon as a heinous offence by these gentlemen, who considered that by obtaining my freedom I had robbed my master of the amount at which I was valued in the slave market.[15]

Success at Last

In view of the disappointing attendance, it was decided to stress the musical aspects of Henry and Smith's show rather than the slavery theme. "Nigger melodies" had crossed the Atlantic quite early. One was sung on the English stage in 1826 what appears to be a burlesque of American life by an

English mimic, who mocked not just the accent of American slaves, but that of the "Yankee character" as well. In his act he also imitated a Frenchman. Musicians from America followed, and by the 1850s, negro minstrel shows, performed by white musicians in blackface presenting songs and sketches, were popular. The four Virginia Minstrels may have been the first to offer a "Grand Ethiopian concert" in England, on June 19, 1843, but as only songs and dances are advertised, this may not have been a full-blown minstrelsy show, which would also include comic sketches. Not much later, in 1844, Messrs. Germon, Stanwood, Harrington, Pell, and White, who were white, formed a group called the Ethiopian Serenaders. Subsequently, a black performer, probably named William Henry Lane but known as Master or Boz's Juba, joined them. Black men also formed their own groups, presenting the same kind of material, but these were rare until after the end of the American Civil War in 1865. Frederick Douglass was ambivalent about these shows, being opposed to white people performing, calling them "the filthy scum of white society, who have stolen from us a complexion denied them by nature, in which to make money and pander to the corrupt taste of their fellow white citizens." However, when he reviewed a performance of Gavitt's original Ethiopian Serenaders, one of the earliest troupes in America with genuinely black performers, his response was more nuanced:

> It is something gained when the colored man in any form can appear before a white audience; and we think that even this company, with industry, application, and a proper cultivation of their taste, may yet be instrumental in removing the prejudice against our race. But they must cease to exaggerate the exaggerations of our enemies; and represent the colored man rather as he is, than as Ethiopian Minstrels usually represent him to be.[16]

The way that the minstrel show was produced and received in Britain was also different from how it was experienced in America. Very few British people had any firsthand knowledge of black people on American plantations. Even in the United States, minstrelsy was not interpreted in a single, fixed way across the country and across time, as Michael Pickering observes in his analysis of the relationship between the blackface clown in minstrelsy and the tradition of clowning and the circus in Britain. Sarah Meer explores how in Britain the minstrel show was seen as a genre with its own conventions. It was judged by how well it adhered to those conventions, not how well it portrayed black Americans. In America performers wore the distinctive clothing of the enslaved there. Slaves were provided with cheap, flimsy clothes and special shoes, known as "Negro brogues." Setting aside the differences in climate, which meant that poor working people in Britain did not, generally, wear flimsy clothes, the performers in Britain, like the early Ethiopian Serenaders, wore elegant formal clothes, not coarse rural costumes.[17] This troupe's particular gimmick was to perform in 18th-century court dress, and

Nov. 13, 1858.] THE ILLUSTRATED LONDON NEWS 455

THE COLOURED OPERA TROUPE AT THE OXFORD STREET GALLERY.

Above and right: The Coloured Opera Troupe performing in London, from the *Illustrated London News* in 1858, and their songbook, both from the collection of Rainer Lotz, Germany. Their elegant dress is typical of the way blackface minstrels appeared in Britain, in contrast to their coarse costumes in America.

what was always emphasized in reviews was their musicianship. They were an example of how skillful musical performances and minstrelsy could be successfully combined without demeaning the performers.

Henry's signature tune in America, "Old Uncle Ned," had crossed the Atlantic by 1850, when it is mentioned in

SONGS SUNG BY THE
COLOURED OPERA TROUPE

No. 1, PRAY EXTRACT THIS BRIAR.

the program of the Ethiopian Serenaders in a concert at the Music Hall in Belfast. With its new lyric celebrating his escape, it had been in Henry's repertoire from the beginning in the United States, where he sold song sheets. He included it in his performances later, so it is likely that it was part of his act from the very beginning of his British stay, and he may also have sold song sheets in Britain. Being genuinely black, Henry and Smith gave audiences the opportunity of "hearing the originals," as a newspaper article noted, and gradually the numbers built. The advertisement for their last week did not emphasize the panorama, which had been reinstated; instead, it said that the pair would sing plantation songs, serenades, duets, and antislavery songs. They made their last appearance in Liverpool on November 30.[18] It had been a struggle, but they had served their apprenticeship in England and were learning to adapt their act to local audiences and cultures.

Moving On

Henry and Smith appeared in Manchester, some 60 miles west of Liverpool, on December 14.[19] The city was to become a special place to Henry. It had grown from a small market town to a city at the heart of the Industrial Revolution. The damp climate (its rainfall is one of the heaviest in the United Kingdom) combined with rivers that provided the power for mills made it ideal for the spinning and weaving of fabrics. Then water was replaced by steam engines, powered by coal, which came only a short distance from mines in Worsley, now within the Greater Manchester area. Its prosperity was built on the manufacture of textiles, and it was nicknamed Cottonopolis. Most of the raw cotton on which the town and its workers depended for their livelihood was slave-grown in the southern states of America and imported through Liverpool. During the American Civil War this was to become important. The welcome of Henry and Smith to this city was enthusiastic, and they stayed on until the New Year. Here the name of the panorama was changed. In America the "Mirror of Slavery" could only refer to local conditions. In Britain there was no slavery, but there were concerns about slavery in colonial India, in Africa, and in other parts of the world in which Britain had interests and influence, so it was necessary to specify that the panorama was about America, and it became the "Mirror of American Slavery." It would later be retitled in response to ongoing events.

In January 1851, Henry and Smith appeared in Blackburn, Darwen, and Preston, smaller towns in Lancashire around Manchester, where they remained for a week. The *Blackburn Standard* commented that although Henry's descriptions were generally good, "some of them appear to exceed the limits of probability," but the local paper in Preston was enthusiastic, calling the panorama "a brilliant piece of art," and later reported that schoolchildren had been taken to see it and "it gave the utmost satisfaction." For the first time, there is a reference to Henry's aim to raise money to purchase the manumission of his wife and three children.[20] This was the stated goal of other lecturers, like James Watkins, and was to become an important issue.

Cheered by their growing success, the two set off for Bolton, Little Bolton, Burnley, and Padiham, on the outskirts of Burnley. These were satellite towns that, like Manchester, were involved in textile manufacture, but Burnley also had a substantial engineering business. Here Henry, who later revisited it, was long remembered. In 1925 the local paper carried a piece about the death of James Fielding, aged 78, who recalled the opening of the town's Mechanics Institute when he was a child. The reporter listed the popular acts that had appeared there, including Henry Box Brown, whom he expected some of the older readers to recall. The pair stayed up to a week in each place, and at the census on March 30, 1851, they were in Burnley at 9 Curzon Street in a small coffee house kept by John Broadhurst. They were the only two visitors, and each was described as an "Anti Slavery Advocate."[21]

Americans in Britain at the 1851 Census

It was not until 1991 that censuses in England and Wales, carried out every ten years from 1801, included a question about ethnicity. From 1851 onward, simply the place of birth was required. This is annoying for historians because it is impossible to make an accurate estimate of the number of people from any ethnic minority in the country. In 1851, more than 7,200 people stated to have been born in America were included in the census, but no indication of their color or ethnic origin was recorded, just their occupations. Some were from Canada, then occasionally called Northern America, and others from South America, but this usually meant the southern states of the United States rather than Latin America, where individual countries are specified.

There are a few references to slaves: some with the surname Slave; a street in Bradford, Yorkshire, called Slave Row; and a few unhappy people, like Mary Round, the wife of a laborer in Stourbridge, whose occupation is entered as "work slave"; James Harward, a patient in a lunatic asylum in Norwich, who was a "butcher's slave"; Daniel Luke, living with his family in Islington, calling himself a "Shop Lad Slave"; and 13-year-old Eliza Cumming in Whitechapel, who was a "Servant or Slave." Young maids-of-all-work were informally known as "slaveys," so this may simply indicate that she was a child servant, of whom there were many. These were plainly white people, some disgruntled, but another whose status was more ambiguous was Emma, living in Hackney with James and Mary Thornton. She is described as a "House Servant, late a Slave," and her lack of a surname and her birthplace in Africa seem significant. Both James and Mary were born in England, but James was a retired grocer from South America, presumably the Southern United States, from where Emma had been brought. It was the householder who was required to fill in the form, and perhaps he was emphasizing her freedom in Britain. She was the only other person in the 1851 census identified as an erstwhile slave, apart from the Crafts. They were staying in Leeds in Yorkshire at the home of Wilson Armistead, a merchant and leader of the local antislavery society. William appears in the census as a "Cabinet Maker *Fugitive Slave*" and Ellen as the "wife of Wm Craft *Fugitive Slave*"; plainly, their host wanted their condition to be recorded officially, and he underlined the description for emphasis.[22]

Henry and James Smith were not in the private home of someone middle-class and sympathetic to their cause but in cheap public lodgings. Presumably they had stayed in similar establishments during the other dates on their tour. Was John Broadhurst proud of hosting men who were at the heart of current debates, or was he just relieved to get paying guests? And how did they cope with being in the intimate surroundings of the small home of a white man and his family who were waiting on them? Smith was a free man but there was still segregation in his homeland; for Henry, the adjustment must have been more extreme. The two must have met similar new situations every day: the first time they found themselves on board a ship with white passengers and staff; the first time they dealt with white customs officials when they got the panorama out of storage; the first time they were called "sir"; the first time they traveled by train in a non-segregated carriage; the first time they went into an eating house, sat down among other customers, and were served by white people. How long did it take to become accustomed to being treated just like everyone else and then to expect or even demand respect (as Henry quite soon after did)? In 1851 in Edinburgh, Wells Brown observed how William Craft reacted to this new environment a month after his arrival and noted that even after 16 months in Britain, he himself had not yet fully adjusted.[23]

In Burnley the audiences were large, and among them were two local clergymen who were asked to provide endorsements, which they willingly and enthusiastically gave. The Methodist minister J.J. Bates wrote:

> I have attended with my family, and feel pleasure in expressing our entire satisfaction with what we have witnessed. The exhibition is well calculated greatly to inform the public mind on the subject of slavery, and to produce a just abhorrence of it. He has been much countenanced by the Clergy and Ministers in Burnley, and I feel much pleasure in recommending him to the notice of the Public.

The incumbent of the Anglican church also praised the presentation:

> The exhibition is calculated to produce a very satisfactory effect upon the spectator, by awakening compassion for the subjects of slavery and condemnation of those who, boasting of their own liberty and refinement, obstinately retain the coloured race, in the southern states of America, in a state of cruel and merciless bondage. Awful as some of the scenes of American slavery are, as represented by Mr. Brown's panorama, they, I believe convey to the mind nothing more than a picture of the exact truth.[24]

The tour continued to Bingley in Yorkshire, some 25 miles from Burnley, where it was necessary to put on an additional performance to satisfy the numbers who wanted to attend. Word of the success of this presentation was sent back to America by someone who had heard about its reception from abolitionists in Manchester.[25]

The Second Edition of the *Narrative*

For some time, Henry had been planning a revised edition of his autobiography. This was probably, as Ruggles considers, brought from America with him, as no event after April 1850 is described in this second edition. There are indications that it had been revised in Boston. For example, among the hymns quoted are two that appear in hymnals there. "Turn! Great Ruler of the Skies!" by James Merrick (1720–69) was a very popular hymn, published in both Britain and America, but "God of Our Mercy and Our Praise" was an obscure hymn by Isaac Watts (1674–1748), which was included in the Service Book prepared for the use of the Church of the Disciples, in Boston, where it was published in 1844.[26] This second edition, printed in Manchester by Lee & Glynn, was, as Henry proclaims, written "by himself," in contrast to the title page of the first edition, which stated that it had been written "from a statement of facts made by himself" with "remarks upon the remedy for slavery" by Stearns. In America, slavery was a firsthand concern; it was a political and legal issue of debate which involved all Americans. In Britain, slavery was not uppermost in most people's priorities. There were a number of other political, social, and religious questions, like the franchise, rights of women, and toleration for non–Anglicans that affected people more immediately, so a different approach was necessary to engage them. The goal here was primarily to engage hearts. On the title page of the second edition was the third verse of a poem, "Forget Not the Unhappy," by Charles Swain (1801–1874), which was directly related to Henry's situation.

Forget not the unhappy
Though sorrow may annoy,
There's something then for memory,

Hereafter to enjoy!
Oh! still from Fortune's garland,
Some flowers for others strew;
And forget not the unhappy,
For, ah! their friends are few.

It shifted the focus to Henry's personal experiences, not the abstract arguments of the abolitionist cause. At this time Swain was honorary Professor of Poetry at the Manchester Royal Institution. Born in the city, his first job had been in a dye works owned by a maternal uncle; then he was, briefly and unsuccessfully, a bookseller. For the rest of his life he worked as an engraver in Manchester, but published a number of books of his verse and became well respected and moderately well known as a poet.[27] Many readers, both in Manchester and elsewhere in Britain, would be familiar with his work. This familiarity brought home to people the human costs of slavery, emphasizing that they shared common emotions. Everyone has, at some time, felt that those around them did not understand their unhappiness and were irritated by it but, although some born in Britain had experienced the depths of Henry's misery, none had suffered the reasons for it. It was an inspired epigraph and must have been suggested by a local person.

This is an oversimplification of the two approaches, but Stearns's edition resembles an academic study; he had a concept, a message, that Henry was used to illustrate. The second edition had no credited writer and the issues emerged from Henry's story; they were not imposed on it. I therefore consider that it was a journalist who interviewed Henry, then edited and rewrote parts of this version in America, but it was further revised in Britain by someone with local knowledge who suggested the poem. The style resembles contemporaneous newspaper reports and is considerably less florid than Stearns's literary grandiloquence, although it does retain some of his original phrasing. There are also passages in the revised edition where Henry's voice strongly comes through, like his account of the crucial event when he saw his children and wife marched south. In Stearns's edition, this occupies one paragraph:

The next day, I stationed myself by the side of the road, along which the slaves, amounting to three hundred and fifty, were to pass. The purchaser of my wife was a Methodist minister, who was about starting for North Carolina. Pretty soon five waggon-loads of little children passed, and looking at the foremost one, what should I see but a little child, pointing its tiny hand towards me, exclaiming, "There's my father; I knew he would come and bid me good-bye." It was my eldest child! Soon the gang approached in which my wife was chained. I looked, and beheld her familiar face; but O, reader, that glance of agony! may God spare me ever again enduring the excruciating horror of that moment! She passed, and came near to where I stood. I seized hold of her hand, intending to bid her farewell; but words failed me; the gift of utterance had fled, and I remained speechless. I followed her for some distance, with her hand grasped in mine, as if to save her from her fate, but I could not speak, and I was obliged to turn away in silence.[28]

The 1851 edition is more detailed, less literary, and more impressionistic:

What should I now see in the very foremost waggon but a little child looking towards me and pitifully calling, father! father! This was my eldest child, and I was obliged to look upon it for the last time that I should, perhaps, ever see it again in life; if it had been going to the grave and this gloomy procession had been about to return its body to the dust from whence it sprang, whence its soul had taken its departure for the land of spirits, my grief would have been nothing in comparison to what I then felt; for then I could have reflected that its sufferings were over and that it would never again require nor look for a father's care; but now it goes with all those tender feelings riven, by which it was endeared to a father's love; it must still live subjected to the deprivation of paternal care and to the chains and wrongs of slavery, and yet be dead to the pleasure of a father from whose heart the impression of its early innocence and love will never be effaced.

    Thus passed my child from my presence—it was my own child—I loved it with all the fondness of a father; but things were so ordered that I could only say, farewell, and leave it to pass in its chains while I looked for the approach of another gang in which my wife was also loaded with chains. My eye soon caught her precious face, but, gracious heavens! that glance of agony may God spare me from ever again enduring! My wife, under the influence of her feelings, jumped aside; I seized hold of her hand while my mind felt unutterable things, and my tongue was only able to say, we shall meet in heaven! I went with her for about four miles hand in hand, but both our hearts were so overpowered with feeling that we could say nothing, and when at last we were obliged to part, the look of mutual love which we exchanged was all the token which we could give each other that we should yet meet in heaven.[29]

This passage could have been composed by a novelist, but the rest of the prose is workmanlike, not creative. These vivid memories were probably taken down in shorthand, as they so closely reproduce actual recollections as Henry relived the event. Factual information is best given by journalists because they can summarize more precisely and succinctly, but opinions, emotions, and anecdotes are best reported in the words of the interviewee, tidied up a little, which seems to be what happened here and in other passages of this edition. Stearns, not a journalist, interposed his own opinions and interpretations. This second edition also has occasional British English idioms, like the use of "underground railway" rather than "underground railroad," which was the American English term. A closer linguistic analysis by someone with specialist knowledge of historical semantics might cast further light on where and by whom this edition might have been produced.

    Additional material included naming people who might have been damaged had they been identified in the previous edition, and a number of song lyrics, including the revised "Old Uncle Ned." The only element added that directly relates to Britain is an endorsement by a group of Sunday School teachers in Blackburn, dated January 1851. Endorsements, attesting to the genuineness and acceptability of the writer, were an essential element of a slave narrative in Britain as well as in America. There were a number of imposters getting money and sympathy from local people, and testimonials to the probity of speakers was essential. The main change, however, was the excision of Stearns's more florid interpolations; the core of this narrative is some six pages shorter.

Few fugitives explored the contrast between their lives under enslavement and their lives in freedom. There is no reflection on how their change of status widened their intellectual horizons or impacted on their emotional state. By focusing on the physical and moral evils slaves experienced, abolitionists hammered home their message in the kind of narrowly focused way that is still most effective when conducting any kind of campaign, but this had the result of limiting the fugitives themselves to symbols. Although some individuality emerges from the narratives, they are mainly representative figures. This does not mean they should be doubted, but it is necessary to bear in mind when reading them that they only tell a small, particular part of a life history. Later in life Douglass and Wells Brown did consider the changes wrought on them by freedom, but from the others, including Henry, there is little or nothing, so an understanding of individual responses has to be recovered from what they did and how that was reported, either by people they encountered or from newspaper accounts of events in which they took part, but these too were mediated by another party with a particular agenda.

Reenacting the Escape

The revised edition was ready in time to sell at appearances in Leeds in Yorkshire on May 22, shortly after Wells Brown and the Crafts had been speaking there at the Temperance Hall. To publicize this engagement and promote his book Henry decided to have himself transported in his box by rail from Bradford, a mill town, to Leeds, about 14 miles away (about 15 km), recreating in miniature his journey to freedom. The box was planned to leave Bradford at six in the evening, arriving half an hour later in Leeds, then going in procession to the Music Hall in Albion Street, where he would be released from the box. It must have been traumatic for Henry to relive this ordeal, although he was accompanied by James Smith and knew he could be released at any point. This reenactment has often been seen as a key event, featured in many studies for its symbolic value. Although it was a dramatic stunt, what no one, apart from Ruggles, has recognized was that it attracted only a small audience to the actual lecture, so in practical terms it was a failure, although Henry did sell some copies of the *Narrative*. Nor did it get much publicity elsewhere in the country; it seems only one provincial newspaper, the *Dorset County Chronicle*, reprinted the *Leeds Times* piece.[30] Henry never repeated this kind of reenactment.

Having seen the box being delivered and Henry released, the onlookers may have thought it was not worth paying to hear him, especially as a few weeks earlier Henry Russell had appeared at the Olympic Theatre in Leeds with a panorama entitled *The Far West*. Russell (1812–1900) was a popular English singer and composer with a powerful baritone voice who visited America between 1836 and 1841. By 1848, but probably earlier, he was including "Negro songs" in his repertoire. His panorama was described as "coarsely painted," which suggests it was hastily put together to cash in on the popularity of the presentations by both Henry and William Wells Brown. It did not have an abolitionist message, being "an illustrated account of the slave trade, from the point at which the negroes are captured, in the interior of Africa, to that at which, apparently reconciled to their fate, they are disporting themselves with dancing and music at a plantation in Carolina." Russell separated each division of the panorama by a song, an anecdote, a philosophical reflection, or a joke and included musical interludes.[31] It would be going too far to suggest he deliberately set out to spoil Henry and Smith's presentation, but undoubtedly he must have reduced their potential audience.

Henry's reenactment was more widely reported in America than in Britain. Some, even in the free states, were not pleased. The *Buffalo Courier* and the *Weekly Raleigh Register* said that England had slavery for white people and they were worse off than black slaves in the United States. The *Oshkosh Democrat* of Wisconsin headlined its report "A Shameful Spectacle," saying that the parade through the street had been preceded by "banners representing the stars and stripes of America," which might have been what caused offense, as the flag was such a powerful symbol of America and was here being used critically. It seems there were other political comments of the kind that the organized abolitionist movement avoided. A local paper in Leeds described the panorama as comprising over 100 views, including some which highlighted American hypocrisies, such as one in which the House of Congress is shown at the top of the canvas, while in the foreground is a slave auction. In another, President Taylor is shown driving in state into Washington with his four grey steeds that were frightened by the cries and groans of a gang of slaves. No doubt, Henry made the point that animals were disturbed by brutality but the President was not. Other scenes portrayed a heartless "Knock-'Em-Off" officiating at a slave auction, at which he calls them "cattle"; a sale of slaves at the same time as the celebrations of America's Independence;

and depictions of the cruelties visited on the enslaved. Some appear to have been added to the original scenes.[32]

It was the kind of stunt that the more austere abolitionists in both America and Britain deplored, not least because Henry seems also to have directly and personally attacked the President of the United States, which was not part of the organized movements' agenda. The abolitionists' strategy, both in America and in Britain, was to attack laws, not to make personal attacks on the lawmakers themselves. This was also official government policy. When Harriet Beecher Stowe arrived in London in 1853 she was lionized. Members of the aristocracy, former Prime Ministers, the great and the good all flocked to meet her, but two notable personages were absent. Neither the Queen nor the Prime Minister of the day, Lord Aberdeen, invited this celebrity to either an official or an unofficial event. The reason was revealed in a letter from James Buchanan, appointed as the new American Minister to the Court of St. James, to Secretary Marcy in November 1853. Buchanan wrote that the Queen had "remarked very sensibly that American slavery was a question with which Great Britain had nothing to do."[33] The head of state could not appear to endorse something that was in opposition to another state's laws. Although those working in the abolitionist cause could criticize policy, a fine line needed to be observed, especially by those, like the Member of Parliament George Thompson, who were part of the British government. This strategy allowed men to save face because it gave them the leeway to admit they were intellectually mistaken, not that they themselves were irredeemably immoral. It is a subtle, but important, nuance with significance that Henry may not have grasped fully or, more likely, did not care about.

Until this point, Henry and Smith had mainly been in the orbit of the religiously inspired abolition movement, and at their presentations a clergyman of one denomination or another would be present, making it clear that they were part of the movement the churches endorsed; a Methodist presided at the lecture in Leeds, for example. Most of the ministers from the dissenting churches, and some Anglican clergy, were temperance campaigners and also disapproved of tobacco. William Wells Brown, a strong advocate of temperance, was the preferred model. To someone whose signature song boasted of his self-emancipation (and who, as will be seen, liked a drink and a smoke), this Puritanism may have started to seem irksome. Although he had only been in England for some six months, Henry was planning significant changes for his future.

The Parting of the Ways

Despite the success of the tour, there were cracks appearing in the relationship between Henry and Smith. As so often in a double act, one must have felt he was the star and the other not contributing much, just a passenger. Henry has left no account of his reasons for his actions, but he probably considered that Smith (who is rarely mentioned in reports of their presentations) contributed little and that Henry was doing all the hard work while they were sharing the proceeds equally, although there were other factors. When the split came, Smith, deeply wounded, wrote back to America to their sponsors, giving his account of events. I have used these letters to reconstruct events.[34] It seems that sometime in May Henry had appropriated their joint earnings, which had been left in Manchester with a trusted woman named Hannah Walton, perhaps when Henry collected books from his publisher. At the beginning of June, Smith found the money mostly gone. There had been almost £100 (equivalent to about £10,000 or $13,000 today), of which Henry left only £10, one-tenth of their earnings, for Smith. Also missing were all the papers that demonstrated Smith's entitlement to half their income, which suggests Henry could by now read quite well, or he had help. Henry (or a helper) had actually picked the lock of Smith's box, the carefully guarded and valued trunk in which itinerant workers and servants kept their possessions. In Britain this box was seen almost as an extension of the person; even employers regarded it as inviolable and did not open it unless in exceptional circumstances. For Smith, this was both a breach of trust and an invasion of his personal space, like being burgled.

Then Henry told Smith that their partnership was finished and gave him a brutally formal notice (I have preserved the original spellings in the following correspondence):

> To C. Smith June 13th 1851
>
> I here by give you notice that I have no further accasion for your services and that in future I shall not supply you with meat, clothe, and other necessaries as I formerly have done as payment for your services. Signed,
>
> H. Box Brown

Smith had not seen this coming, and his letters back to America to Gerrit Smith and William Lloyd Garrison are redolent of his pain and shock at the betrayal by someone "whom I have done much for": "I have spared no pains nor lost any time in doing what I could for [the exhibition's] progress." Initially, he gave a long description of the way Henry had broken with him, after all he had done. To stress his fundamental loyalty to the man who had rejected him and to retain the moral high ground, Smith reiterated that he was sorry to have to say these discreditable things about Henry: "Brown have behave so bad that I feel ashamed to tell it"; "But I must tell the truth tho. it may be [word deleted] Brown has behaved very bad sence he have been here—and indeed his Character is that bad I am ashamed to tell it"; "I am sorry that I have nothing to write which is good."

I do not intend to be flippant, but Smith sounds like a rejected first wife. During the lean years of Henry's enslavement in Richmond, then touring in the northern United States and finally in Britain, he had been a loyal friend, associate, and partner, working in the background to support his friend, and now, just as the rewards were coming in, he was being dumped. Henry stood firm, despite pressure from others:

> To prevent an exposure and for the Sake of the Cause these [Thomas Barker, Hannah and Rebecca Walton, James Bryce and Dr. Lees] and other friends went and talk to Brown to see if they could get to terams without making it any more Public than what it was. And it was with much difficulty before they could make him confest the truth or any thing like it, all tho. they give him his own words. After two or 3 weeks bother he mad an acknowledgment that we were equal Partners—but the money was all made away.

Smith and these friends eventually realized that there was no way of rebuilding the partnership, and an announcement appeared in the British government's official publication, the *London Gazette,* on July 29, 1851:

> Notice is hereby given that the Partnership heretofore subsisting between the undersigned, Henry Box Brown and James Cæsar Anthony Smith, in the business or profession of Exhibitors of a Moving Tableaux [*sic*] or Panorama, carried on by them in different parts of England under the firm of Brown and Smith, has been this day dissolved by mutual consent. The business will in future be carried on by the said Henry Box Brown alone, who will receive and pay all debts and sums of money respectively due or owing by the said late firm.—As witness the hands of the parties this 25th day of July 1851.
>
> H.B. Brown
>
> J.C.A. Smith

Although money must have been a factor, in a postscript to his letters Smith added that he thought Henry's actions might have some ulterior motive, because initially Henry claimed he wanted to redeem both his wife and children but had recently been speaking of the children only:

> You may wonder how such a change could have taken place with Brown. But I will tell you the reason. He have got it into his head to get a wife or some thing worst and I used to be teling him that he ought to try and get his wife and children which was in slavery before he thought of anything else. That has given some offence to him I surpose. And further more he have been telling the people that he could not get his wife if he had the money to buy her with. And a number of persons asked me how was the case that Box. Brown says he could not get his wife but could buy his children if he could raise a cirtin amount of money. I did not wish to do no hurt but I could not tell a willful lie and know it—therefore I said—that the man who owned Box Browns wife wrote me a letter in answer to one I sent—to know what he would take for Browns wife and children. And the master of his wife said he would take $1500 for her and the children if Henry Box. Brown would promise to treat them kindly. This Brown has never

acknowledge to any person, and I used to ask him why he did not tell when he was asked the name of the man that owns his wife and where she lived he said be cause the abolitionist would fret the man so much he would refuse to sell his wife. I believe that un till I know better. He have told the people that the man who owns [h]is wife wrote him word that he would not sell the woman but said he will sell the three small children for fifteen hundred dollars and all belong to the same person. And a number of persons do not believe no tale like that. And be cause I told the truth—this is the reason he have thus treated me cruel.

The major reason for Henry's reluctance to redeem his wife emerged some time later (and is revealed when that time is described here), but he had plainly not confided in his partner at this point, probably because, as the letters make clear, Smith had been discussing with other people personal matters that made Henry uncomfortable. He had also nagged Henry and now realized he had gone too far. Perhaps feeling slightly guilty at the pressure he had been piling on, he tried to excuse himself by slipping in the possibility that Henry was not looking for a respectable wife, but something *worse* (underlined). Presumably Henry had found that in England his color was no bar to enjoying the company of white women. It may have gone no further than being friendly and flirting, but this was something that straitlaced, middle-class abolitionists, some of whom in Britain as well as in America disapproved of interracial relationships, would abhor, and Smith would have known how damaging such a suggestion was.

Wives of Enslaved Men

There is another consideration. Nancy was very much the product of the slave system in the southern states of America. Like Henry, she had had no chance to become literate or to learn about the wider world, but he was now in a very different society. John Broadhurst, his wife, and customers at the coffee house and other places where Henry lodged must have chatted with him about current affairs, and he would have met many other people at events who made him realize he was socializing with better educated, more sophisticated, white people, both male and female. The southern states, as Frederick Law Olmsted, John Franklin, the Genoveses, and many others have observed from different perspectives, were at that time places of isolation and stultifying limitations.[35] Southerners prided themselves on their hospitality— what they offered was food and comfort, not intellectual stimulation. Those who wanted to attend cultural gatherings to widen their horizons had to travel long distances, and in any case there was less available than in the states of New England. In tiny, crowded England, on the other side of the Atlantic, events and experiences that would widen the horizons of even the poorest, most ill-educated men and, sometimes, women were within walking distance, especially in towns and cities. Churches, charities, and secular organizations arranged occasions, like lectures, that could be attended for free or for very little money with minimal traveling. Poor men were encouraged to improve their knowledge and situation in life by the provision of classes and libraries. The more advanced could share their knowledge with their wives and daughters. How would Nancy, enslaved and kept in ignorance, cope in Britain or in the northern states were Henry to return? How would she be received? Might she become an embarrassment to him?

Other fugitive slaves faced similar harsh moral dilemmas. Both Douglass and Wells Brown married young, before they had earned their success and acquired status as role models. Like many successful men, they outgrew their first wives. Anna Murray, who married Frederick Douglass in 1838 when he was about 20, was an illiterate laundress whom he met while he too was uneducated and doing manual work. He considered remaining in England but, as well as missing people he knew in America, realized that he could not ask Anna to relocate to such a different culture. Undoubtedly, Douglass loved his wife and appreciated her unfailing domestic support and expert housekeeping, but after his sojourn in Britain he found intellectual companionship elsewhere and set up *ménages à trois* (or more), which must have hurt Anna. Whether or not these involved extramarital relationships is not known. The first one of significance was with Julia Griffiths, a white Englishwoman, and then with the German Ottilie Assing, also white. She introduced him to her country's culture but was disparaging about Anna. His second marriage, two years after Anna's death in 1882, was to Helen Pitts, a white American who was a campaigner for female suffrage and for abolition, and Assing, ill with cancer, committed suicide. Rumors of impropriety dogged these relationships and others, and he was severely censured by both black and white people.[36]

William Wells Brown married Elizabeth Schooner in 1834, when he too was 20. Left alone in Buffalo for extended periods after he started public speaking tours, she became involved with another man, and Wells Brown moved his family to another smaller town, some 100 miles away. Here Elizabeth was still neglected, and in 1847 she told him she was leaving. He took custody of their two surviving daughters, Clarissa and Josephine (a third had died young). A year later Elizabeth, with a baby, came to the offices of one of his then employers, the Massachusetts Anti-Slavery Society, demanding that he support her. All this was embarrassing to both Wells Brown personally and to the cause, and this must have been one of the factors that decided the Massachusetts Anti-Slavery Society to send him on a lecture tour of Britain in 1849. Because of the Fugitive Slave Act he remained away from America until 1854, and while he was still abroad Elizabeth died in 1851 or 1852, allowing him to remarry without the public scandal of divorce.[37]

After he had purchased her freedom, James Watkins's wife joined him in Britain in 1854, but she did not remain. She returned to America, ostensibly because of ill-health sometime around 1862. She must have found it hard to adjust to life in Britain, away from an environment she understood. The last report of Watkins in Britain that I have found is in 1865 when he was speaking in Milfield, near Berwick-on-Tweed in Northumberland.[38] In the intervening period, he was still raising money but not, it appears, to return to America and not for his wife's passage back to Britain.

Douglass, Wells Brown, and Watkins all needed to maintain a respectable image, presenting a virtuous face to a world on both sides of the Atlantic that was too ready to condemn black men and women as licentious and lacking morality. Henry did not have the level of fame and approbation of either Douglass or Wells Brown, but at this stage he was taking a perilous chance by splitting from Smith. It was not simply for being reluctant to redeem his wife that Smith criticized him. Henry, Smith added in a further postscript, had been drinking, smoking, swearing, and gambling. Smith was aware that these allegations would be regarded critically by abolitionists, in both America and Britain, who were determined that their representatives show themselves as morally impeccable and unimpeachably respectable. Smith was honest enough to add that Henry's drinking did not involve strong spirits, rum, or brandy. He listed "Rasbury wine, pop, peppermint, Sampson, Jinny Lind, soabrity, gingerrote, ginger Beer, gingerale, Blackbeer and many other things of that nature." Some of these were unexceptional, like pop, a sweet, nonalcoholic drink with bubbles usually produced from carbonated water. Sobriety was a teetotal drink made of carrageen, also known as Irish moss. Sampson may be another temperance drink, as God told the biblical Samson's mother not to drink wine and that her son should be a Nazarite, who abstained from wine and even from touching grapes (Judges 13:4). Beer, however, was not mentioned in the Bible, so this was possibly a strong beer (there is one on the market at the moment called Samson). Black beer, also known as spruce beer, was and still is made from conifer needles.[39] It could be made with or without an alcoholic content, and the others, like raspberry wine and the various ginger drinks, would have had a low alcoholic content. In the days when water in British towns came from pumps in streets where the water supply was often contaminated with fluids draining from graveyards and abattoirs or with other domestic and agricultural waste, it was healthier to drink mildly alcoholic beverages, as bacteria could not survive the brewing process, or hot drinks like tea or coffee because boiling water would serve the same purpose.

Nor is it surprising that Henry, who had previously worked in a tobacco factory where he needed to test the quality of the goods, was a smoker and used snuff. As Smith did not give any specific details about the swearing, this

Present-day English counties, following a reform of local administration in 1974. Britain is about half the size of California, but was, and is, much more densely populated. The counties are broadly the same as the Box Browns would have known, with the major difference of the creation of Greater Manchester, incorporating many individual towns that he and later they toured. Greater London was created in 1963, incorporating Middlesex, a historic county to the northwest.

Some of the counties are abbreviated: Beds = Bedfordshire, Bucks = Buckinghamshire, Cambs = Cambridgeshire, G. Mancs = Greater Manchester, Herefs = Herefordshire, Herts = Hertfordshire, Lancs = Lancashire, Leics = Leicestershire, Northants = Northamptonshire, Shrops = Shropshire, Staffs = Staffordshire, Wars = Warwickshire, Worcs = Worcestershire.

may just have been an all-purpose slur. It is also impossible to know whether the gambling was confined to an occasional flutter. The games Smith listed—dominoes, draughts, bagatelle—were commonly played in public houses for small stakes. None of these activities was illegal, but they were strongly disapproved of by the more fundamentalist wing of the abolitionists who wanted to ban not only slavery but also alcohol, tobacco, and fun. Because some people misused them, they must be forbidden to all. Henry was trying activities that had been hitherto prohibited, either by his masters or by the censorious mindset of abolitionists in America. In the southern states of America he had been enslaved; in the North he had legal freedom but was constrained within the limits determined by abolitionists and segregation there; now in Britain he had liberty. The only restrictions on his actions were the laws and local regulations that applied to everyone. Unshackled, it is only surprising he did not celebrate more riotously.

Whether Henry knew of Smith's correspondence is an open question, but it seems unlikely. Subsequently he seems to have behaved honorably, keeping to schedules, fulfilling engagements, and no reports in the press or elsewhere of any similar transgressions against other people have been so far found, so this one incident was exceptional, especially as it came such a short time after his arrival. To reject the support he had received and might still need seems foolhardy, but as well as constantly reminding Henry of the need to redeem his wife and children, Smith probably voiced criticisms of his drinking, smoking, and gambling and lectured him on the need to behave in a way acceptable to their sponsors. Henry finally decided to split from a partner who was not just contributing less but also nagging him and discussing his personal business with outsiders who now added their strictures. One of those who urged Henry to remain, Dr. Frederick Lees, was an abolitionist and temperance campaigner as well as a Chartist (supporter of a bill of rights and the franchise for working-class men) and a vegetarian, who must have emphasized the need to behave in a way the more fundamental and censorious abolitionists like himself deemed appropriate. Wanting to break free from this restrictive environment and the intrusion into his affairs is understandable, but nevertheless it was a brave move and took some fortitude to resist over a period of two or three weeks the importuning of Lees and other people, who no doubt warned Henry of the perils of going it alone without the backing of their movement.

Going Solo

It is not clear when Henry fulfilled his first solo engagement. After Leeds in Yorkshire, the panorama was shown in Huddersfield and Dewsbury, but there is no mention of Smith being there. The first show after the official dissolution of their partnership was a visit to Halifax, Yorkshire, in June 1851, where Henry appeared at the Odd Fellows Hall, not apparently under the aegis of a religious organization. This may be the occasion on which he joined the organization. Friendly societies, legalized in 1793, were made up of groups of workers who paid a weekly sum into a general fund from which they could draw in the event of illness. They also had regular meetings, usually in public houses, to socialize and network. Some remained small, local concerns, while others, like the Odd Fellows, grew into national companies that were particularly attractive to itinerant workers, since assistance could be accessed across the whole country while people were traveling and looking for work. Henry probably calculated they could provide an alternative to the abolitionists' network. Smith stayed on for a while in Britain—he was in Ashton-under-Lyne near Manchester in 1854—but his story was not compelling enough to draw audiences. He was a free man in America so there was no reason to remain, and by 1861 he had left Britain. Although Henry alone was generally well received, not everyone was bowled over. In Dewsbury his exhibition was "but indifferently supported," but in Halifax audiences were "very large and crowded."[40]

Surprisingly little detail about Henry's actual performances was given. The content of the panoramas comes from his own advertisements, and most of the accounts of his appearances simply stated the subject of his talk. Only rarely were there insights into his appeal for his audiences. Shortly after his arrival in Britain, Henry was described as having "a plain unvarnished manner," or giving a "plain homely description." One reporter commented that the "scenes exhibited were beautifully described." As he gained in confidence and his audiences responded to him, he felt able to introduce a more personal style, speaking with "much eloquence and effect" and allowing his emotions to show.

> If there be one fault, the voice of the exhibitor is raised often to too high a pitch and his utterance is rapid but as he proceeds in depicting the cruel scenes to which he been an eye witness, he becomes excited which may account for the loudness of his delivery.[41]

It was observed that "Mr Brown is not so accomplished a speaker as Frederick Douglas [sic] or Mr W.W. Brown but he narrates his story in a way which tells on his auditory." What Henry could do above all was move his audience. In America it was the moral and political aspects of the slavery system that were paramount, but in England, where slavery had not existed since medieval times, it was emotional identification and sympathy that drew audiences. "Mr. Brown's descriptive powers are truly great; he speaks from the heart—there is no mistaking a single sentence—every word comes from the fountain of truth and finds its way into the bosom of his hearers"; he "painfully affects his hearers as the tears shed by his hearers of the gentler sex plainly show"; "the description he gives of slavery is heartrending."[42]

The ending of the partnership marked the beginning of the end of Henry's involvement with religious groups and the wider abolitionist movement, but this was achieved gradually. In Rochdale, Lancashire, a bastion of high-minded reform, he tried a new gimmick, offering prizes for the best antislavery essays. There were 21 entries. On October 2, 1851, John Ashworth, a painter, received the first prize, a family Bible; the next day the second prize, Fleetwood's *Life of Christ*, was awarded to George Bull, a wool sorter; and on the third evening a copy of *The Pilgrim's Progress* rewarded a factory operative, Abraham Howard. Spreading out the presentations meant that people had an incentive to return. Where they were held is not stated, but it is most likely, given the prizes, that this was under the aegis of a religious denomination. The winner, John Ashworth, was a Methodist preacher. His essay, *The Horrors and Curse of Slavery*, was written in the overblown, rhetorical style of the day, much like Stearns's prose.[43] Later Henry revived the distribution of prizes but with less high-minded tasks and trophies.

He remained in Rochdale for some three weeks, where as well as the religious theme he tried out a political one, and news of this went back to America. In November 1851 the *Morning Star*, published in Limerick, Maine, carried a letter drawn from a report in a British newspaper entitled "Kossuth and Cotton" (which I have been unable to trace). Following an uprising in Hungary in 1848, Lajos Kossuth had been appointed regent-president in an attempt to mediate between the royalist and the republican factions but was forced to go into exile in 1851. He, like so many other political refugees, had come to England but also spoke in America, where at this time he was on tour and being rapturously received.

> At Rochdale Mr. Henry Box Brown the fugitive who committed treason by riding from Richmond to Philadelphia, shut up in a box, held an exhibition of his panorama of American slavery on upwards of 50,000 feet of canvas for the benefit of those Polish and Hungarian refugees now residing in Rochdale who served under Kossuth and his generals in the late Hungarian struggle. Mr. Brown explained the several scenes presented on the canvas and made appropriate allusions to the case of the Hungarians.
>
> ...
>
> But the thought of a fugitive from American slavery who cannot stay in this country, making such an exhibition for the purpose of aiding the fugitives from Austrian tyranny, whom the people of this country are doing so much to honor, is an impressive commentary on the strange mixtures that exist in human affairs.—*Ib.*[44]

The writer was unsure what to think. By saying Henry had committed treason by escaping, he seems to condemn him, yet the concluding paragraph is more open-minded, suggesting he was not entirely clear what he should make of this parallel between slavery in America and the support Americans were giving to political freedom in Europe.

In December Henry was in Stockport, near Manchester, making an unadvertised and unreported appearance, which is only known because on December 31 John Leucy was charged at a local court with stealing 87 books from Henry. He had been hired as a scene shifter and, after several weeks in Stockport, on December 13, while the presentation was being moved to Hyde some seven miles away, it was discovered that 27 copies of the *Narrative* and 60 unbound copies of the *Anti-Slavery Harp* were missing. Leucy was not suspected until he absconded and was traced to Huddersfield. He had sold the books, either in Huddersfield, as one newspaper reported, or in Stockport, according to another. The *Anti-Slavery Harp* was a collection of 48 songs for antislavery meetings, compiled by William Wells Brown and originally published in 1848. He had another edition produced in England in 1851. Henry may have intended to get them bound and sell them, but this collection was never mentioned in either his advertisements or reports of his performances. He was probably distributing the loose sheets among the audience to sing along.[45] Despite this minor setback, all seemed to be going well. He was managing without the support of James Smith, and the split from his erstwhile partner did not yet seem to have damaged his bookings, so his future must have looked bright.

Scene 2

Wolverhampton, 1852

After Henry's appearance in Hyde, presumably in early 1852, there was then a period of around two months until the next recorded presentation in Wolverhampton, Staffordshire, in the Midlands in March 1852. He may have been making other unmentioned appearances, but the link with abolitionists in England could by now have been damaged by correspondence from America repeating Smith's accusations. Some (but, as will be seen, not all) religious organizations might have been unwilling to host Henry, as Smith himself was still in England and probably spreading the word about Henry's dishonorable conduct toward someone who had been a good friend and done so much for him but who was now abandoned. At this tricky time, Henry needed to think carefully about what kind of patrons and audience he was hoping to attract. He would have heard about, and could have attended, the talk that James Watkins, a fugitive slave from Maryland, gave in Bolton on December 16, 1851. This was some 27 miles from Hyde but the train service in this area was good. The local paper, the *Bolton Chronicle,* carried a very long and detailed report of the typical pattern of the antislavery lectures that were being delivered under the aegis of local churches all over Britain. Here Henry could have seen the kind of event that produced crowds, book sales, and donations.

Between three and four hundred people attended, including a number of children. The meeting was in the local Temperance Hall, and the chair was taken by a Baptist minister who directed and controlled the proceedings. Several members of the Society of Friends were also on the platform. The minister first detailed the provisions of the Fugitive Slave Act, which, he said, had made "the whole of the United States and its free citizens ... into a huge slave-hunting mob," and then castigated the churches in America, including his own, that supported slavery. "Only one denomination of Christians existed in America—the Friends (applause)—whose hands w[e]re not stained with the blood of slaves." Then Watkins, "who was received with much cheering," spoke at length about his experiences, his escape to the northern states and his final move from Connecticut to Canada following the passing of the Fugitive Slave Act. His freedom had been purchased for $250 dollars but he felt he could not live in America, where any man could arrest him, put him in prison and drag him into slavery, "Shame Americans in sending 3,000 miles for Kossuth! Let them set free the Kossuths of their own country, and then it would be consistent to sympathise with others." The proceedings closed with a motion, "That this meeting expresses its deepest abhorrence at American slavery in general, and the recent Fugitive Slave Act in particular; and that it calls on American Christians to repudiate it in every possible way, and that the Christian churches of this country be advised to hold no fellowship with any clergy or laity who give to slavery their sanction." The motion was seconded and carried, and followed by a vote of thanks to the chairman. The meeting ended with Watkins singing two songs on slavery.[1]

Those on the circuit of nonconformist churches speaking about abolition and/or temperance were largely preaching to the converted. Their listeners came to have their beliefs confirmed, not challenged, and both the content and the program were predictable. Control of the proceedings was by locally influential white people, undoubtedly on the right side, undoubtedly well-intentioned, undoubtedly charitable, and also undoubtedly convinced of their own virtue. It is difficult to see how it could be otherwise; all campaigns that achieve results operate like this. Henry, however, presented his panorama alone, and he directed proceedings, so he was challenging the hierarchy and the authority of the abolitionist movement. Even if Smith's allegations about him had leaked back from America to Britain, at this stage he could easily have rebuilt a connection with the religious wing of the movement by presenting himself as a reformed sinner (the best kind). Was this, however, where he wanted to be? He was skeptical of organized religion of whatever denomination and was not a fan of temperance, although he was not, to judge by the beverages Smith listed, a heavy drinker. Although the Church of England Temperance Society recognized that total abstinence was a hopeless task and concentrated on getting people to moderate their alcoholic intake and avoid spirits, most dissenters were strong advocates of teetotalism.

Henry, as his break from Smith and his later life showed, truly wanted to be free of other people's demands and expectations, aiming to become independent without limitation on his personal self-direction. The manumissions of Watkins, Douglass, Wells Brown, and others were purchased by sympathizers, but there is no record that Henry was offered this, or requested it. He did not look for middle-class approval or support, which would have placed him under an obligation, and he seems to have decided that he would not return to the United States, where there was nothing for him. In June 1851 Frederick Douglass had appealed to various people, listing James W.C. Pennington, Henry Highland Garnet, Alexander Crummell, Josiah Henson,

CORN EXCHANGE, WOLVERHAMPTON.

THE AMERICAN KOSSUTH!!!

For Six Nights!!! On the Evenings of Monday, Tuesday, Wednesday, Thursday, Friday, and Saturday, the 15th, 16th, 17th, 18th, 19th, and 20th of March, 1852.

MR. HENRY BOX BROWN, the celebrated American Fugitive Slave, who escaped from Slavery, packed as luggage, in a box 3 feet 1 inch long, 2 feet wide, and 2 feet 6 inches high, travelling a distance of 350 miles! from Richmond, Virginia, to Philadelphia, Pennsylvania, the journey occupying 27 hours, will OPEN FOR PUBLIC EXHIBITION, in the CORN EXCHANGE ROOM, his unrivaled PANORAMA of AFRICAN and AMERICAN SLAVERY!!

Mr. Henry Box Brown is traveling under the patronage of the Ministers, Superintendents, and Magisterial authorities of Lancashire, Yorkshire, Cheshire, and Staffordshire, endeavouring to raise the sympathies of the people of England in behalf of his, traveling a half of his race, in a state of degradation and slavery in America!

The Panorama is painted on 50,000 feet of canvass, by Wolcott, Rose, and Johnson, of Boston, U.S. and has been exhibited to three hundred and sixty-five thousand persons since its arrival in this country!

The scenes will be accompanied by the celebrated ITALIAN HARPISTS. The celebrated Italian Minstrels will introduce several Italian Duets, &c.

Admission. — Front Seats, 1s.; Second Seats, 6d.; Back Seats, 4d.

Exhibitions.—Doors will open at seven; Panorama commence moving at eight precisely.

CORN EXCHANGE, WOLVERHAMPTON.

UNRIVALLED TREAT!

Under the distinguished Patronage of the Ministers, Superintendents, and Sabbath-School Teachers of Lancashire, Yorkshire, Cheshire, and Staffordshire.

MR. HENRY BOX BROWN, the celebrated American FUGITIVE SLAVE, who escaped from Slavery, packed as Luggage, in a box, 3ft. 1in. long, 2ft. wide, and 2ft. 6in high, travelling a distance of 350 Miles!—from Richmond, Virginia, to Philadelphia, Pennsylvania, the journey occupying 27 hours, will exhibit his unrivalled American

PANORAMA OF SLAVERY,

On the Evenings of Monday, Tuesday, Wednesday, Thursday, Friday, and Saturday, March 15, 16, 17, 18, 19, and 20.

The Scenes will be described by Mr. Henry Box Brown.

Signor Antonio Abecco, Signor Michelangelo di Lonardo, and Vincent Abecco, the celebrated ITALIAN MINSTRELS, will introduce several splendid pieces from the Italian Opera of "Sonnambula," "Puritani," "Romeo e Giulietta," &c., &c. Duetto from the Opera of "Il Matrimonio Segreto," by Simarosa. Duet, "Suoni Ia Tromba," Bellini.

At the conclusion of the Exhibition Mr. Brown will sing a Song descriptive of his escape, and several other Plantation Melodies, and exhibit the identical box in which he made his escape.

This Exhibition has been visited by 365,000 persons since its arrival in this country.

Admission.—Front Seats, 1s.; Second Seats, 6d.; Gallery, 4d.

Doors will be open at Seven; Panorama commence moving at Eight precisely.   5521

Newspaper advertisements for Henry's appearances in Wolverhampton were carefully targeted at the local newspapers' different readerships. The *Wolverhampton Chronicle* (left) was more radical than the *Wolverhampton Herald* (right). *Wolverhampton Chronicle.* © The British Library Board. All rights reserved. With thanks to the British Newspaper Archive (www.britishnewspaperarchive.co.uk). All rights reserved/Bridgeman Images.

the Crafts, and Brown (presumably William Wells Brown), to come back to America to "rouse the slumbering conscience of this nation to out wrongs."[2] There is no mention of Henry; did Douglass know such an appeal was useless, or was he even in mid–1851 considered out of the abolitionist movement and of no use to it?

Where and how Henry spent this hiatus is not recorded, but if he was not making appearances he had a sum of money to live on, consisting of the accumulated savings he had taken from the partnership with Smith and his earnings since the breakup, which gave him time to rethink his approach and try out new themes to see which best suited his act. In October he had been awarding prizes for worthy essays, but now he decided to represent himself as a fiery political orator when he advertised his forthcoming exhibition at the Corn Exchange in Wolverhampton, an important industrial centre, where he was booked to make six appearances between March 15 and 20, 1852, and he placed advertisements in both the local newspapers. Perhaps he had seen Watkins's presentation and realized how topical Kossuth still was, as in the *Wolverhampton Chronicle* he called himself "The American Kossuth!!!"

Kossuth's oratorical skills were admired and he was honored on both sides of the Atlantic; barely a day passed without some report in the British press of what he was doing and saying in America. In this advertisement, Henry claimed 365,000 people had seen his panorama (contents not listed) and said he would be accompanied by a band of Italian harpists. The whole performance would be "Under the distinguished patronage of the Ministers, Superintendants, and Sabbath-School Teachers of Lancashire, Yorkshire, Cheshire and Staffordshire."[3] He was not yet prepared to break completely out of the influential religious orbit.

The advertisement in the *Wolverhampton and Staffordshire Herald* in the issues of March 3 and 10, 1852, made no mention of Kossuth. The notice was medium sized and did not list the contents of the panorama, which Henry claimed 350,000 people had seen. He listed the extracts from various operas that a band of Italian musicians, named as Signori Antonio Abecco, Michelangelo di Lonardo, and Vincent Abecco, would perform. He himself would sing the song of his escape and several plantation melodies and would exhibit his box. As in the advertisement in the *Chronicle*, he listed his patronage, both secular and religious. This advertisement appeared on the front page at the top of the right-hand column, immediately under the masthead, a good position for which he would have paid premium rates. These two advertisements reflected the interests and politics of the local population. Most counties had at least one progressive Whig and another conservative Tory paper. The minor differences between the advertisements suggest that the *Herald* did not favor radicalism and was more interested in music than political oratory.

Henry's intelligence was often mentioned in the press, perhaps because this was not expected of a black man, especially one who had been enslaved: "Mr Henry Brown's a remarkable fine specimen of the mental as well as the physical powers of Africa's sons"; "Brown is a fine, intelligent-looking man"; "the clever ex-slave vividly describes the incident poutrayed [*sic*]"; "Mr Brown is an intelligent man"; "a very intelligent man."[4] He used his intelligence to assess his market and to decide best how to advertise to it and to present to his audience, but the editor of the *Wolverhampton and Staffordshire Herald* was not impressed by what he did.

It is puzzling why Thomas Brindley was so aggressive in his review, which was published on March 17, 1852. The easy answer is racial prejudice, but Brindley's primary objection seems to have been to the style and contents of Henry's presentation, although there was undoubtedly a strong element of bigotry. This review, although overstated, started with what could have been a legally justifiable opinion.

Mr. Box Brown's panorama [is] without a feature of resemblance, and his so-called "eloquent and poetical address" a jumbled mass of contradictions and absurdities, assertions without proof, geography without boundaries and horrors without parallel.

Brindley claimed that both written and pictorial accounts contradicted Henry's portrayal. Among the artists he cited was Banvard, presumably the John Banvard whose panorama of the Mississippi, first exhibited in Boston in 1846, was the one that William Wells Brown found "too mild" on slavery. He was therefore basing his criticism on evidence from other sources. The next section, too, might have been defensible, as he emphasized that this was a personal view. It is also worth noting that Brindley did not say that Henry's deficiencies were because of his race. This was not pure racism, saying that his behavior was innate that he acted like this because he was black, that black people were inherently inferior, but it was Henry's manners and style he found offensive.

> The representation to our thinking, instead of benefitting the cause of abolition, is likely, from its want of *vraisemblanche* [*sic*: presumably *vraisemblance*, meaning likelihood] and decency, to generate disgust at the foppery, conceit, vanity and egotistical stupidity of the Box Brown school. To paint the devil blacker than he is is, certes, a work of supererogation and to make the slave states a series of inquisitorial chambers of horrors—a sort of Blue Beard, or giant despair den, for the destruction, burning, branding, laceration, starving and working of negroes; and the owners of slaves a class of demi-fiends, made of double distilled brimstone—is about as reasonable as giving his satanic majesty a coat of black paint to increase his hideousness.

In the section that formed the main grounds for the ensuing libel suit, Brindley used a journalistic trick. After describing "an intelligent American gentleman, who has won a name throughout the civilised world, by our side at this exhibition, and who has visited the slave states often, and seen the development of slavery in every phase," he says that "a gentleman present" questioned Henry about the Dismal Swamp, whether it was in Virginia or Carolina. This juxtaposition implied that this authoritative and knowledgeable American spoke, but it was actually Brindley who asked the question. The reply was given in the stereotyped language of minstrelsy shows, and it was a combination of this misrepresentation and the statement that Henry was ignorant of the place's location that led to legal action.

> "Well, he daint sacly know; taint somewhere in de middle of de state." "But," continued the interrogator, "is it not on the borders of North and South Carolina?" "Well, he daint know; you might put it in Carolina but he taut it was in Virginny." Much laughter followed this confab ... the proprietor [Henry] said "there was a swamp in Virginia but not *the dismal* swamp," a fact which we may presume may be predicated of every state in the union [italics in the original].

In his summing up, Brindley again emphasized that it was the presentation, not the principle, to which he objected:

> We deeply regret that the public should be gulled by that which can only give them a very partial, unfair, and decidedly false view of American slavery. The bondage of slavery is bad enough and the principle is wicked enough without evoking from the bottomless pit shades dark and gloomy, and auxiliary horrors to dress up and horrify with, this foul blot on the star-spangled banner.

He admitted that slavery was "wicked" so would probably have been able to sit through and applaud a polite, reasoned lecture on moral grounds, illustrated with a few examples of cruelties discreetly expressed and some humor, as Douglass and Wells Brown delivered. Knock-about satire, funny stories that mocked slave owners and ministers of religion, as well as dramatic, emotive descriptions of the brutalities inflicted on slaves and the sexual exploitation of females, were too much.

These must also have offended Brindley's American friend Alfred Hobbs (1812–91), a locksmith who had come to London for the Great Exhibition in 1851 in order to promote his company's products. He exercised his lockpicking skills on products made by the Bramah and Chubb companies, then claimed to be the most impregnable, and managed to open them, forcing them to improve their designs. He remained in Britain after the Great Exhibition and accepted other challenges. His successes and failures were often reported in the press, making him well known to the public. The majority of the readers of the *Herald* would have been unaware that Hobbs, born in Boston, had no particular connection to Virginia; what they saw was a celebrity with apparent authority simply because he was American, although his expertise was in a specialized area totally unrelated to the subject. Although Hobbs was from a non-slaveholding state, he seems not to have been a friend of abolition and was undoubtedly made uncomfortable by the sarcasm directed at America and Americans.

In the next issue, a week later, Brindley revisited the subject, welcoming the drop in audience figures in Wolverhampton. In this second piece, headlined *The "Nigger" Panorama*, Brindley showed indications of class snobbery, saying that the only people to whom Henry's act appealed were juvenile ragamuffins and describing him as "the bejewelled and oily negro, whose obese and comfortable figure and easy *nonchalance*, reminds one of various good things and sumptuous living." He referred to Henry's "ludicious [*sic*] and semi-baboonish agility" and gave examples of parts of the act, like Henry's story about masters giving slaves rum so they did not go to church, in minstrelsy style to ridicule his performance. In his 1851 *Narrative* Henry had published a fable of how black people became subservient to white, which must be what he used in this presentation. At a time when there were four people on earth, two white and two black, and Nature provided everything necessary with no need to work, two bags dropped from heaven. The black couple, being faster and stronger, grabbed the larger bag. It contained a shovel and a hoe.

The white people were left to open the smaller bag, which contained pen and ink, which enabled them to write what they said God declared. The paths in life of the two races were fixed. It is easy to see how this could be expanded with asides and comments to make it amusing, but at the heart was a bitter sting and a message against organized religion. Brindley distorted this fable by suggesting that it illustrated the laziness of black people and made other disparaging comments on aspects of the entertainment. He added that Henry's "truth and pathos" made Niobes of all the shoeless daughters of the slums and alleys, suggesting that only women of the lowest level of the poor and uneducated would be moved to cry at the presentation. After repeating the common assertion that American slaves were better off than the English laboring classes, Brindley claimed that every educated person, like him, was now too sensible to believe that anyone would destroy their valuable property.[5] This unsympathetic account provides some information about the content of Henry's presentation. He had left behind his original, unadorned descriptions and was now introducing more savage humor. He was satirical about those who preached to the enslaved, and was telling jokes that could leave a barb in his audience's minds.

Legal Action

Brindley may have rejoiced that between the appearance of the first and second newspaper articles audience figures plummeted, but Henry decided to sue the owner of the *Herald*, William Smith, as the publisher of a libel that had caused him to lose income. Henry would not have had enough knowledge of Britain and its laws to have done this on his own initiative. The legal system in Britain was complicated, and he would have needed help not only to realize he had a case but also to bring it to court. Whether he was advised by abolitionists, a schoolmaster in the audience who later gave evidence for him, or his then assistant or he was approached by an opportunistic lawyer, the lawsuit came to Warwickshire Assizes in July 1852. Although the *Herald* was produced in Wolverhampton in neighboring Staffordshire, the publisher, who was also the proprietor of the *Birmingham Mercury*, lived in Birmingham, some 17 miles away in Warwickshire, which is why the case was held in this county. It would also have been explained to Henry that only barristers, not local attorneys, pleaded cases in the higher courts. His attorney Mr. Fleetwood hired two counsel, Kenneth Macaulay, QC, and Mr. Field as his junior. A Queen's Counsel was (and is) a senior barrister, appointed by the monarch on the recommendation of the Lord Chancellor. William Smith's attorney hired Mr. Sergeant Miller, another high-profile (and therefore expensive) barrister, and Mr. Hayes.[6] This must have brought home to Henry the stakes he was playing for to defend his honor and his reputation. Bringing a case to court was a risky move because he would have to meet the costs of both sides' legal fees if he lost.

This was an unusual case so would be of national interest, not least because the plaintiff was a black man, the first I have found to bring such an action to the English courts. This was unrecognized then. In the event, both *The Times* and the *Morning Chronicle*, London newspapers with a national distribution, reproduced most of the original articles. The *Morning Chronicle* also reported the various witnesses' evidence very fully and the proceedings were copied in other provincial newspapers, spreading the derogatory descriptions beyond a limited geographical area, which Henry might never need to revisit, to the whole country and even back to America. He must have been warned about these dangers. James Smith was right: Henry was a gambler, but not just for small stakes in pub games. In his escape he had gambled with his life, in splitting from Smith with his security, and now it was his image and money that were on the line. If he lost, he would become a laughingstock and his career, if not finished, would be severely damaged. He decided to press on; he was not going to take this meekly.

The hearing was on Wednesday, July 28, 1852, at the Assizes in Warwick, the county town, in Court No. 2 in the Shire Hall. This imposing building was built in Corinthian style in the 1750s to house two courtrooms, lodgings for judges, the cells for prisoners, and a military barracks. As Henry entered the court he would have been struck by the elegance of the octagonal room with its finely decorated domed ceiling supported by pillars. The judge presided under the coat of arms of England with the motto of the Order of the Garter, *Honi soit qui mal y pense* (Evil be to him who thinks it). To the judge's right was the jury, to his left the press benches, and the defendant faced him. The witness box was at the end of the jury's seating and slightly in front, so the jury could only hear the evidence. The legal representatives and their assistants sat below in a circular pit. The clerk to the court, who administered oaths and made a record of the proceedings, was also present. A gallery for the public encircled the courtroom above. It was, and is, a surprisingly intimate space. When he took the stand, Henry could have reached over to touch William Smith in the adjacent defendant's box but did not need to look at him unless he turned to his right. Directly in front of him on the opposite side of the courtroom were the press benches. For this day they were his audience, not the jury, whom he could not address without turning around.

Henry was called to give evidence and to prove that the libels had caused him to close early after he had planned to spend a total of three weeks there and also that he had had to cancel other local appearances in and around nearby Birmingham. Before the first review was published his accounts showed

Rory Rennick in the witness box of the No. 2 Court in the Shire Hall, Warwick, where Henry stood to give his evidence. Mr. Rennick is a few inches taller and on the right, many pounds lighter than Henry was, but this gives an indication of how Henry also appeared in the box. The jury sat in the seats on the right of the image, slightly behind the witness box. The railing on the left is in front of the box in which the defendant, William Smith, sat. The air-conditioning units on the public gallery above are anachronistic but cannot be removed because they were in place when it became a listed building.

that receipts on the first night were £7, and £9 9s for the next. The third and subsequent nights were usually the most profitable, but he had only taken 19 shillings on the fifth night, suggesting an audience of fewer than 30 people. Henry needed to hire about a dozen men, costing £13 per week, so that each was getting the average wage of the time. The venue cost £3 3s for the first night, £2 2s the second, and thereafter £1 1s. Advertising was budgeted at about £4 per week. A visit to Bilston, also in Staffordshire, had produced disappointing results: only £7 over six nights, which was not enough to cover his costs. To compensate, he had been forced to travel outside the area covered by the newspaper, and presumably to pay for the expenses of the band and other employees to accompany him. In Tyldesley in Lancashire, some 100 miles from Wolverhampton, he had taken £50 in a week, and in Leigh a few miles away in the same county, £60, which was the average for his appearances. His trip to Kendal in Cumbria had also netted £50. All these places were outside the territory of the *Herald*, so potential audiences would not have been influenced by Brindley's reviews. In consequence of a notice from Smith's lawyer, he had also had the expense of having the panorama transported from Carlisle, which suggests it had been planned to use the visual representation in evidence. No doubt Smith's team hoped to prove that the images were excessive, but must have been disappointed as the panorama was never produced in court. Henry admitted he had referred to this review of his appearance to audiences in other places but he denied he had verbally abused the editor, nor had he called him a "base calumniator."[7]

Since August 1851, after the split with James Smith, Henry's accounts had been delegated to a trusted assistant, and it was Walter Glynn who actually produced the receipt book to corroborate his evidence. There are only a few young men of this name or similar in the 1851 census, so he must be the Dublin-born letterpress printer, aged 22, then living in Manchester with his widowed father and siblings. It was the company of Thomas Lee & Walter Glynn that had printed the British edition of Henry's revised autobiography. Their partnership was dissolved on June 24, 1851, a few months after this publication and at the time of the dissolution of Henry and Smith's partnership.[8] It looks as if Henry had met him in Manchester, they bonded over preparing the new edition for the press, and Glynn decided to throw up the prospect of a solid career to go on the road with the charismatic performer. Henry, with his limited literacy skills, needed someone who could read, write, and keep accounts to replace James Smith. Walter Glynn, who was not in a position to nag him, fitted the bill and may have been the person who told Henry about the libel laws, something printers needed to understand because it was the publisher of a libel, not the writer, who was held legally responsible.

Henry deposed that "a servant" had written a reply to Brindley's accusations, starting off "He who steals my purse steals trash," a quotation from Shakespeare's *Othello*, Act 3, Scene 3, which would have been very familiar to an educated audience. Henry was unlikely to have come across it before; perhaps Glynn had suggested this, too. Iago's speech begins,

> Good name in man and woman, dear my lord,
> Is the immediate jewel of their souls.
> Who steals my purse steals trash.

It concludes,

> But he that filches from me my good name
> Robs me of that which not enriches him
> And makes me poor indeed.

The reference to Othello, the "noble Moor," is apposite. Henry, another maligned black man, was making the point that it was his reputation and good name that were important to him. However, the loss of money was crucial.

To the credit of Smith and Brindley, the case was covered in the *Herald* but it did not report, as the *Morning Chronicle* and other newspapers did, that when Henry gave evidence "though his dress was rather fine and he displayed some jewelry about his person, his manner of giving his evidence was quiet and creditable and his pronunciation altogether very correct." If he was intimidated by his surroundings, he gave no evidence of this. The *Leamington Spa Courier*, published in a town three miles from Warwick, even said Henry "appeared to be an educated man," which must have given him enormous pleasure (barristers are as hungry for good reviews as any performer, and Macaulay would have read the local press reports and fed them back to his clients). Other local newspapers reported the proceedings much as appeared in the national press but added more details of the evidence of a Wolverhampton schoolmaster, William Yateman, which the *Herald* included in abbreviated form. Yateman had been at the presentation and had challenged Brindley over the question about the location of the Dismal Swamp. According to the *Herald* and other newspapers, he reproved both Brindley and Hobbs when they ridiculed Henry. Brindley responded to Yateman by threatening him with a "bonneting," a way of shaming and silencing a man by pulling down his high-crowned hat over his face to the shoulders, breaking the crown and making the speaker both look ridiculous and unable to see or to be heard coherently. Yateman added that he had never known "a grosser misrepresentation than these articles."[9]

In the course of his evidence Henry revealed that he sometimes traveled first class between engagements while his employees went second class, and this caused amusement in the court. Smith's counsel, Sergeant Miller, seems to have attempted a joke and also to mock Henry. According to one account, he asked Henry whether he traveled in a horse box, but the *Herald* reported that he said "a horse box would have been good enough for him" and this "drew upon him a general hiss from the court, and manifestly aggravated the case in the minds of the jury." When Yateman mentioned that Henry sang a song, Miller read out the words of the "Escape of Henry Box Brown" to the hilarity of the court (reading song lyrics in a deadpan voice always gets a cheap laugh). Nor did Miller call witnesses for the defense, relying on the claim this was a personal opinion and saying it "was not only the right but the duty of the press to expose improper exhibitions; that the criticism was a fair one, although severe," remarking "with some severity" on what he termed the indecency of the exhibition, and the positive propriety of exposing it, and concluding by ridiculing the "jewellery bedizened obesity of the runaway slave," declaring that his character had suffered nothing by the criticism.[10]

The judge, Baron Alderson, summed up, saying that the question for the jury to consider was whether the article was a mere criticism on the work of the plaintiff, or whether it was holding him personally open to ridicule, hatred, or contempt, giving examples of Brindley's comments about his appearance and the way he spoke. According to the London *Express*, he "expressed rather a strong opinion with respect to the attacks upon the person of the plaintiff, and made some jocular critical observations on the style in which the notices were written," but even the *Herald* admitted, "His lordship summed up in an able manner." Miller's attempts to mock and denigrate Henry did his client's cause no good with the jury. They took only "a minute or two" to reach their verdict, finding for Henry, who was awarded £100 damages and 40s costs.[11]

For Henry it was a vindication and a great deal of publicity. Coming less than two years after his arrival in the United Kingdom, it was a sweet moment for an ex-slave. In Rhode Island he had won an assault case, but this was his first encounter with English law. He had been brave enough to bring the case, the jury had taken him at his own valuation, and he had come out triumphant. This gave him confidence; he now demanded (not just expected) respect, and in the coming years he was to appear in court several times, both as prosecutor against those who damaged his interests and as defendant fighting his case, rather than submit to what he saw as injustice.

Reactions in Britain

There is no question that Brindley, for whatever reason, allowed his social and racial prejudices to go far beyond reasonable bounds, especially for a journalist who should have been well aware of the libel laws. Although Smith did not immediately dismiss Brindley, he seems to have demoted him; nine months later an announcement that he was leaving the *Herald* described him as the advertising canvasser and collector, not the editor. Brindley's response shows that he had been given notice by Smith, not resigned, and had lost the house that went with the job. In 1853 Brindley seems to have set up another newspaper, the *Wolverhampton Journal*, but not long after he parted from its proprietor Jesse Ascough, in May 1854. This and his threat to bonnet Yateman suggest a man of volatile temperament who did not get on easily with others.[12]

Nor were other journalists pleased at the outcome of the trial. The *Critic*, which reviewed theatrical performances, was concerned about the restrictions on genuine adverse opinions and potential censorship of performers. It covered both Henry's libel case and that of another actor, Benjamin Webster, who had brought a suit against the owner of the *Manchester Guardian* but lost.

Not unnaturally, the *Critic* was dismayed that such cases should be brought to court. The *British Army Despatch* also had reservations about possible censorship but was mainly concerned about what the editor saw as the sentimentality of the abolitionist movement:

> Now, we apprehend in a case like this, malice ought to be shown. Otherwise, who is to set bounds to criticism? Supposing that the *Times* had condemned an exhibition of the sufferings of sweeps, or Manchester mill-slaves, as exaggerated, indecent and absurd, we should like to know what damages would be accorded.... In the case to which we allude, there appears to have been some honest indignation, but no malice. The editor of the Wolverhampton paper is no slave-owner, nor has he, we fully believe, a share in an opposition exhibition of wax-work murderers, or a stuffed mermaid. He merely participated in sentiments we expressed last week, and hates the exaggeration of an unnatural philanthropy, and a mischievous interference in other people's affairs. He does not want to see the common people prepared here by such exhibitions as that of Mr. Box Brown's, for the top-dressing to be administered by Mr. George Thompson, intended to grow a crop of hatred towards our transatlantic children. He does not believe in the cruel stories related of Yankee slaveowners any more than a sensible American believes that we are a nation of Rushes and Tannings, because he has read of murders happening in England. Moreover, he had an intelligent American, Mr. Hobbs, the locksmith, at his elbow, to assure him, rightly or wrongly, that it was an unfair and grossly incorrect representation, calculated to mislead the British public. Under such circumstances he penned a strong article. If the honest belief of a journalist be thus condemned, we must indeed be careful. We are exceedingly glad, for instance, that we did not visit this panorama, and shall take care not to do so; for, if we did, we should certainly speak out. We might have the satisfaction of being tried by a jury of philanthropical cheesemongers, directed by a full-blown attorney from the bench, the sole sentiment of whose life should be a maudlin leaning towards abolitionists; and have thus had to pay a round sum to the portly identity of their black brother, in the well-dressed, jewelled, and intellectual person of Mr. Box Brown.[13]

Again, class prejudice played a part. Juries were composed of householders, generally shopkeepers, and to call them philanthropical cheesemongers indicates Victorian aristocratic prejudice against trade, earning an income through buying and selling, rather than from landownership or service as officers in the armed forces, both of which were regarded in these social classes as far superior occupations. The writer also thought that the "common" people should not be stirred up to hate Americans. Presumably, uncommon people like him were too clever to be swayed.

Reactions in America

Jonas Pekel, who said he was a Briton writing from New York, was happy to report the verdict in a letter to *Frederick Douglass's Paper*. Some American newspapers, like the *New England Farmer* of Boston, Massachusetts, simply reported Henry's case and his victory in a single paragraph, although they slightly misrepresented it, saying it was a critical review rather than a libel:

> Henry Box Brown, a Fugitive Slave, and owner of the panorama representing Southern Slavery, had brought a suit against the proprietor of the Wolverhampton Herald for making a severe criticism on his exhibition. Brown gained a verdict of $500 damages.[14]

Others were more disapproving but restrained:

> We see by the London *Observer* of August 1st, that Henry Box Brown, a fugitive slave, who has figured in some of the Eastern States, and latterly in England at abolition conventions, was plaintiff in an action for libel, brought against an English paper, which had exposed the mendacious character of a panorama which he was exhibiting, purporting to be an illustration of American and African slavery.[15]

Initially the *Boston Post*, like a number of others, carried the one-sentence report, "Henry Box Brown, fugitive slave, and owner, of the panorama representing southern slavery, sued the proprietor of the Wolverhampton Herald for making a severe criticism on his exhibition, and gained a verdict of $600 damages." But a week later it published the most vituperative reaction to appear in any publication, in a lengthy account from someone who must have been present. As there was no chance that Henry would be able to sue this newspaper, the editor was confident he could republish the libelous original articles, as well as insulting attacks on Henry, on abolitionists, and on English people who, like the jury, were sympathetic to slaves. It may also reveal something about the politics of the abolition movement and the contents of Henry's presentation, but as this is such a hostile witness the account needs to be read with caution.

> Mr. Henry Box Brown, who escaped from Richmond to Philadelphia, packed up as luggage, some three years ago, and who was shown off for a hero at several abolition conventions, has been in England, exhibiting a panorama illustrative of slavery, since the spring of 1850. This exhibition he accompanies with oral explanations. For a time he was taken in hand by the leaders of Exeter Hall—then by the provincial abolition societies—then by the George Thompson sect—all of whom consecutively dropped him as rather too dirty a specimen of niggerdom to exhibit out of the zoological garden. For a twelvemonth he has now worked on his own hook, visiting many of the principal towns in both England and Scotland, where he has found a degree of encouragement that is truly surprising, when it is considered that a more dirty specimen of stupidity, vulgarity and indecency, could not well be found under a wooly-head from Boston to New Orleans. He has lately seized upon the nomination of General Pierce as one of the subjects of his caricatures, and the English rabble have been amused with stories about the power of the "slaveocrats," as he styles them, and

their cunning in gulling the north, which, without the cleverness, are on the same level of truth with Baron Munchausen's escapes from imprisonment.

After travelling through the principal towns of Yorkshire, he came to Wolverhampton in Staffordshire, where he met with one sensible man, at least, in the person of Mr Smith, editor of the Wolverhampton Gazette, whose opinion of him is given in the following notices.

Then followed a more or less verbatim republication of the articles in the *Herald* that had provoked the lawsuit. Finally the writer reported the hearing:

Upon these he instituted a suit for libel, and though the whole appearance of the plaintiff on the stand corresponded with the description given of him in the publications, and the summing up of the Baron Alderson was clearly leaning to the opinion that the article in question did not transcend the fair limits of criticism upon a very trashy and mischievous exhibition, but an English jury could not divest itself of the sympathies awakened by a black skin, a verdict of £100 damage was rendered for the plaintiff. It is through the slanders of Brown and such as he, that the fire of hatred towards the United States is kept burning among the lower classes here. Talk of charity for the slaves! Why, from George Thompson down to Henry Brown, or vice versa, for it is difficult to tell which is uppermost, it is purely a money making business, from which all the elements which constitute a respectable method of livelihood are excluded. George Thompson is rich,—Box Brown is getting rich; but for the appropriation of any of their wealth for the relief of a suffering slave—you might as well look for gold mines on Hampton Beach![16]

The correspondent is not identified, but the use of American expressions, like "on his hook," suggests this was a native of the United States. He made some errors: Smith was not the editor of the paper but the publisher, and it was the *Wolverhampton Herald*, not the *Gazette*, that was fined. Brindley would not have made these mistakes. There is evidence that the writer had attended Henry's presentation because no mention of Franklin Pierce appeared in the original newspaper articles. Pierce had been selected as the compromise presidential candidate by the Democratic Party and wanted to maintain the unity of the United States at all costs so had supported the Fugitive Slave Act, which would have given Henry scope for satire.[17] This kind of direct comment on current political issues and attacks on the presidential office was something that mainstream abolitionists avoided, and it may be the element that justified Henry's claim to be the American Kossuth. The most likely author of this piece is Alfred Hobbs, the Bostonian who did not intend to return to his home town to be greeted by ridicule for being bested by a fugitive slave.

The letter writer also falsified the judge's summing up, as "Baron Alderson was clearly leaning to the opinion that the articles in question did not transcend the fair limits of criticism upon a very trashy and mischievous exhibition." The judge did no such thing, which even the *Herald* acknowledged.

Had he expressed this kind of personal view in his judgment, that would have been grounds for an appeal. Alderson stated that while criticism of a performance was justifiable, a personal attack on an individual was not, citing examples which he appears to have treated sardonically. This was suppressed by the writer, so was something the American readership would never have known. There must have been a substantial readership of the publication, perhaps including some abolitionists, who were angered by how America was being represented in Britain so had some sympathy with the writer.

The Abolitionists' Response

It might be expected that such a momentous event—an ex-slave defending his reputation and his integrity and winning a case against a white man who had insulted him—would be supported by his fellows and widely publicized, but there was a deafening silence from abolitionists on both sides of the Atlantic. There was not even any attempt to rebut the *Boston Post* account. It seems that this letter writer was correct: Henry had been dropped by the abolitionists in Britain. Although the motive ascribed was deliberately discreditable to both sides, it contained a kernel of truth. The break from Smith and disassociation from the movement itself by such a popular figure must have seriously angered them.

It was not just Brindley who objected to Henry's personal style. In a private letter to Wendell Phillips in America, William Wells Brown criticized Henry's dress sense, saying that his gold ring on every finger, the gold and brass round his neck, the ruffles on his shirt, and his green dress coat and white hat made him look like a "well dressed monkey" and added that he was to be "pitied." Henry was contravening the image of restrained, gentlemanly decorum that the abolitionists wanted to project. His flashy clothes were too reminiscent of the Zip Coon figure in minstrel shows, the gaudily clad townsman who provoked mockery for his attempt at sophisticated speech, and Wells Brown may have feared that people would see Henry as some kind of parody of himself. Because of the similarity of their names, they were occasionally confused. Ten years later, in 1862, an American publication, the *Independent*, copied an item from another publication that muddled the two and *The Liberator* sent a correction, carefully distinguishing between them. Henry Box Brown, it said, "confined his attention to looking out for No. 1, a work for which he was as competent as any Yankee," while Wells Brown, "beside supporting himself and his family, has always assiduously laboured in the twofold work of overthrowing slavery and inciting the free people of color to aspiration and improvement." Even a decade after Henry had split from the abolition movement, a section at least harbored resentment and spite against him.[18]

Although they had some things in common beyond their surnames, the two men differed in a number of more significant ways, and they must have compared themselves and their receptions by audiences in both the States and Britain. Wells Brown commented on Henry, but there is no record of what Henry thought of his competitor. From comparison of their itineraries, they seem never to have been in the same place in Britain at the same time, and in his accounts of his travels Wells Brown only mentions the Crafts, who often spoke on the same platform. He claimed to have seen Henry but may have been relying on what was being reported to him by contacts in Britain, since Henry would have been soberly dressed in America, where the two did meet and when he was not rich enough to buy jewelry.

The jewelry that Wells Brown deplored served a double purpose. In America there had been, and still were, wildcat banks that took investors' money and then collapsed, leaving them with no recourse to the law or to their money. Wells Brown related his experiment with setting one up.[19] Henry carried his wealth on him so, were he in need of ready cash, the jewelry could be sold or pledged with a pawnbroker until finances improved, which is still a practice among the poor around the world. In addition, dressing extravagantly was expected of people entertaining the working classes, who themselves took pains over their appearance. "No need to be poor and look poor too" was an oft-repeated mantra. Louis Hayes described the orchestral conductor Monsieur Julien, a local star in Manchester, who "always dressed very lavishly" with "a massive gold chain, like a miniature cable, a large diamond shirt stud and a handsome gold watch."[20] As well as emphasizing his newfound prosperity, Henry was showing his largely working-class audiences that he was making an effort to look good for them. Like royalty he dressed up, not down, for his public.

Interpretations

I have recounted the events surrounded the libel case in such detail because it was from many perspectives an important and complex event. It is the first example I have been able to find of a black person bringing a suit for libel in Britain, let alone winning.[21] There may be some complaints of slander (which was spoken) or defamation by black people in the lower courts that heard more mundane matters, but this seems to be another area in which Henry was a trailblazer.

Although described with hostility, the details of the content of his presentation at this stage in his career appear nowhere else so far found. The response of newspapers, in both Britain and America, indicate both his fame and the different points of view that sections of the populace on both sides of the Atlantic held on the abolition question. Everyone who has written about Henry in Britain has described this event, partly because it is so sensational and partly as an illustration of their particular thesis. Unfortunately, very few seem to have looked at the original accounts, either in the *Herald* or in the many other newspapers that covered the court case.[22] The most common response has been that it proves British racism. On this spectrum in Victorian Britain, Brindley was at one end and, although the individual prejudices of the jury are irrecoverable, at least twelve men swiftly opposed one man's bigotry, and the judge, while maintaining professional standards, seems to have been sympathetic. The public watching the proceedings also took Henry's side, hissing Smith's counsel when he made a distasteful joke. Granted, not everyone approved of everything Henry did, but as anyone working in a job requiring public approbation soon realizes, the only way to be uncritically loved is to get a dog. A range of reactions is the norm for any performer, and to concentrate solely on a single, high-profile example of extreme, untypical hostility risks sensationalism and misrepresentation.

Daphne Brooks does recognize that Brindley was a lone and extreme voice but, like other commentators, focuses on this exceptional event and the reenactment of Henry's escape in Leeds (discussed earlier). As the subtitle of her book *Bodies in Dissent* indicates, she is interested in "Spectacular Performances of Race and Freedom." She offers thought-provoking arguments about how entertainers from a variety of backgrounds used different ways to present their bodies to challenge standards concepts of color, but because she is interested in the remarkable and exciting she does not look the other hundred or so run-of-the-mill appearances that Henry made without any similar degree of hostility or of libelous remarks, even, as will be seen, when his appearance became more fantastic than the green coat and white hat that Wells Brown condemned.[23]

John Ernest cites Brooks and others who make claims of racism and discrimination on the basis of very little evidence. Although he admits Henry was "greatly popular throughout England" he says that he "often met with considerable disapproval," but is able to cite only this single, extreme example of the *Herald* case.[24]

Marcus Wood rightly looks at the "distance between what the English and American abolitionists wanted to take from Brown, and conversely what Brown wanted to make of himself," and observes that in Wolverhampton Henry "drew on commercial and creative resources which white abolitionists shied away from." However, he does not refer to the content of the libelous articles, but just footnotes Blackett's *Building an Anti-Slavery Wall* and states that there were two publications that carried the story, calling the first the *Wolverhampton and Staffordshire Gazette*, a publication that never existed, and then saying that the *Herald* went further. This and other references, like saying that Henry jumped out of his box as part of his act (I have found no report of this), further suggest he did not consult original sources and made unsupported claims. These claims are repeated by Britt Rusert, indicating that she used his account.[25]

Audrey A. Fisch is the most emphatic, seemingly regarding Brindley as typical of the British public. She acknowledges the verdict but she considers that it "illustrates the complexity of British racism." Although she notes that Henry was popular and quotes other, laudatory, pieces, she shares Brindley's patrician disdain for what she calls Henry's "buffoonery," contrasting it with Sarah Parker Remond's "ladylike" presentations. Like Brindley and the writer of the *Boston Post* piece, she condemns the fact that Henry made money. Her format to examine the reception of various fugitive slaves in Britain (not just Henry) is fresh and interesting. The opening of each chapter consists of an extract from a letter, a newspaper article, a novel, or a speech, which she uses to critique British society. The piece she uses to look at Henry's reception is a letter to the New York *Express*, reprinted in the English *Anti-Slavery Standard*. Like the writer to the *Boston Post*, who said the English jury "could not divest itself of the sympathies awakened by a black skin," this correspondent also said that, having run through fashions for Chinese, Asiatics, Turks, and Moors, "nothing goes down, now, with her [Britannia], so well as the genuine black." Although recognizing this was bombastic and ungenerous, Fisch concludes it was in essence true and attributes the verdict in the court case and the praise for Henry's performances elsewhere to three factors: Britain's smug expression of moral superiority, the British public's unhealthy "Negrophilism," and/or its fascination with the exotic.[26] However, she makes no mention of the influence in both America and Britain of the American Phineas T. Barnum (1810–98), the premier showman presenting the exotic and the freakish at this time, nor of the 1851 Great Exhibition, which had awakened the public's interest in different cultures across the world, especially in the British Empire, which encompassed all skin colors.

I have another, more important, reservation about her conclusions. The American letter writers to the New York *Express* and the *Boston Post* claimed that a black skin was enough to win sympathy in Britain, and they are not isolated examples. This assertion provided both a comforting narrative and a distraction for members of the American public, sensitive to criticism of their society where, in both the South and the North, black people faced prejudice and segregation. If criticism of these moral issues could be dismissed as the credulity and ignorance of people who were influenced by a single, literally surface, factor, Americans did not need to confront the true underlying concerns. It is an example of the kind of logical fallacy called *ignoratio elenchi* or, more popularly, a red herring.

As events, especially court reports published in British papers, demonstrate, color alone made little or no difference; the crucial factor in gaining public sympathy was enslavement. The transcripts of his evidence in Warwick that were reported in newspapers show that Henry's counsel wisely got him to recount his experiences as a slave at length, emphasizing the selling of his wife and children, and this must have been an element in the jury's verdict, rather than his color alone. The details of his income and expenditure and how hard he worked for his money would also have resonated with trades-men, who had similar considerations. They saw in him someone like them-selves and one who had suffered not because of the color of his skin but because of his enslavement.

Black people were not apparently (but more research needs to be done) treated any worse by the courts, but nor were they favored. It was only those who said they had been enslaved who got public sympathy and money, as many newspapers reports about fraudsters attest. Their skin color did not allow them to escape punishment. In 1858, for example, *The Times* reported that Charles Williams, "a tall black man," had been begging with a sign round his neck saying he was a fugitive slave. His Irish wife said he was a sailor but had recently taken up begging, claiming to have been enslaved. Women too tried to profit. Sarah Amelia Rosa Mungo was said to have attacked a woman with a poker, and in the course of the hearing at a magistrates' court in Lon-don it was alleged she was someone who had previously elicited "so vast an amount of sympathy at one of the police-courts by stating herself to be a fugitive slave." She was sent to trial.[27]

Others carried out more successful scams, like George Brine, self-styled King of the Beggars. He and another itinerant were in competition to accom-pany a black woman who came from New Orleans with her young son to try to find her British seafaring husband because both realized how profitable this appealing couple could be. Brine won and concocted a story about the women being a fugitive slave that was successful in raising public sympathy and money in a way a woman, of whatever color, searching for an errant hus-band would not be.[28]

Alfred Wood conducted a different fraud. He seems to have been a gen-uine Baptist minister and claimed to be raising funds for his church in Liberia where, he said, among his congregation were George and Eliza Harris, char-acters from *Uncle Tom's Cabin*, and he said that he had attended the deathbed of another, Cassy, who had died shortly after her arrival in Liberia. Not only were the British public generous, they were credulous, seeming to accept the novel as truth.[29]

This kind of exploitation of public sympathy was why genuine refugees from enslavement needed to carry references and endorsements from figures of authority, like church ministers. If a black skin alone were enough to elicit support and money, there would be no need for such testimonials. In citing the case of another fraudster, Reuben Nixon, a free man from New York who traveled Britain using a variety of aliases and was extremely successful, Fisch does not seem to consider this. Instead, she links Nixon to criticisms made of Frederick Douglass and tries to make a case (I think but I cannot entirely follow her line of argument) for this being another example of her thesis that Victorians wanted to consume horrors.[30] It was never just Victorian Britons who liked their news sensational. News consists of the exceptional, and dramatic reporting has always been the nature of a section of the media both in the past and today, whether in print, in broadcast radio and television, or on the Internet.

The revolution of 1776 when Americans had made liberty from Britain a rallying cry still had a potent legacy, but now Britain was genuinely morally superior in the matter of the kind of liberty from tyranny on which America prided herself. Members of the British public had every right to feel a little smug; their slave trade and then slavery in their colonies had been abolished because of public pressure. The government had devoted resources to suppressing the trade, then following abolition in 1834 paid out substantial sums to compensate slaveholders.[31] Fisch might have acknowledged that there was some justification for this self-congratulation, but she could also have observed that Americans were equally justified in pointing out that conditions for the poor in the mines and factories of Britain were not much better than enslavement, on which the British were open to similar moral criticism, as Brindley said.

Scene 3

New Directions

Wells Brown may have pitied Henry, but Henry was not pitying himself. He had won the libel case and must have been reveling in his freedom. In 1849, according to Mr. McKim, who was present when Henry arrived in his box in Philadelphia, he weighed about 200 pounds. At five feet, eight inches tall, this gives a body mass index (BMI) of 32, which is today defined as clinically obese.[1] Even if the weight were overestimated, he was still very heavy for his height. In England he could indulge himself not only in the drinks Smith listed but in good food, which was cheaply available in towns. Meat, often denied to slaves, formed a large part of the meals in eating houses. Wells Brown lists the menu recited to him by a waiter in London: "Ox tail, Sir; gravy soup; carrot soup, Sir; roast beef; roast pork; boiled beef; roast lamb; boiled leg of mutton, Sir, with caper sauce; jugged hare, Sir; boiled knuckle of veal and bacon; roast turkey and oyster sauce; sucking pig, Sir; curried chicken; harrico [*sic*] mutton, Sir." The variety of dishes on offer might have been a reflection of the size of London's population, but in the provinces there was also a great variety available. Louis Hayes recalled the foods of his youth in mid–19th century Manchester. Pigs' trotters and tripe (cows' stomach, cooked with onions, often in milk) were sold from stalls in the street, and there were cookhouses and eating houses "where the windows were always filled with an abundance of savory pies in fins, cut in squares and huge legs of underdone roast pork, absolutely bursting out with stuffing of sage and onions. Everything in the shop looked greasy and swimming in rich gravy."[2]

Being what today is called overweight and having a large "corporation" or stomach was then considered better for a man than being underweight. Not only did extra weight protect from tuberculosis, a scourge at the time, it also gave reserves to support the body during a long or debilitating illness, again common before the mid–20th century, and it displayed wealth, being able to afford good food and a lot of it. Henry's size is occasionally noted in reports of his appearances, and what they mention is his girth, his waist measurement. The word "portly," as Brindley described him, was also used by other journalists, and in the portrait used in the first edition of his *Narrative*, the buttons of the waistcoat over his stomach seem to be under some strain. This portrait also showed him looking bulkier than other fugitives of the time, but this may be partly from muscles developed in his work in the tobacco factory. One British reporter later called him "brawny."[3]

Wells Brown might have been critical, but all the publicity around the libel case did Henry no harm at all. It probably helped. He brought out another issue of his *Narrative* and continued touring. One effect the Wolverhampton case had was to focus interest on his command of English, which was afterward occasionally mentioned. This might be because of the stereotyped language used in minstrel

Engraving of Henry Box Brown in 1849, from the first edition of his *Narrative*. By the time he had been in Britain for 18 months he was dressing more extravagantly, but this was said to be an accurate likeness, the only one so far found. British Library, London, UK. © British Library Board. All rights reserved/Bridgeman Images.

shows and by what were called nigger comedians, but it may also be because the libel case had been a salutary lesson for journalists: "His pronunciation is clear and his language at times good. A few grammatical errors are overlooked by his hearers"; "his description and anecdotal matter, spoken in most excellent English, is much admired"; "well versed in his English diction"; "Mr Brown is the best Negro speaker of the English language we have ever heard, and he has mastered the subject of his lecture exceedingly well."[4]

Scotland and a Revelation on Tyneside

Perhaps hoping that the furor caused by the case in Wolverhampton, which was reported by newspapers in every county of England, would not

have been as widely reported in Scotland, Henry set off north of the border.
In August he was in Kirkcaldy and in September some 12 miles (20 km) to
the south in Edinburgh, the capital of Scotland. In both places he seems to
have stuck to his standard presentation with no gimmicks. After the libel
case he probably felt the need, especially in Presbyterian Scotland, to show
himself to be a sober, respectable, antislavery advocate. However, he did
not completely escape the echoes of the Wolverhampton case. The *Greenock Advertiser* briefly mentioned his success in the libel case and reported
his appearances in Edinburgh in a single paragraph but could not resist a
sneer:

> Mr. Box Brown, the man of colour who recently figured as prosecutor of the
> Staffordshire *Herald* in action of libel, is at present in Edinburgh, with his
> panorama descriptive of the details of slavery in America. Mr. Brown is in good
> physical condition, looking more like a sable alderman than itinerant dealer in
> notions.[5]

Aldermen, who administered the local government of large towns and
cities, were notorious for living well at public expense. Calling him "an
itinerant dealer in notions" also made Henry seem like a peddler of cheap
trifles.

Only reports of these two appearances in Scotland have been found.
Henry may have made others, publicized locally with handbills rather than
in the press, but he never returned. His style must have been too exuberant
for straitlaced Scots. By October he was back in northeast England, appearing
in Newcastle-upon-Tyne and neighboring South Shields and North Shields
on either side of the river Tyne in the present-day county of Tyne and Wear.
Newcastle was the home of the Quaker Richardson family, active in the abolitionist cause, and it was sisters-in-law Ellen and Anna Richardson who had
led the campaigns to purchase the freedoms of both Frederick Douglass and
William Wells Brown. Anna sent out digests of antislavery stories to British
newspaper editors to keep the issue in the news, and one of her leaflets had
first made the British public aware of Henry's story, a year before his actual
arrival. He might not have been, as a local paper observed, "so accomplished
a speaker as Frederick Douglas [*sic*] or W.W. Brown," but he was received
with what looks like universal approbation in an area that prided itself on its
abolitionist credentials. Walter Glynn was still working with him and joined
Henry in singing "Negro Melodies."[6]

He went south along the coast to Hartlepool, Co. Durham, in November
and then on to Hull in Yorkshire in early December. At the end of November
he sent a letter to a local newspaper, the *Sunderland News and North of
England Advertiser*, in response to some comment by the newspaper's editor.
Unfortunately, issues before May 1855 are no longer extant so there is only

Henry's reply, because it was reprinted in numerous local and national newspapers:

There is no man, I care not who he be, black or white, has felt the loss of his wife and children more than I. I have borne the galling chains, the tyrant's threats and more than that, I have seen my wife sold and bartered from one villain to another, and still clung to her and my children as long as they remained in Richmond. At length a fatal hour arrives: my wife is sold off to a wretch, not to work in the cotton field or rice plantation but, as she was handson [sic], for a purpose I cannot here name, but leave you and the public to judge. Bereft of my wife and children and all the comfort that even the hapless slave enjoys, I resolved to be free. I obtained my liberty. I travel in the free states, and denounce slavery and slaveholders. I appeal to the public for assistance to buy my wife and children. I obtain the money: I offer it; I am refused. I raise more money; I offer twice their commercial value, and the reply of their owners is—You shall not have them. I have tried, sir, and others have tried and the remorseless slaveholder still holds her and my children in bondage; and before I left the States, behold my wife gave birth to another slave: the master is, sir, its father![7]

Immediately after his escape he told Lucretia Mott he had heard from or about Nancy and the children two or three times. Unfortunately, he seems not to have told her what he had heard.[8] The most likely explanation is rape, but it was not unknown for enslaved women to calculate that sexual relations with masters could improve their treatment and that of any resulting child. Although Henry had stopped saying he wanted to redeem his wife as well as his children early in his period in Britain, James Smith's letters to abolitionists in America at the time of their split made it clear that he could then have purchased them. This letter might therefore be questioned as Henry's attempt to start again with another wife (as Smith had stated he wanted to do), but that would be too easy to disprove. Both slaveholders in America, sensitive to claims of immorality, and the abolitionists in America and Britain who were displeased at Henry's declaration of independence from them had cause to deny the truth of what he claimed. But none did, even though this account was widely reproduced.

Why Henry chose this time and place to give this startling information is a matter for speculation. He must have been asked about purchasing his wife and children by members of his audiences since so many other fugitives, like James Watkins, made this a major point. At the time of their split James Smith claimed Henry was looking to marry again, although, according to Smith, Nancy's master was prepared to sell her if Henry "would treat her kindly." This could be interpreted as evidence of previous domestic abuse, but in the light of this letter, indicating that Henry had known about the master's child before he left the United States, it is more likely that the master was trying to ensure that Henry would take her back and even pay for the freedom of the child. But this must have been a step too far for Henry. His masculinity, newly discovered in Britain, would be again belittled by this constant reminder of the control of a master over a female slave and whose power to cuckold so arrogantly her husband would reduce him to figurative impotence.

In America, according to Moses Grandy's autobiography, it was common practice to allow slaves to remarry if they were separated.

> It will be observed that the narrator married a second wife, without having heard of the decease of the first. To explain this fact, it is necessary to state, that the frequent occurrence of cases where husbands and wives, members of Christian societies, were finally separated by sale, led the ministers, some years ago, to deliberate on the subject: they decided that such a separation might be considered as the death of the parties to each other, and they therefore agreed to consider subsequent marriages not immoral.[9]

Certainly Henry's autobiography makes it clear he believed his marriage was over when Nancy was marched away with their children, and his master also believed this, telling him he could get another wife. Although this may have been accepted practice in America, it was far harder to defend in Britain, where cases of bigamy were regularly brought to court and severely punished with imprisonment.

Henry would have been well aware of the need to present himself as respectable in such an important center of the abolition movement as Newcastle-upon-Tyne was at this time. It was led by the Richardsons, who, through the Quaker network, would have been in touch with abolitionists across Britain and in America. James Smith's allegation that Henry was not intending to redeem his wife but to get a new one in England by now must have arrived back in Britain and may have been communicated to the editor of the *Sunderland News and North of England Advertiser* when reporting his appearance. Henry could not at this moment afford to sacrifice the good opinion of any section of the public, and it was no use arguing that to regard a marriage as dissolved when the spouse was sold was normal in America. Quaker women, who had a near-equal status with men within the Society of Friends, raised the main female voices, loudly and constantly, and the Richardson family abounded in them. If he were confronted by people with a strong local power and contacts in the antislavery movement around the whole country, Henry may have felt pressured to reveal something so deeply painful to justify and exonerate himself. It is still a matter of shame for men if they cannot protect their women from sexual abuse and also if they are humiliated by a partner's betrayal, so it is understandable that he never told James Smith what he had heard, especially as Smith seems to have been happy to discuss Henry's personal matters with outsiders and semi-strangers.

A New Subject

Although Henry must have been kept busy by the need to vindicate himself both in the press and to people to whom he was speaking, he would have heard about the literary sensation sweeping the country. Harriet Beecher Stowe's *Uncle Tom's Cabin; or Life Among the Lowly* started in 1851 as a serial in an abolitionist periodical in America. His hosts and members of his audiences would have spoken of it and questioned him about how realistic it was. Even before the end of its serialization in the *National Era*, an American abolitionist periodical, so popular was *Uncle Tom's Cabin* that it was published as a novel in Boston, Massachusetts, in March 1852. It was an immediate bestseller and two months later appeared in England, where it was given a different subtitle, "or Negro Life in the Slave States of America." British reviewers were lavish in their praise of Mrs. Stowe's work. In their notices there was often a subtext of smug congratulation that Britain was morally superior in having abolished slavery. Some of the reviews in British newspapers mentioned Henry. He was not the only fugitive slave speaking at this time, but he was, in part thanks to the Wolverhampton libel case, the one with the highest profile.

By September a dramatization of Mrs. Stowe's work was being advertised at the Great National Standard Theatre, the largest in London, and the Royal Olympic Theatre, also in London, put on a rival production. There were at least eight different dramatic versions in the following few years. A reviewer observed that in order to put a story that was not easy to dramatize on stage it was necessary to distort characters and events in the novel quite significantly, so that in the end "universal bliss reigns." He also noted that in this production "the piece is made up of the ordinary buffooneries of the stage nigger." Nevertheless, the audience greeted the announcement that it would continue until further notice with "vociferous cheering."[10] The story became a firm favorite with both readers and theatergoers for decades, although the usual presentation, with minstrelsy songs, made it much more of a musical than a straight drama. It also created some persistent stereotypes: the loyal, faithful servant, Uncle Tom, the maternal mammy, and the cheeky "piccaninny," epitomized by Topsy. The strong emphasis on Christian faith and the sentimentality of many of the episodes, especially the death scenes, were entirely in accord with the fashions of the time but now make it of historical literary interest only.

Copyright law was not yet internationally defined or implemented. As well as unauthorized dramatizations, pirated editions were published. A number of British publishers produced different editions at prices to suit all purses and purposes. Stowe herself came to England in April 1853, largely to negotiate about copyright on her next novel, *Dred, a Tale of the Great Dismal Swamp*, another story about slavery in the South. Henry never got the chance to meet her. As far as can be ascertained, of the fugitive slaves in Britain at that time Wells Brown was the only one invited to meet her, a few months after her arrival. Harriet Beecher Stowe attended events organized by prominent women, like the Duchess of Sutherland, but seems not to have spoken publicly about her book or any other matter because that was regarded as unwomanly. Although the more famous of the couple, she was often reported as a mere appendage to her husband, "the Rev. Beecher Stowe and his accomplished lady." A *Key to Uncle Tom's Cabin* was published about the same time to answer Stowe's critics, who claimed that this teacher from Connecticut had never visited a Southern plantation. She said that the memoir of Josiah Henson, a slave in Maryland who had escaped to Canada, was one of the major sources of her novel.[11] Although he never seems to have met her, Henry was planning to profit from her work.

A Foray into Acting

After York, Henry went on to Preston in Lancashire, where he advertised that his first appearance of six would be on February 28, 1853. He was very popular in this town. He had visited it two years earlier, but enthusiasm was undimmed and he prolonged his stay, claiming that this would be his farewell exhibition of the panorama before retiring.[12] There was then a two-month gap until the end of May because he needed to take time off to prepare for a momentous change of direction. James Scott, the lessee of the Royal Adelphi and Parisian Promenade Concert Hall in Blonk Street, Sheffield, must have seen Henry present his panorama and been impressed by his personality and delivery, and Scott asked Henry to perform in an entertainment based on *Uncle Tom's Cabin* at the Adelphi Theatre in Sheffield. The statement that his appearance in Preston would be the last indicated that he was planning to give up touring with the panorama for an entirely different role.

Henry would not be the first black actor on the British stage. As a young man, Ignatius Sancho (c. 1729–80) considered treading the boards but had a slight lisp or some other vocal peculiarity that militated against this. In the 1770s a young black actress played Polly in a production of *The Threepenny Opera* in Lancashire and also Juliet in *Romeo and Juliet*. The African American Ira Aldridge (1807–67) is the best known. By 1825 he was playing leading roles on the London stage, but at this time he was touring Eastern Europe. In Britain productions of *Uncle Tom's Cabin* were being performed by white players in black makeup, so although he would not be the first black actor, Henry would be rare, and to the impresario this must have seemed a winning combination. But Scott was nevertheless cautious. The actual agreement was only finalized at the last minute in May, meaning Henry was not being paid for two months. He was hired for two weeks for a total fee of £34, which was considerably lower than the amount he could expect to earn from his panorama. He must have been willing to take this sum to gain experience and another possible form of income. Henry was probably not aware that Scott was an unscrupulous entrepreneur, who had been involved in legal wrangles with the proprietors of other Sheffield theaters. In fairness, it must be added that all the theater managers in the town were frequently in dispute with each other, arguing over activities that ignored or tried to exploit the differences in the laws covering theaters and other places and forms of entertainment.[13] Scott hired Henry to appear in an entertainment based on *Uncle Tom's Cabin*. It was not a full-scale drama, in order to evade the legal restrictions on his kind of venue, but probably included theatrical scenes, or monologues, interspersed with songs.

Getting Henry to perform in scenes from the current bestseller must have looked like a smart move on Scott's part, but there were factors he had not thought through. Two years after Aldridge's London debut, in 1827 Leman Thomas Rede (1799–1832) published *The Road to the Stage, A Practical Manual for Aspiring Actors*. As well as a directory of theaters and managers, the costumes performers were expected to supply, and tips on makeup, he also gave advice on acting itself. Rede offered an early Stanislavskian *aperçu*, "If the actor cannot feel what he utters, it would be useless to attempt to make him run the gauntlet of emotions by rule," and described the recognized methods of conveying specified emotions, by which audiences were made aware of what was being represented in the way that classical Japanese Noh plays employ stylized gestures. Grief, advised Rede, is conveyed by "beating the head or forehead, tearing the hair, and catching the breath as is by choking; also by screaming, weeping, stamping, lifting the eyes from time to time to heaven, and hurrying backwards and forwards." Such contortions were necessary on stage, where subtle facial expressions would only be seen by those in the front rows of the audience, but contemporary parallels can be found in the exaggerated style employed in television soap operas. Rede added that the gestures, "if not well contrived and equally as well executed, frequently [fail] of the desired effect."[14] As Henry's account of parting from his wife and children shows, real heartbreak manifests itself in a bleaker, less overt way. Charles Dickens, a talented and experienced amateur actor, gave highly successful readings of his novels because he could conjure up his characters so they appeared before his audiences, but he had learned his craft over a long time and it was how he wrote his novels, acting out the events and the characters' emotions in his study. Henry, however, had had no practice in the established theatrical conventions for conveying grief, so he probably looked as awkward as he no doubt felt when required to convey this or any other strong emotion. It was different when he was simply speaking to an audience. His emotions were genuine as he recounted his experiences, and he could also use stillness and silence to allow his listeners to put themselves in his place.

Moving from the kind of dramatic lecturing Henry did with the panorama and his box to acting looked like logical step, but there are significant differences between these types of performance. Lecturers have a script, but they appear as themselves. They may tell anecdotes or read from a document in a semi-dramatized fashion, but that is a long way from inhabiting another character, which is not necessary; their audiences are in general more interested in the content than the delivery. It is clear from reports of his speaking engagements that Henry was amusing, which is always a bonus in a lecturer but is not essential.

There is no description of the entertainment in which Henry starred and there are no further details about who wrote it. Scott may have fancied himself as a writer or may have hired a local person with whom he had worked before. Whether it was the script or the delivery, or more likely a combination of the two, this interpretation of *Uncle Tom's Cabin* did not engage the enthusiasm of the public in Sheffield. After five days, Scott refused to allow Henry to perform any more. Henry continued to show up at the venue as his agreement required but was refused entry and was not paid anything at all. This resulted in a court case to recover the agreed sum, which was heard on July 28, 1853, in the County Court. Scott countersued him for £50, alleging breach of agreement. When he presented no evidence of this, judgment was given in Henry's favor and he was awarded £40, plus expenses and costs, but it was an empty victory because Scott was declared bankrupt a few months later and one of his many creditors was Henry, still owed £34.[15]

Underemployment

After this court case there are no reports of any appearances for the rest of the year, apart from a report in October that Henry had given his musical entertainment with his "troupe of negro harmonists" in Rochdale and in November that Mr. Box Brown's troop of Sable Harmonists from Vauxhall (in London) was performing in the Philosophical Hall in Huddersfield, Yorkshire, some 20 miles (32 km) to the northeast. There were a number of minstrel groups under this or a similar name. A few months earlier the Sable Harmonists, or American Serenaders, had caused "an immense sensation, unintermitted applause and roars of laughter" on the bill of an entertainment in Dublin. There were six singers in the group, but none is named in any of the advertisements or reviews. They appeared on the same bill as the Ethiopian

Ballet Troop and remained there until September. When in the following year the Ethiopian Ballet appeared in Whitehaven in Cumbria, it was billed as "real Negroes," so these Sable Harmonists may also have been black. Henry perhaps decided after the strains of the year to join a singing group and have a rest from the responsibility of managing a demanding schedule. He could have stored his panorama with a sympathetic person and joined these Sable Harmonists or another group trading on its name. In Macclesfield, Walter Glynn was mentioned as the manager of the Sable Harmonists troupe, which does suggest Henry was involved with them, and probably singing as well. Here they appeared for a week and had a good audience, except on one day when money had to be returned.[16]

Although this is speculation, it may suggest how Henry got through periods without any lecture bookings. He had a good voice, and in Victorian England this would have always been a way to supplement his income. The diary of Charles Rice, a young man who worked at the British Museum by day and at night supplemented his earnings with singing in taverns in London, detailed how much casual employment was available. Rice's repertoire was mainstream, and he mentioned Sambo Sutton (c. 1817–1851), a popular black prizefighter who enlivened his matches with songs and tricks. He performed on several occasions at a pub in Soho.[17] I have found no newspaper reports of performances by either Rice or Sutton in public houses; it is clear that a lot of entertainment and many of the entertainers in Victorian England were simply not newsworthy. Henry may well have done some casual tavern singing, or joined ensembles in order to keep money to live on coming in.

It must have been a bleak period in his life. After the theatrical failure in Sheffield, it would have been galling to see that *Uncle Tom's Cabin* was everywhere in some form or another in the latter part of 1853. During December, to take advantage of the Christmas market, there were exhibitions of scenes from *Uncle Tom's Cabin* on display in Sheffield, Lancaster, Milnthorpe, and Chelmsford. At the same time, a dramatization "as acted at the Theatre Royal Drury Lane" came to the Theatre in Cardiff and a touring company was visiting Herefordshire, going on to Monmouth and Ross and neighboring Abergavenny in Wales. Dramatizations were also staged in Hanley and Portsmouth on the south coast. Another was in Ireland. Beyond dramas based on the novel, others jumped on the fashionable bandwagon. In Poole, Dorset, a local composer entertained an audience with his own compositions based on the novel. On his travels Henry could have had a drink in an Uncle Tom's Cabin. There was one in Dewsbury, one in Stoke-on-Trent, and one in Bristol, and there must have been others. Even William Wells Brown responded to the sensation. On December 12 he appeared at Hereford near the Welsh border and on the following day in nearby Leominster, delivering a lecture on

American Slavery and another on *Uncle Tom's Cabin*, illustrated with "splendid dissolving views." A full account of his lecture occupied nearly three columns in the local newspaper there.[18]

Henry could not now afford to retire from lecturing, as he had intimated in Preston. At this time the system of support for the poor, unemployed, and sick in England and Wales was administered through a complex web of legislation under the umbrella term "the Poor Laws." Henry did not qualify under any of the provisions: he was not born in England or Wales; he did not have a place of residence where he had lived for more than a year; he had never served an apprenticeship in Britain; nor had he worked for wages for more than a year in a single parish, nor been employed as a parish official. Although if he were to become ill he would be taken into the workhouse infirmary as a matter of common humanity, while he was a fit, single man he would be expected to scrape a living by doing any work that came along or by begging, but that was legally problematic.

It was a situation many fugitive slaves faced. Wells Brown met one of these refugees near Temple Bar in the City of London in 1849. He had escaped from slavery in Maryland but had not felt himself secure in New York so had traveled to Liverpool "by the kindness of the captain." In Liverpool he had been unable to get work and had come to London but had no success there either; his skill, like Henry's, was in tobacco.[19] Britain had more than enough agricultural laborers. Even William Craft, who was a cabinetmaker and carpenter, had problems gaining a living that could support his wife and growing family.

Uncle Tom's Cabin Revived

There was nothing else on the horizon, so at the beginning of 1854 Henry got back on the speaking treadmill, but with a new subject. His free time, however miserably spent reflecting on his failed acting ambitions, had given him time to prepare it. This was unveiled in Hanley in Staffordshire on January 23, 1854; he too was going to present *Uncle Tom's Cabin*, but in a format he was familiar with. His advertisement said that he would be exhibiting pictorial illustrations painted by Signor Antonia [*sic*] Abecca and Signor Vincenti di Lonardo, late artists of Naples, for two nights. These were actually musicians who had appeared with him in Wolverhampton, and they appear in no catalogue or directory of professional artists. Most likely they had some experience of scene painting in theaters and, multitalented, had done the work to help an old friend. Perhaps Henry had been occasionally singing with them in the intervening 18 months.

Then he moved on to Newcastle-under-Lyme in Staffordshire, where he announced that after visits to Tunstall, Hanley, and Burslem he would be making his farewell to towns in England. His last day in Burslem was scheduled for February 4, but he did not announce the subject of the presentation. This new panorama had proved to be a costly failure. The audiences expected him to talk about himself, and the difference between his firsthand experience, which was in a factory, not on a plantation, and Stowe's sentimental literary creation was too great. Wells Brown was able to blend the two more successfully. He was well read and wrote fiction himself and could even speak with authority about the author, as, with his daughters and the Crafts, he had attended a soirée for Harriet Beecher Stowe in Oxford in June 1853. For at least the next six months, *Uncle Tom's Cabin* formed a regular element in Wells Brown's speaking engagements and he used illustrations of some of the scenes. The last reference to Wells Brown's "dissolving views" comes in Leominster in December, but whether this was his slavery panorama, which he was still using at this time, or scenes from *Uncle Tom's Cabin* is not specified. Then the association between Wells Brown and the novel seems to have ended. The reason that both Henry and Wells Brown did not have much success with lecturing about the novel may simply be that audiences almost anywhere could see more exciting dramatizations on stage. As the review of a London production, already described, showed, it was not considered a great work of literature, just a sensational page-turner, so audiences would be less interested in hearing a discussion about it rather than seeing it.[20]

Henry appeared in Longton, near Hanley, in mid–February 1854 and announced another farewell appearance in Birmingham, where he would be presenting his original panorama at the Odd Fellows Hall in April, at a tea party to celebrate the fifth anniversary of this Friendly Society.[21] Henry may have needed their help because he was having problems. He announced a further farewell entertainment in Derby in April. Although news was highly local at this time, he was pushing his luck, constantly drumming up audiences by suggesting this was their last chance to see him. After the failure of the entertainment and the lectures on *Uncle Tom's Cabin*, he may genuinely have thought his career was finished. Maybe he was bored after three years of saying the same thing night after night and getting in and out of his box, which would be more difficult if good living had further increased his girth. Traveling alone may have become wearisome. Wells Brown seems to have stayed with people in the abolitionist movement, who were prosperous and middle class with room in their houses for guests and probably for free, or he stayed in good hotels, the cost of which may have been met in part by abolitionist organizations or individuals. Even with the costs of traveling with his panoramas, he seems to have been able to afford better accommodation and more congenial company than Henry. At the 1851 census Wells Brown was one of nine people staying at the Bull & Mouth Hotel in Leeds, Yorkshire, one of the busiest coaching inns in Leeds and with more staff than guests, while Henry was in a small coffee house in Burnley.[22]

Whether in 1854 Walter Glynn was still traveling with him is not known, but it looks as though by this time he had left the act. There is no more mention of the two singing together, and the musical acts billed with Henry in Hanley were Jacob Somes and S. Chettle, players of the accordion and flutina. At the 1861 census Private W. Flynn was in Farnborough Barracks in Hampshire, so he had probably left his service at the time when Henry was experiencing problems and planning to leave the business. Henry may have been feeling lonely, but by May 1854 he had recovered from whatever had triggered his plan to retire. He was in Nottingham "being nightly visited by large, respectful and delighted audiences" and received enthusiastic reviews of his performance:

> Mr. Brown delivers his lecture on the history and horrors of slavery with much eloquence and effect, and calls down repeated bursts of applause … his descriptions and anecdotal matter, spoken in most excellent English, is much admired.

Maybe all he needed was to be appreciated and to have company. He was invited to speak by the Working Man's Improvement Society in Loughborough on four evenings at the end of June, where he was accompanied by two accordionists, and sang his "Escape from Slavery" to the tune of "Uncle Ned." With Thomas Frodsham in place of Chettle, the three appeared in Leicester at the beginning of July, where not just his performance was praised but also his personality:

> We have seen and conversed with him, and find him highly intellectual, and possessing those pleasing powers of conversational eloquence which at once attract, as his personal appearance and manners do, attention to him as a man far beyond the general appreciation of his class.

There was no more talk of giving up. In September he appeared for a few days in Oxford, but his performance was not reviewed in the press.[23]

Henry may have spent some time singing with an ensemble somewhere or appearing in venues that were advertised by handbills only, because his next recorded presentation of the panorama of slavery was six months later in January 1855 in Cardiff, where he pasted bills to advertise his appearance, cheaper than a newspaper advertisement. *Uncle Tom's Cabin* had been translated into Welsh a year earlier, and he thought his presentation might be worth reviving. He had kept his pictures, and when he went on to Newport, in addition to the slavery panorama he exhibited "several well painted pictures of the chief features in Mrs. Beecher Stowe's celebrated work." Although the newspaper reviewer was generally approving, he added that the exhibition "would, perhaps, be improved by Mr. Brown doffing the gold-frogged and be-laced coat and cap of the mere showman … and assuming the quieter gait of the respectable and enlightened society among which he nightly appears." He was also accompanied by a local brass band.[24]

Henry was still trying to find a way to incorporate fashionable *Uncle Tom's Cabin* into his entertainment. In Bristol, where he appeared in April, he presented both the slavery panorama and the *Uncle Tom's Cabin* pictures, but when he went on to nearby Weston-super-Mare and Taunton, only the panorama was advertised. By this time, he estimated that his original panorama had been seen by two million people, which must be a showman's exaggeration, and after the first week presenting this, he added *Uncle Tom's Cabin* before going on to Exeter in Devon, where his life was to be changed in a dramatic way.[25]

Act 2: Partnership

Scene 4

Love in the West Country

Although James Smith claimed Henry was looking for a wife in England in 1851, it was not until 1855 that he married. He may have met someone earlier, but any romantic involvements came to nothing until he encountered Jane Floyd, the daughter of Cornish tin miner John Floyd and his wife Ann. Jane was born in Perranuthnoe, a small settlement on the southern coast of Cornwall on the opposite side of Mount's Bay from Penzance, and baptized in the parish church in nearby St. Hilary on May 24, 1834, so she was 21 when they married.[1] Henry was about 40.

Tin mining has a long history in Cornwall. In the mid–17th century there were 22 households in Perranuthnoe, but over the next century as prices for tin fell some inhabitants emigrated in search of a better living. Then in the middle of the 18th century copper mining also took off in Perranuthnoe and the combination of tin and copper brought prosperity. Wheal Neptune, a mine near Perranuthnoe, became so successful the owners issued their own bank notes, but this was not the only mine in the region. It was claimed that 100 windlasses turning above shafts could be seen there. Miners from South Wales and Cornwall migrated in both directions across the Bristol Channel as the prices for coal mined in Wales and metals mined in Cornwall rose and fell. The Floyd family originated in Wales (Floyd is the English version of the Welsh name Lloyd), but Jane's father was baptized in nearby St. Hilary, suggesting the family had been established in the Perranuthnoe area for a while. By the time of the 1841 census, the prosperity of the copper and tin mining had increased the population of the village to 1,438. The Floyd family, John, 47, his wife Ann, 46, and their daughters Mary, aged 10, and Jane, five, were living in the part of the parish known as Perran Downs.[2]

Before about 1850, miners effectively agreed a contract for extracting ore from a site based on an assessment of the likely yield and costs of processing it. A wage system gradually replaced this but, as might be expected, the Floyd family's income had fluctuated. In poor families the eldest children had to work as soon as possible so their contribution to the family budget, however small, would help to support the younger ones. Most took unskilled work or went into service, and they could be as young as seven when their working lives started. Jane was lucky to be the youngest survivor of a small family. By the time she emerged from childhood the family would have been relatively comfortable financially. Her father had a steady job in a flourishing industry and, with most of the children off her hands, her mother could have been earning a supplementary income. Usually girls from this background would become servants or take some other unskilled job about the age of 12, but Jane had the luxury of pursuing her education and becoming a teacher. From 1846 there was a system whereby bright children were encouraged to stay on at school to become pupil-teachers, who, while still taking lessons themselves, taught the younger children. In 1851, at the age of 17, Jane was still at home, so it must be assumed she was continuing her education.[3]

Until 1870 education in Britain was provided almost entirely by religious denominations, and National Schools were run by the National Society for Promoting Religious Education in accordance with the Church of England. The Floyd family were firmly Church of England, which suggests they were of a higher social standing than the average miner, to whom dissenting denominations, especially Methodism, appealed. At some point Jane was appointed to the National School in Phillack, a suburb of Hayle on St. Ives Bay on the northern coast of Cornwall, some eight miles from her home town. There was a Floyd's Hotel in Hayle, so she may have had relatives nearby, but the name is common in this area. The school was situated in the area known as Copperhouse after the foundry there. Most of the National Schools were built next to the parish church and had very strong links with it. Jane may have been teaching in Phillack when, in February 1852, the children of the Sunday School were regaled with tea and cakes by the Rev. H.S. Wright, who was leaving the parish. Afterward they walked to the church for a sermon, which the schoolmistress would have been expected to attend, as well as to take part in other church-sponsored events. The Hayle Mutual Improvement Society held regular lectures in the schoolroom.[4] From the 18th century, the port of Hayle had developed as a mining town and industrial center, and later it contained two of the three largest mine engine foundries in the world. Although today Cornwall is largely seen as a holiday destination, a peaceful rural backwater, in the 19th century it was an industrial powerhouse. The Cornishman Richard Trevithick built his steam-powered road carriage here in 1801, and one of the first railways in the world ran from Hayle to Redruth. Jane was no wide-eyed country bumpkin; her upbringing and work in this town were good preparation for later touring the industrial towns of the North and Midlands. She knew the people in these audiences: their daily working lives, the hardships they suffered, and their need for entertainment, as well as their desire for self-improvement.

Black People in Cornwall

People of African origin were not unknown in Cornwall. Since the 18th century they had been settling in the county. The best known is Joseph Emidy, the composer and violinist, who was born in Africa. He had been a player in the King of Portugal's orchestra in Lisbon when a British sea captain, in need of an onboard fiddler, kidnapped him. In 1799 he came to Falmouth, where he married a local woman, and later settled in Truro with his wife and their family. He played an important part in the county's musical life. The reports of his death in 1835 were laudatory: "His talents as a musician were of the first order and he was enthusiastically devoted to the science." The items about concerts held to benefit his widow and family do not mention his color, simply his "long and unwearied public services."[5] Most other people of African origin in 18th-century Cornwall seem to have been mariners in the coastal parishes or servants.

Henry Box Brown was not the first fugitive American slave to speak in the county. Although some mariners or other visitors must have spoken informally of their experiences of enslavement to local people, it was in 1851 that the first known lecturer, John Brown, came to Truro from America. John Brown, born into slavery in Virginia around 1818, worked in the cotton fields of Georgia near Milledgeville before being sold on to planters in other states. At Milledgeville he met John Glasgow, a sailor from British Guiana (today Guyana), who had married a Lancashire woman and had two children and a small farm when he sailed to Savannah, Georgia's main cotton port, in 1829. Slave states in the United States had strict controls on their black residents, and in ports free black sailors on French and British ships were regarded as a potential source of trouble. In several places it was usual to put black seamen into prison until their ship was ready to depart and the captain had paid money to release them. For some reason, John Glasgow's captain left him in prison and he was sold at auction for $350, to a planter near Milledgeville. There Glasgow met John Brown, and his stories of life in England prompted Brown to escape. His route went via Michigan to Canada and then on to England, where he arrived in 1850. It was reported that he hoped to meet up with Captain Joseph Teague of Redruth in Cornwall, who had promised to help him, but on his arrival Brown found that Teague had died in America. In England Brown worked initially as a carpenter, gave talks on his experience of slavery, and sought funding to go to Natal, South Africa, where he thought his knowledge of growing cotton could be useful, although he later abandoned this plan. Louis Chamerovzow, the secretary of the British and Foreign Anti-Slavery Society who edited its *Anti-Slavery Reporter*, also wrote down Brown's dictated memoir, *Slave Life in Georgia*, which was published in London in 1855.[6]

In 1853 John Brown was in Cornwall and attracted a large and interested audience when he spoke in the National School Room in Redruth. He related his escape "in a very clear and forcible manner." Redruth is only 11 miles from Phillack, and it is possible that the young schoolteacher attended. A month later Mr. Thomas, "a man of colour," appeared in St. Austell town hall to speak about slavery, but nothing more is known about him. Brown later settled in the West Country, where he married a Wiltshire-born woman named Mary (surname unknown) and practiced as botanist.[7] His path was some years later to cross with Henry's.

When and where Henry and Jane Floyd met is not known. His tour of the West Country had started in Bristol, followed by Weston-super-Mare, Taunton, Exeter, and Newton Abbot, which he reached in July 1855. Three months later, in October, he crossed the river Tamar, which divides Devon from Cornwall, and arrived in Penzance, in the far west of Cornwall, to make his only appearance there. It seems a long way to go with the panorama and the diorama of Uncle Tom's Cabin for a single appearance. A month after his presentation in Penzance, the nearest large town to Perranuthnoe on the opposite side of Mount's Bay, he and Jane were married. This seems too much of a whirlwind courtship. Most likely she had traveled to see him in Exeter in June and there was introduced to him by a minister or someone from the National Schools organization. In Exeter Henry exhibited his panorama for two nights and extended this for another four in response to public demand. Then he announced that he would also be showing the diorama of Uncle Tom's Cabin before discontinuing his tour due to ill health. He did, however, fulfill his last obligation in Newton Abbot, a small town 17 miles from Exeter, at the beginning of July.[8] Whether he was genuinely ill or had made this an excuse to court Jane in peace, he had nearly five months, apparently without performing, before he went to Penzance.

What was the attraction for Jane Floyd? At 21, she was not yet regarded as on the shelf and overly keen to marry. In addition, she was well educated and had a good job, for which she would be respected and have some status in her town. There were ambitious, aspiring young men whose prospects in local industries were excellent, and that was the kind of marriage for which her family would have hoped, but Henry had the knack of attracting the adventurous. His old assistant and fellow performer, Walter Glynn, gave up a promising career and steady job as a printer, and now Jane Floyd was going to leave teaching for the uncertainties of the entertainment world, which was not regarded as entirely respectable. Young men often feel threatened by clever, strong-minded women, but Henry was 40 and his experiences had put him past that stage of callowness and insecurity. He might not have had Jane's level of formal education, but his intelligence was often mentioned in reports of his appearances, and there is not always a correlation between academic learning and intelligence: the ability to think logically, to solve practical problems in a creative way, or to respond flexibly to events. Also, he was amusing, which is usually a winning attribute for women. Whatever the factors that drew them together, Jane and Henry decided to marry, and the next stage was for him to be introduced to her family and to ask her father formally for her hand, as was the practice then.

It is a matter for speculation how Henry indicated his personal interest in Jane and how she indicated she was not averse to his courtship (or perhaps vice versa, as not all young Victorian women were shrinking violets), but this was another area of life where he would have found a bewildering difference between the United States and Britain. In the southern United States, sexual relations between the races were illegal, although this illegality was frequently disregarded by masters with their female slaves, but even in the free states miscegenation was rejected, as the Englishwoman Harriet Martineau found when she casually remarked in Philadelphia that she saw no reason why black and white should not intermarry. Men in the South, even those with black mistresses, violently protected what they saw as the virtue of white women and opposed any relationship with a black man, whether enslaved or not, so behavior around women must have required even more self-abasement and the maintenance of a wider distance, both physical and verbal, than they were required to show their masters. Frederick Douglass described how his mistress Sophia Auld, who was from a non-slaveholding family, found the "crouching servility" he had shown toward her disturbing. Nor was she troubled if a slave looked at her directly. He found this disconcerting and did not know how to interact with her.[9] Henry would have internalized such manners since childhood. He must already have understood that failing to meet a man's eye when speaking to him made him appear untrustworthy and shifty to the British, but how to negotiate the elaborate rules that governed male–female dealings in Victorian England was another new learning curve, one he had by now completed.

Mixed-Race Relationships in Britain

While touring Lancashire and elsewhere, Henry must have realized that in Britain interracial marriage was not uncommon, but it is impossible to give any figures or statistics since certificates and other official documentation did not require ethnic classification. A small, but very vociferous, number of British people condemned miscegenation. In the 18th century it was those with economic interests in slavery who were loudest in their objections, and in the 19th century the espousers of scientific racism denounced racial mixing. There were in Britain no laws against miscegenation, and although it was not welcomed in the middle and upper classes, the people who were most likely to read and believe the racists' publications, the working classes seem to have had no problems with it. The publication of racist theories makes them easy to research, so they are probably given too much emphasis by historians. Douglas A. Lorimer, whose *Colour, Class and the Victorians: English Attitudes to the Negro in the Mid-Nineteenth Century* is rightly considered a classic study, is cautious about assuming that all classes shared the same racial beliefs and he distinguishes between attitudes in Britain and in its colonies. He admits that when he was writing historians could work only from a small and possibly unrepresentative sample. "In spite of efforts to get at popular views of the Negro, the bulk of sources material remains the reports of an articulate minority from the respectable ranks of society." He also explores the differences in attitude and behavior between Britain and in its colonies, where there was much more racial prejudice from officials. His conclusion, that "the relationship between individual blacks and respectable Victorians continued to be governed less by a consciousness of racial differences between black and white than by the reality of social disparities between rich and poor," seems to hold true when the kinds of records that were not easily accessible 40 years ago are now examined.[10] It is, however, time-consuming to trawl through thousands of scattered references in newspapers, court reports, and other sources to investigate what was actually happening in the country, rather than to read what a small, academic elite thought ought to happen.

A number of other fugitives married white women, as did John Brown, previously mentioned; Moses Roper married Ann Stephen Price of Bristol (who, like Jane Floyd, was a teacher); the actor Samuel Morgan Smith's second wife was Harriet Goldspring, an actress, born in Norwich in East Anglia; Nelson Countee's wife was a Londoner named Maria. Another less prominent black American was Joseph Freeman. In 1863 he married Sarah Farrow, a widow with five surviving children, and their daughter Sarah was born in 1865. He published no narrative and delivered no lectures; almost all that is known of his life comes from his gravestone in a cemetery in Chelmsford, Essex:

> Erected by his Christian friends to the memory of JOSEPH once a slave in New Orleans who escaped to England and became also a FREE MAN in Christ. He was employed for several years at the London Road Iron Works until his death at the age of 45 on the 28th Novr 1875. Reader! Have you been made free from the slavery of sin?[11]

Africans and other migrants from parts of the British Empire also found white brides, as did Charles Williams, previously mentioned, who had claimed to be a fugitive slave. There is no indication of his original country, but his wife was Irish. The color of the spouses or fiancées of those who appeared in court was not given: Irish is a nationality, but in other similar cases, where color was not specified, the participants must be assumed to be white. In 1859 a "coloured" seaman, John Pieza, was lodging in Walworth, south London, with his girlfriend's family when her brother sold his gold watch and chain while drunk. That Pieza was staying under the same roof as his girlfriend shows how unremarkable such a situation was. Her mother accepted him and his courtship. Black women, too, married white men, but they are much harder to identify because on marriage they took the legal status of their husbands and were far less likely to come to official notice. Most, like Mattie Lawrence of the Fisk Jubilee singers who in 1890 married a businessman, Henry Thrift, disappeared into quiet domesticity, but Zilpha Elaw, a freeborn American Primitive Methodist preacher who came to England in 1840, had a successful speaking career both before and after her marriage in 1850 to Ralph Bressey Shum. He was a butcher whose German father had been naturalized in 1811–12.[12]

Meeting the In-Laws

Henry's appearance in Penzance must have been so he could meet all the family there. John Floyd had nine siblings, at least three of whom and their offspring were alive and living in the area at this time. It is likely his wife had a similar network of relations, so Henry would have found himself amid a large extended family. He gave four performances in

MR. H. BOX BROWN,

THE CELEBRATED AMERICAN FUGITIVE SLAVE,

BEGS most respectfully to inform the Nobility, Gentry and Inhabitants generally, that he will exhibit his GRAND

PANORAMA

OF AMERICAN SLAVERY.

The Narrative of H. B. Brown's Life will be Sold at the Hall.
Illustrated Views from Uncle Tom's Cabin, painted on 50,000 square feet of Canvas.

PART FIRST.—The Nubian Family—Seizure of the Slaves—Religious Sacrifice—March to the Coast—View of the Cape of Good Hope—Cape Felucca—Interior of a Slave Ship—British Frigate in chase of a Slaver—Spanish Slaver at Havanna landing Slaves — Interior of a Slave Mart,—Gorgeous Scenery in the West India Islands—Nubian Family at Auction.—The Grand Fourth of July Celebration—Separation after the Sale of Slaves —Grand Slave Auction—March of the Slave Gangs.— Modes of Confinement and Punishment—Brand and Scourge—Interior of Charleston Workhouse.
PART SECOND.—Sunday among the Slave Population—Monday Morning, with Sugar Plantations and Mill —Woman at work—Cotton Plantation—View of the Lake of the Dismal Swamp—Nubians Escaping by night —Ellen Crafts Escaping—The Whipping Post and Gallows at Richmond, Va.—View of Richmond, Va.—H. B. Brown escaping—View of the Natural Bridge and Jefferson's Rock—City of Washington, D.C.—Slave Prisoners at Washington—Washington's Tomb at Mount Vernon Fairmount Waterworks—H. B. Brown released in Philadelphia—Distant View of the City of Philadelphia— Burning Alive—Promise of Freedom—Grand Industrial Palace—West Indian Emancipation—Grand Tableaux— Universal Emancipation.
Mr. H. B. Brown will give a Song descriptive of his escape, and exhibit the Identical Box in which he made his escape. Mr. C. Westoni will go through a series of Operatic and Nautical Songs.
ADMISSION.—Reserved Seats, 1s.; Second ditto, 6d.; Back ditto, 3d. Tickets to be had of Mr. T. BEARE, Bookseller, &c.—Doors open at Seven in the Evening, to commence at a quarter to Eight.
Dated Octobe 30, 1855.

Newspaper advertisement placed by Henry in the *Cornish Telegraph* of October 31, 1855, to make public just how he could support his intended bride. © The British Library Board. All right reserved. With thanks to the British Newspaper Archive (www. britishnewspaperarchive.co.uk).

Falmouth, circa 1850, where Henry Brown and Jane Floyd were married in the parish church of King Charles the Martyr.

Penzance between October 29 and November 1 in the Union Hall, where he exhibited both the *Grand Panorama of American Slavery* and *Uncle Tom's Cabin*. His newspaper advertisement gave a full description of the panorama, listing all the illustrations. He also said his *Narrative* would be on sale and he would sing.[13] His advertisements in Exeter and Newton Abbot had been smaller and much less detailed, suggesting he was determined to prove his worth to the prospective in-laws and to impress their friends and neighbors.

On November 28, 1855, the couple were married by license in Falmouth parish church by the curate William Wood.[14] At this time Falmouth was often the first port of call for ships returning from long voyages and was the town from which a packet service, dispatching mail to the British Empire, operated, but it was still small and relatively undeveloped. Docks were not constructed there until 1858 and there was no rail service until 1863. It must have reminded Henry of the New England towns he had toured when promoting his auto-biography. Why the couple chose the town is unknown; neither seems to have had any connection with it and it was customary for couples to be married in the bride's parish. Henry was probably making an unadvertised appearance here; he also seems to have visited Redruth without this being mentioned in the press.[15] At this time there was no local paper in Falmouth, although those published in Truro and Penzance covered events in the town.

Henry must have thought it was not financially worthwhile making a journey to either of these towns, paying both for travel costs and for newspaper advertisements. He could have stuck up posters and paraded through Falmouth, handing out playbills advertising his performances, which would have been cheaper and simpler.

The marriage certificate shows that John Floyd, probably Jane's father but possibly an older brother, was one of the witnesses. She was over 21 and did not need her father's permission to marry, so having a relative sign the certificate shows there was no family opposition to the wedding. Henry gave his residence as Falmouth, his status as widower, and his occupation as a lecturer. When Henry heard that his wife Nancy had become the kept woman of another man by whom she had a child he regarded his marriage as finished. Had he now heard she was dead? His appearances were now mainly in public places of entertainment under the aegis of the mayor, not a clergyman who might be involved in the abolitionist movement, so how was he getting news from America? Or was he gambling that the authorities would not have the time, resources, and inclination to make enquiries? He stated that his father's name was Edward and he was a farmer. This was the first time he named his father in any record, and it raises the question of whether he chose "Old Uncle Ned" as his signature tune in tribute to the man who all his life had used the shovel and the hoe that Henry had escaped, as the lyric he now sang boasted.

Throughout his dealings with authorities in Britain, as will be seen, Henry told half-truths that disguised or misrepresented his status. As anyone

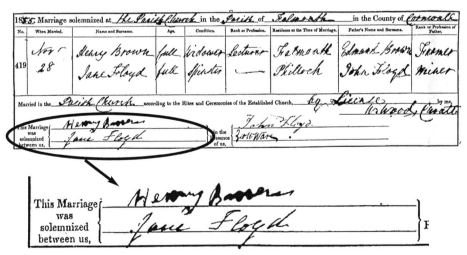

Certificate from Truro Register Office. Henry's signature on the marriage certificate indicates that he had learned to sign his name.

who had attended one of his lectures or had read his *Narrative* would know, he had been a slave, born into slavery as the child of slaves. Yet here, when information was being recorded for posterity, he could not bring himself to say that his father was a field hand or agricultural laborer. In 1851, he said in his *Narrative* that both his parents were free but he gave no indication of how he knew or how this came about. It was often a condition, or a legal requirement, that freed slaves left their home state. In America a one-time enslaved field hand would be very unlikely to attain the status that the description "farmer" connoted in Britain. Among the enslaved themselves there were gradations of rank. As the Rev. R.M. Johnson, who had escaped slavery to study at Edinburgh University, put it during a lecture, the "house slave associated with the family circle was more civilized than the common field slave." Henry himself seemed to have been destined for field work. He was raised on a plantation and his first master thought he might make a plough boy or a gardener.[16] His life had turned out very differently, but he perhaps still felt defensive about his status, especially in relation to his wife's solid background.

Another way in which his life had changed was in literacy. Slave owners prevented their people from becoming literate, fearing they would be given ideas above their station and, more destructively, be able to disseminate them widely. In Virginia it had actually been illegal to teach slaves to read and write. Both Jane and John Floyd wrote easily, and by now Henry too could write his name. His signature is not practiced but it is cursive, so he had learned to sign fairly fluently. Unfortunately, he was the first to sign and the ink flooded his signature. The pen may have been old and damaged as well, so it is difficult to estimate exactly how easily he wrote. By now he was probably able to read well. He was bright, eager to learn, and had had opportunities in North America, where there is mention of a text being written for him, to acquire the necessary skills.[17] After that, reading is a matter of practice. Many people, as various records of the time show, could read but were unable to write beyond signing their names. Even in Britain the more reactionary members of the upper classes were quite happy to have children taught to read the Bible to make them obedient but not taught to write in case they spread more revolutionary ideas.

A wedding notice was inserted in the local papers in the standard format. No mention was made of the groom's color or ethnicity.

> At Falmouth Church on Wednesday last, Mr. Henry Box Brown, Proprietor of the Panorama of African Slavery, to Miss Jane Floyd, late mistress of the National School, Copperhouse.[18]

Losing up to five months of income had undoubtedly put a dent in Henry's finances. A week later, on December 10, he was in Hampshire, appearing in Southampton, then at Christmas in Winchester.[19] What role his new wife played in his career at this point is not clear, besides providing emotional support and company on the road. Without a settled base, always on tour, he had had no time to form friendships. Although he needed other people to move, set up, and operate the panorama, he must have hired the majority of the stage staff in each place because it would have been cheaper. He had been employing 13 men at the time of the court case in Wolverhampton, and although he was paying accommodation costs and travel (second class) for at least some of these people, it would have been too expensive to do this for all. Being constantly friendly and cheerful to a succession of strangers, who could spoil his presentation if he annoyed them, must have been stressful. One had even stolen from him. Although Henry had been able to call on two of his employees to give evidence when he sued the theater owner in Sheffield for reneging on a deal, there was a professional distance. At least one person, Walter Glynn, had traveled with him for a while, keeping his accounts and singing with him in his act, and he must have given Henry some companion-ship. But now he had someone who was totally committed to his welfare and with whom he could share the pains and pleasures of touring. For nearly five years Henry and Jane Box Brown were able to enjoy and develop their rela-tionship before they started to raise a family.

Jersey

In January 1856, two months after their marriage, the couple went to Jersey on what would be the first of three visits. Traveling to the island may have been intended as a belated honeymoon, combining work with a visit to what must have seemed a slightly exotic location. The Channel Islands off the coast of Normandy became English territory with the advent of William the Conqueror in 1066. Even though the islanders spoke a variant of Norman French and their legal system retained medieval French elements, they remained loyal to Britain over the centuries whenever the French tried to regain possession. As a black man, Henry would not have been a new sight in Jersey. John Copley's famous painting of 1783, depicting the death of Major Peirson, who died in 1781 defending Jersey from a French invasion, shows his black servant prominently and in a heroic posture. Many local people displayed in their homes prints of this painting or of a similar work done by Edward Burney a few years after Copley's work.

According to the *Dictionnaire Jèrsiais-Français*, at the end of the 18th century or beginning of the 19th there was a black man living in St. Brelade. He had come to the island when very young and spoke Jèrsiais perfectly. He was nicknamed, ironically, Jean L'Blianc (John White). There is no further information about him, but he was probably the servant of a wealthy family, perhaps one with estates in the Caribbean. There may have been others; color and ethnic origin are not always recorded in official records. Jersey's laws were, and still are, different from English laws, but on this matter they were agreed; there was no legal discrimination against black people. The main port, St. Helier, must have seen black mariners, as there were a number in both the Royal Navy and the merchant navy. The "white negresse" visited, probably around 1760. This must have been the woman known professionally as Amelia Harlequin, although the name is not given in the local newspaper advertisements. She was born about 1742 in Jamaica, the daughter of house slaves of African origin, and was remarkable because she had albinism. She was brought to England as a child in 1753 and later exhibited herself for her own profit. John Jea and a Mr. Benson had preached in Jersey in 1817 and 1853, respectively. John Jea was born in 1773 in Calabar in present-day Nigeria, and was taken to New York, where he became the property of a Dutch couple. On gaining his freedom, he became a preacher both in the United States and in Britain. The other speaker was probably Mr. A. Benson, a "gentleman of colour" from New York reported as delivering a speech about temperance and teetotalism in Stourbridge in Worcestershire in September 1851[20] and in other locations.

Abolition was not the primary message of John Jea or Mr. Benson, who visited in 1817 and 1853, respectively. They considered themselves first and foremost men of God or advocates of temperance. When he arrived in January 1856, Henry was apparently the first antislavery speaker to make an appearance in Jersey, and he was certainly the first to bring a panorama with him. He appeared at Cornwall's Riding School in Gloucester Street, which was on the site of the present-day Opera House.[21]

The show was both advertised and reviewed in the local French-language newspaper. Although by this date English was overtaking Jèrsiais as the language of the majority, there were still many who spoke it as their first language, so Henry must have thought it was worth paying to attract French-speakers. His appearance

a attiré une foule de curieux. Ce Panorama est un œuvre de mérite, il dépeint fidèlement et sous des couleurs effrayantes le triste état de ces milliers de créatures humaines qui gémissent sous le poids du sort le plus cruel. Nous dirions à tous ceux qui veulent se faire une idée des tortures physiques et morales auxquelles sont condamnées les compatriotes de M. Brown : "allez voir le panorama et jamais vous ne le oublierez."[22]

[has drawn a crowd of the curious. This Panorama is a work of merit, it faithfully depicts in shocking colors the sad state of these thousands of human creature who moan under the weight of the cruelest fate. We say to those who want to get an idea of the physical and moral tortures to which the compatriots of Mr. Brown are condemned: "go and see the panorama and you will never forget it."]

From this is it clear that Henry did his standard antislavery presentation, but he added personal touches, as one of the English-language newspapers revealed. This was one of the rare accounts that gave details about the humorous elements of his act.

> This interesting exhibition has been well patronized during the week. We may with all consistency state that we have been much amused. Mr. H.B. Brown is a funny fellow; he does not like Parson Brown's inconsistency at all, and particularly as it applies to the sale and exchange of Slaves. The American Ladies are no favorites with him; he quotes *outré* specimens of their behavior after having received what is called in America—"a Boarding School Education"; still he cites paragraphs from "Uncle Tom's Cabin," which was edited by one of them—Mrs. Beecher Stowe. He tells his audience how he made a gentleman of Mr. Brindley, a newspaper editor, and has not a word to say in favor of Mr. Hobbs, the celebrated American locksmith. He gets into the box in which he was conveyed 250 miles by steamer and rail and allows himself to be tumbled over on the stage. He sings a good Yankee Doodle tune and seems perfectly satisfied with himself after he has done it. He is as full of bounce and fun as a bottle of wine is full of wit, and his heart seems to bound within him as he feels the satisfaction that he is "free." Go and see his panorama, we say, go and hear his speechification and explanation and if he does not amuse you and give you your money's worth of fun into the bargain we are deceived. Next week is to be the last, as Mr. Brown is announced to exhibit his panorama in Guernsey on the following Monday.[23]

Plainly the libel case in Wolverhampton four years ago, in which Mr. Hobbs had played such a prominent role, still rankled with Henry. Making fun of Brindley and Hobbs may well have been part of his act in the intervening period, but he might have felt that in Jersey it was unlikely there would be any repercussions so took the opportunity to give his feelings full vent. The island is far from mainland Britain and not a center of lockmaking, so there would be no one to report his satire to Hobbs. Possibly his failures connected with *Uncle Tom's Cabin* made him less than enthusiastic about Harriet Beecher Stowe, but she would have been revered by most of his audience so any implicit criticism of her would have been a misjudgment. Nowhere else is any criticism of women mentioned in any other review; he may have dropped it if his audience objected to this lack of gallantry.

This report does not, however, give a complete description of his act. Who Parson Brown might be is not stated; he is unlikely to be a local clergyman being satirized. Although Jersey had had 18 plantation owners who had been compensated by the British government following the abolition of slavery in the Caribbean colonies in 1833,[24] this was no longer a live issue in the Channel Islands. Henry, in the persona of Parson Brown, probably performed a mock sermon, satirizing the clergymen he had encountered back in Virginia. And why would his heart not bound at his freedom to go where he chose, to be applauded for entertaining people who welcomed him, and to have his marriage to a young, white woman accepted without comment?

What is missing from this account, and from his advertisements, is the sale of his *Narrative*. This was last mentioned at his appearance in Penzance, just before his marriage. It seems Henry stopped selling it about this time. Although other speakers found a good market for their autobiographies— Moses Roper's *A Narrative of the Adventure and Escape of Moses Roper, from American Slavery* went into 10 editions between 1837 and 1856, selling more than 33,000 copies—there seem to have been no further editions of Henry's printed after 1851. His escape continued to form part of his act, but the reason for it was not mentioned in the press, so presumably he either left it out or minimized it. Now that he had remarried he wanted to look forward. The trauma of the end of his first marriage would not have disappeared, but it would have been considerably modified by the news of Nancy's subsequent child and eased by his remarriage. And Jane might not have wanted to hear every night about how happy he had been with his first wife and their children. Henry was willing to sacrifice income for her.

Back to Britain

The Box Browns went on to Guernsey, also in the Channel Islands, where Henry showed only the American Slavery panorama. They returned to Britain, visiting Portsea on the south coast at the end of March 1856, afterward crossing the Solent to the Isle of Wight for an extended stay. Here Henry showed both his original panorama and the *Uncle Tom's Cabin* presentation, which were well received: "All persons were highly gratified with the splendid views but the description he gives of slavery is heart rending." When he sang "a Negro song," his audience joined in with the chorus. There was time for sightseeing in Ryde, Newport, and Ventnor while they stayed on the island until the end of July 1856. In Ryde one of his stagehands, John Delamare, got drunk and mistakenly broke into the house next door to his sweetheart's, where he smashed crockery. It was an introduction for Jane into not only the joys but also the problems of touring. Then they visited Brighton, the fashionable bathing resort on the south coast, where the Prince Regent's Royal Pavilion, an extravagant Regency interpretation of Asian architecture, was an exotic sight to share. Here Henry appeared in the Upper Room of the Town Hall, and the *Musical Gazette* reported that "in addition to depicting very vividly the horrors of slavery, he gives some amusing anecdotes of the Americans. His pronunciation is clear and his language is at times good."[25]

Henry's performing schedule in a location could be demanding, but there were periods that could be given over to leisure. At this time he was visiting one location per month. Transporting the 50,000 square feet of the original panorama was time-consuming and could be worrying, as it consisted of "upward of one hundred magnificent views," as well as *Uncle Tom's Cabin*, which he was still occasionally showing, as he advertised in Arundel, about 20 miles from Brighton, in July. He also needed to ensure that the escape box was transported undamaged, to negotiate with venue managers, to organize publicity, and to find accommodation. Jane must have taken on some of the work of arranging visits, replacing Walter Glynn as assistant and keeper of accounts. In smaller towns, like Guildford in the neighboring county of Surrey, where they traveled next, he would only be speaking on three or four occasions with the rest of the time free. On nonperforming days Henry and Jane could stroll around, seeing the sights. However, no showman could afford to miss an opportunity to publicize himself, so he probably dressed in his eye-catching, theatrical clothing and distributed handbills to passersby on their promenades. Even though he was no longer appearing in religious venues, he still wanted to attract as many people as possible, and he included this endorsement from a clergyman in his advertisement for a two-day appearance in Godalming in late August:

> Among the many and most recent Testimonials, Mr. Box Brown has been honoured with the following from the Vicar of Sompting: The Vicar of Sompting is much obliged to Mr. Box Brown for his most interesting exhibition, which he considers most interesting its tendency, and calculated to impress on the minds of the young especially the blessings of Christian Liberty.[26]

Sompting is a small village near the coast in Sussex and the visit there may have been at Jane's instigation, to speak at the local Church of England school. Henry was probably not paid for this appearance; like all celebrities he did occasional charity appearances, especially for children.

In September they moved on to Maidstone and in October to Faversham, both in Kent. In these towns Henry did his customary few days but in cities the schedule was more intense and he might spend ten days performing, as he did between November 3 and 13 in Canterbury, followed by three days in Dover in December. At the beginning of 1857 they were still in Kent. February was unusually busy: Henry appeared in Sheppey or Sheerness (the source is not clear), then went to Woolwich, Greenwich, and Deptford on the southern outskirts of London, with an appearance at nearby Blackheath at the beginning of March. Josephine Brown, William Wells Brown's daughter, had been headmistress of a school in Plumstead, only four miles away, in 1854. She was at this time in America with her father so, alas, there is no record of his performance that she might have described to him. Then, after a brief show in Cheshunt in Hertfordshire, he returned to Kent to stay in Margate.[27]

This unusually heavy schedule may have been necessary to build up resources while Henry prepared to return to acting. He must have been too busy to keep up with what was happening elsewhere in the world, but there were two events that would later have considerable influence on his professional life. In America on March 6, 1857, in the case of *Dred Scott v. Sandford*, the Supreme Court of the United States ruled that black people, despite the Constitution, were not citizens and that slaves could not sue for freedom. This judgment became a factor in the outbreak of the American Civil War. In May, a rebellion against British rule in India started.

Scene 5

More New Directions

Henry would have heard about the *Dred Scott* case and the mutiny in India, but at that moment he was busy with other new plans so they were not at the forefront of his mind. On June 28, 1857, the *Era* announced that he would soon make his appearance on the stage of the London theaters, appearing in three new dramas, *The Fugitive Free; The Nubian Captive or, Royal Slave*; and *Pocahontas, or, The English Tar and the Indian Princess*. It added that communications should be address to the Royal Hotel in Margate, where he would be staying until the end of summer. All three dramas were written by a Margate man, Edward Gascoigne Burton, who, like James Scott in Sheffield, must have seen Henry's ability to engage an audience and wanted to display it.

The Royal Hotel was located in Cecil Square, where the well-to-do of Margate lived and attended events in its elegant surroundings. On the first floor was a large mirrored ballroom, and other assembly rooms included card rooms and a billiard room and of course a bar. Although called a hotel, it was mainly a place of entertainment; at the 1851 and 1861 censuses there were no guests. Presumably there were some rooms for occasional favored customers, so Henry and Jane lodged with Thomas Gardner, the licensee, and his family, as he had lodged in a coffee house in 1851. Now he was no longer an obscure lecturer but a celebrity, which was reflected in his more upmarket and gracious accommodation.[1]

While he was staying there Henry would have enjoyed the amenities of this fashionable spa town, but he mainly needed to learn his lines. Between 1737 and 1968 all plays had to be submitted to the Lord Chamberlain's office for a license to be performed, and the manuscripts are in the British Library in this extensive collection. On the title pages of these new plays Burton listed other plays he had written. Some had had a few performances, but none appears to have been published in print. The most successful was *The Warrior Boy or Innate Heroism*, which was licensed by the Lord Chamberlain in 1850 and

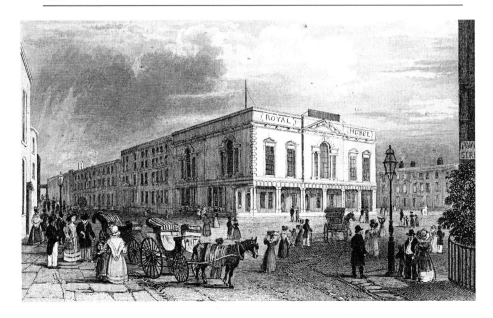

The Royal Hotel Margate, engraving circa 1850. Henry stayed in this establishment while preparing to act in the Royal Theatre here.

performed at the Pavilion Theatre in East London. It was revived more than a year later, in July 1851, when it appeared at the Victoria Theatre in London with Sarah Thorne in the title role, and then repeated in October. Thorne was a talented child actress and her abilities must have helped to get the play put on again at the Pavilion Theatre in November and the following year at the Marylebone Theatre also in London. She played Bobby in *The Lad of the Village or the Sporting Boots of the Inn* (*Bobby the Boots* is probably an alternative title). It was performed at the Grand National Standard Theatre in London in 1853, after the main drama of the evening, but it did not have the success of her previous role: I have found no other reference to it. She also starred in *The Blind Child of Africa or the Last Prince of Abyssinia and the True British Seaman*, which had a successful run at the Pavilion Theatre, where other plays by Burton were also performed from 1846 onward and where he himself acted.[2]

The same tropes seem to recur in all Burton's works. There is a comic lower-class character, cheeky but loyal, who knows his place and the hero and heroine's love story is mirrored in a subplot of a romance among the lower-class characters. In all three of the plays in which Henry appeared there are a villain and his henchmen, who bring apparent defeat to the ruler or master but are thwarted, and all ends happily. This basic plot line, and its variants, is one of the standards, from medieval mystery places via Shakespeare to contemporary soap operas; the skill, then as now, is disguising its predictability and making the script attractive. I am not a particularly good judge of drama on the page, but even I can see the major faults. The quality of Burton's writing is not high. There are redundant words and phrases, which make the dialogue seem slow and flabby; much verbiage serves neither to advance the action nor to delineate personality. Beyond the comic and the villains, the characters are noble, well spoken, and indistinguishable. People simply stand and speechify at each other and there is little stage business beyond fights. The plays also contain, as was the practice then, songs and a dance sequence. This was the pattern of many mid–19th century plays on the British stage, generally agreed to be a dramatically barren period, but by this time this style of drama was becoming old-fashioned. Although prolific and feted Tom Taylor was still turning out melodramas with the same elements as Burton's works, but more skillfully written, Dion Boucicault and Tom Robertson were beginning to work on plays that dealt with contemporary issues in a more naturalistic style.

In August the local newspaper reported the season of plays at the Royal Theatre in Margate, including Burton's works. *The Fugitive Free*, though said to be based on Henry's own life, is very different from actual events. It is set on a plantation, where Henry Brown, his sister Jane, and mother Betsey are enslaved. The plantation owner, Captain Ambler, is implausibly good-hearted. Every year to celebrate his daughter's birthday he frees a slave. As the action opens, preparations for Amelia's coming of age are in hand and she asks her father to free all three Browns, to which he consents. However, his agent, Mr. Allen, is plotting to impoverish Ambler and take over the plantation, which he does on the day of the celebration, before the papers to free Henry and Jane can be signed (mother Betsey is freed), and they are sold. Cottrell, Nancy's master, sells her to Allen, and Henry is bought by Parson Brown, a business associate of Allen. While in prison waiting to be taken south, Henry is flogged and appears to die, but this is used to rescue him. Ambler's groom, David Dobbs (the comic character), blacks up to take his place, so Henry is able to leave and is put in a trunk, which travels with Captain Ambler to Philadelphia, where Henry is freed. Allen's machinations are overcome by a stranger arriving from the English business house with which Ambler deals, and all ends happily. In the three plays in which Henry performed, the villain is defeated due to the intervention and heroism of someone British. The only good thing to say about it is that Burton does not represent the slaves speaking in minstrelsy style—they are as well-spoken and verbose as the white characters.

The fact that Henry was happy to act in this unnatural farrago with its patently absurd, sanitized picture of slavery and distortion of his own experiences suggests he was a playgoer himself and knew this was what pulled in the punters. As Smith had hinted when they split, he was taking opportunities

The Nubian Captive*, written expressly for Henry, by E.G. Burton. This was never published and is in the Lord Chamberlain's plays archive in the British Library, Add. Ms. 52,966 W. British Library, London, UK. © British Library Board. All rights reserved/Bridgeman Images.*

to try all kinds of new experiences, and playgoing, as well as being pleasurable in itself, showed him what his audiences liked. Outside London, he would have had a limited exposure to innovative drama, so his tastes were probably relatively unsophisticated. He himself must have enjoyed this kind of tale in which the good triumph after a period of tribulation. The character Parson Brown is a business associate of Allen who purchases Henry. From early in his speaking career, Henry delivered a sermon in the style of Parson Brown, and now one turns up as a villainous and hypocritical dealer in slaves on a large scale. Perhaps this was Henry's way of getting revenge on a real person, the Methodist minister to whom he believed Nancy and the children had been sold. While performing in Jersey he had taken the opportunity to crow over Brindley and Hobbs, and this may have been another such act.

After appearing in *The Fugitive Free*, Henry performed in *The Nubian Captive*. On the title page of the manuscript and on the pages dividing the acts, Burton notes that this play was written expressly for Henry, but it is hard to see why, or how it was thought so apposite. Hameh, a prince of Nubia, marries Medora. He is betrayed by a kinsman, Konac, and both he and Medora are sold into slavery. They are taken to Cuba, where Hameh initially works in a cigar factory while Medora is enslaved on a plantation owned and run by Englishmen. Three years later Hameh's master sees an advertisement for the sale of a very superior slave and Hameh thinks it may be his wife. They visit the plantation and it is Medora. Her master makes advances to her but she remains faithful to Hameh, who arrives in time to shoot him. They flee and hide in a swamp. Slave catchers set off in pursuit. Von Clatz, a Dutchman, shelters them, but all three are captured and put on a slave ship. Rescued by a crew from the Royal Navy, Hameh is released and with Medora restored to his princely state. Here are other familiar elements of all Burton's plays. The comic is Von Clatz, who uses standard clichés to advertise his nationality. The British sailors are bold and resolute. To give Burton some credit, he does not use the flowery, pseudo–Arabic clichés used by other playwrights; his Nubian characters, though they occasionally refer to Allah, speak in a resolutely English style. Their speeches could be almost seamlessly interchanged with their counterparts in the other plays.

Nevertheless, a local paper was impressed: "Mr. Brown's powerful acting in this new piece is really worthy of the highest commendation." Henry also gave readings from the plays on September 14 in nearby Ramsgate but the event was "thinly attended," despite being supported by a brass band.[3] He had been due to appear for six nights in the theater, but after the first two nights the audience was so small that there were losses. This venture was a repeat of the fiasco in Sheffield and, despite the praise of his acting, resulted in disappointment and a court case.

Henry sued Richard Thorne, the manager of the theater, for £2 16s 5d, his share of the two nights' earnings, and the suit was heard on 14 September at the County Court in Margate. Henry claimed he was due to receive half the receipts, after the manager had deducted £6 per night expenses, and also to receive a benefit (a performance at which he would receive all the seat money), but Thorne had denied him the benefit by delaying it until it was too late to advertise it so he had refused to take part. Thorne replied that the agreement for expenses had been a total of £36, not £6 per night, and Burton the playwright (whose other plays were staged by Thorne, the father of Sarah) testified that Henry himself had told him it was the total sum, not a nightly deduction. Burton also denied there had been any agreement for a benefit. The case went in Thorne's favor.[4] What this episode does show, as well as his continued confidence in getting involved in litigation, is that Henry could by now read well enough to be willing to do so in public and was able to learn a script rather than extemporize in a lecture. None of the other actors seems to have sued Thorne; they were used to failures and probably took it as part of the ups and downs of theatrical life.

Undeterred by his defeat, Henry traveled north, where at the beginning of October he appeared in *The Nubian Captive* in Liverpool's Royal Park Theatre. His performance was described as "satisfactory." He was due to act in the third play during the season and to have a benefit on October 9, and in preparation the October 4 issue of the *Era* carried a long biography of him, mostly drawn from the *Narrative*. It stated, erroneously, that this was his debut on the English stage and that he had written the plays himself. As the local newspapers in Kent, where he had already performed, and the manuscripts licensed by the Lord Chamberlain made clear, he was not the writer.[5]

The Royal Park Theatre had been opened in 1852 in Toxteth, to the south of the center of Liverpool. This new theater put on plays and pantomimes. Not everyone welcomed its presence. The Rev. Henry Postance of Holy Trinity Church complained that "when the Church was completed and open [in 1859], we had to encounter a most serious difficulty in having the Royal Park Theatre, one of the lowest of all places of entertainment, right opposite to it in Parliament Street." It also caused a "serious disturbance" to the evening services he held.[6] Henry's visit came shortly before the completion of the church, but Mr. Postance's strictures suggest the audience here was drawn from working-class people who would be unlikely to attend a more straitlaced lecture of the kind Wells Brown delivered and were unlikely to be regular churchgoers. Then, as now, the locale had a large black and mixed-race community, drawn from the Americas and Africa. The Irish potato famine of 1844 had brought other settlers and there were Greek and Chinese communities, as well as people from the Indian subcontinent. When he looked out at his audience, Henry would have seen black faces next to white and people whose skin color and features showed their mixed ancestry.

His performances in the plays there were well reviewed, but the engagement of a well-known Liverpudlian comedian, Charles Rice, to act in *The Fugitive Free* must have helped. Rice presumably played the role of the groom, David Dobbs. The run here was successful enough to go to nearby Wigan, where on October 17 Henry acted in both *The Nubian Captive* and *The Fugitive Free*. Next the plays transferred to Hanley, a suburb of Stoke-on-Trent in Staffordshire, where in early November Henry performed at the Royal Pottery Theatre. He was advertised to give two performances of *Pocahontas or the English Tar and the Indian Princess*, which the local paper called "Mr. Brown's Drama."[7] *Pocahontas*, in which Henry played Powhattan, father of Pocahontas and the chief of the tribe, is in dramatic terms probably the best of the plays, although the part of Powhattan is relatively small and the character is dim and ineffective, which may be why Henry chose not to perform it often. The best roles, as the full title of the play suggests, are Pocahontas, who is feisty and brave, and the comic role, here Jack Hanway, an English sailor, who appears in many more scenes than summarized in the following.

The original story of Pocahontas, a Native American woman, was well known in America by the mid–19th century and had been told in novels, plays, and poems there. Burton either got a garbled version of it or, more likely, chose to alter it to fit into his standard plot. In the original tale (which is not entirely accurate) she saved the life of John Smith, a English settler at Jamestown, by laying her head on his when he was about to be executed by her father Powhattan, the chief of the tribe. Later she converted to Christianity, married John Rolfe, another settler, had a son, and came to England, where she died at age 20 or 21 in 1617. She was buried in Gravesend, Kent, westward along the coast from Margate.

Burton's play is set at the founding of Jamestown in 1607. Horatio, the son of the governor Sir Edward Smith, and Pocahontas fall in love at first sight. When Jukka, her cousin for whom she is intended in marriage, attempts to shoot young Smith, Pocahontas stands in the way, and later when Jukka puts poison in a cup from which Horatio is about to drink she knocks it from his lips. Jukka rebels against Powhattan, seizes Horatio, and takes Horatio to his camp. Pocahontas flees to the cave of Agar, an English recluse who has lived there for 25 years, because she fears for her life, but she is soon back to convince her father of Jukka's ill will. Powhattan tells his daughter she can never marry Horatio, as it is against the law of their tribe. Horatio is rescued by Jack Hanway, Jukka is defeated, and finally Agar reveals that Pocahontas's mother was his daughter, so she is half English and the marriage can go ahead.

Henry also gave two more performances of one of the plays, not specified in the advertisement. He finished the week in Hanley with *The Nubian Captive*, and his acting aspirations also finished here. There was no transfer to London, as the *Era* had said he was aiming to do. This episode may also have caused Burton doubts about his abilities as a dramatist. About this time he published a well-received poem, *The Wreck of the Northern Belle: Or, the Life of a Ship from the Cradle to the Grave*, and then a local guidebook. A few years later, however, he wrote one last play, which was licensed in December 1862. *Retributive Justice, or, Mabel the Avenger*, was given a performance at the Victoria Theatre (now known as the Old Vic) in London in January 1863. The original title was *The Ocean Straight*, suggesting a familiar nautical element.[8] It did not merit a review and seems never to have been performed again.

The notices of Burton's plays in which Henry appeared speak of the acting, or the "creditably placed staging" and the "effective" scenery, but there is no mention of the quality of the script. Although this was in accord with the practice of reviewing Victorian theater, when the performers and their acting were the focus of the production, it does seem significant that there is no mention of any memorable speech or scene in the play. Henry did not play the comic role in any of these plays; he was one of the upright, dignified characters. Although a very good and experienced actor can do wonders with a mediocre script, ultimately a production stands or falls by a combination of the quality of the dialogue and its delivery. Henry was not an experienced enough actor to use tricks to disguise just how dull and plodding the words he had to speak were, although the reviews suggest he had some talent. Being a black actor was not remarkable enough to be a draw by itself; there were a number of black actors and performers working on the Victorian stage and in entertainment generally at this time, and some were very successful.

Black Actors on the Victorian Stage

Samuel Morgan Smith (1832–82), generally known as S. Morgan Smith, was a middle-ranking actor. Born in America, he had a long career in Britain playing a range of roles, not just those traditionally reserved for black actors, but he never became a draw on the London stage. Although a technically good actor, he seems to have lacked that additional ingredient that makes a star, which Ira Aldridge possessed. Another factor against him may have been his height. At five feet, six and one-half inches, he was not especially undersized for that time, but this did limit the range of performers he could work with, especially heroines.[9]

George Dunbar (c. 1831–before 1881?) also acted in the provinces for a long time. Something disastrous must have happened to his career, because by 1875 he and his wife were no longer giving theatrical performances of full-length plays but were appearing in music halls, on the bill with variety artistes. His last recorded appearance with his wife was in Redditch Warwickshire, in

August 1879.[10] He was one of the many actors whose careers, then and now, end in diminished parts in minor venues, but at least Dunbar had a period of success.

Paul Molyneaux (c. 856–1891) also had an unremarkable career as a middle-ranking actor. The son of Aaron Molyneaux Hewlett, a physical education instructor at Harvard, he came from a relatively comfortable background, and his sister married one of Frederick Douglass's sons. He toured America with Taylor's Jubilee Singers before coming to Britain in the hope of making his name and had arrived by 1881. He made his debut in February 1883 playing Othello and Richard III in North London but the self-financed productions were inept. He rejoined Taylor's Jubilee Singers, now touring Britain, and became their speaker, talking about the conditions for black people in America, but by 1886 he was out of work and advertising for pupils who wanted to learn self-defence. It was a low point in his career but plans to return to America were shelved when he was offered a minor part with a company touring Scotland with that old favourite *Uncle Tom's Cabin*. His engagement lasted for three years until early 1889. Shortly after he returned to America and died in 1891.[11] Although he was, like so many others, limited to one production, *Uncle Tom's Cabin* was so popular on the Victorian stage that genuinely black actors were at a premium, as regular advertisements in the *Era* attest. Performers who could stand the rigours of long provincial tours were virtually guaranteed employment.

There must have been a number of aspiring actors who, like Henry, did not get beyond the lowest rungs of the ladder. George Gross was a young American who had a keen sense of self-publicity. In 1868 he made his first appearance in England and was optimistically called "the only successor to the celebrated African Tragedian, Mr. Ira Aldridge" and "the great South American Tragedian" when it was advertised that he would play Othello and Richard III at the New Royal Adelphi Theatre in Liverpool. He did not appear there again, nor indeed anywhere else for some time. At the 1871 census in April, he was living in Wapping, in the East London docks, with his wife Emma, 21, a local woman. A few months later he was on the bill at the Oriental Theatre in Poplar, another dockside settlement a short distance from Wapping, but there are no other references to him in the theatrical press and no one of that name born in the United States appears in the 1881 census. Presumably he (or Emma) decided that his youthful ambitions would not be realized in Britain and moved on, most likely returning to America.[12]

Gustavus Allenborough, the "Coloured Tragedian," advertised himself in 1866 as having concluded highly successful engagements at Woolwich and Northampton and to be available for work. His repertoire, he said, consisted of "Othello, Black Doctor, Slave, etc." Allenborough seems to have spent some time "resting," as actors called being unemployed, as it was not until a year later that he played Othello in Redhill, Surrey. Nothing more is known about his life and there is no other trace of him, not even a death registration, in English records.[13]

The combination of his own limitations and the quality of his material meant that Henry joined the ranks of those who, like Gross and Allenborough, were less successful. He had not been the focus of attention in any of these dramas; in all three there were characters who would have received a better response from the audience, notably the comics. Even in *The Nubian Captive*, written for him and where Henry played the hero, Mustapher [*sic*], who was in charge of the slaves in the Nubian court, was a more engaging character. Henry was used to being the center of attention and to making people laugh. He must also have realized how uncertain the life of an actor was and how little money there was in it, compared to what he could earn on the lecture circuit.

The Holy Land

Aware that he was not ultimately an actor although he was a performer, Henry went back to lecturing in his entertaining way. Lecturers who can enthuse and engage an audience are rarer than actors. Although people will turn out for the most boring of speakers if the subject is one of interest, there are some people who attract a sell-out audience through their style of delivery, and Henry was becoming one of these select few. Unfortunately, he has left no indication on whether he regarded his foray into acting with regret or as a useful lesson when he went back to his familiar profession.

All this time, Jane had not been just an admiring member of her husband's audience and consoling him in his disappointments. She must have been planning a change of direction for them. Henry's religious education had been scanty. His mother had spoken to him of God, corrected his childish belief that their master was God and his son was the Savior, and also impressed on him the need to behave honestly, but like all other enslaved people in America, the main message he received from white ministers was the need to obey his masters. Obedience was also a major theme preached to the working class in Britain, but there were more opportunities to hear and explore alternative views. Many ministers published their sermons on a range of subjects that British people could read or have read to them, and the need to engage people was a major theme of the growing literature on preaching.[14] In America Henry had been unable to read religious works, and his experience of the gap between those who professed to be Christians and their actions left him with a cynical attitude to formal religion. His Parson Brown sketch probably satirized these hypocrites. By the time he could read, he was unlikely to want to pursue religious knowledge for its own sake and in any case was too busy. Jane, however, was a member of the Church of England and, as a schoolteacher in an Anglican school, would have been expected to teach her pupils knowledge of the scriptures, which was tested by the local minister; part of her salary depended on how well her pupils did. When Henry unveiled a diorama entitled *The Holy Land* at the beginning of 1858, this must have been at her instigation. Both of them would have known that the public is fickle and always seeking a novelty. She knew that religion was more important than color in Britain and could persuade him that this was worth doing. For the opening, the seats were priced slightly higher than usual, at 1s 6d and 1s, but there was a two-for-the-price-of-one offer. Dioramas of the Holy Land based on various travelers' artwork had been around since the 1840s and were still popular in the 1850s. The *Spectator* described a diorama of Jerusalem and the Holy Land, which, in May 1851, was the third the reporter had seen in two or three months.[15]

The Box Browns' diorama is later referred to as a panorama, but the term diorama was also used for the presentation of scenes painted on transparent cloth, through which lights could be shone, rather than on canvas. Victorian theaters were equipped to hang multiple backdrops and produce lighting effects, so this type of presentation would be confined to places with the necessary equipment. Their pictures included St. Peter's in Rome, the Holy Sepulcher, the Crucifixion of Christ, His Resurrection, and the Destruction of Jerusalem. Henry was still showing his original panorama of slavery, which, as it was on a roller within a portable frame, could be presented in almost any venue with a large enough stage. It was the only exhibit on display when he visited Braintree, Essex, in February,[16] and the Holy Land presentation did not reappear for a while.

It may not have been solely the limitations of the venues that caused this break in its presentation. Although he had attended a church in Richmond, prayed for help when in difficult situations, and believed in a supernatural force that would respond to prayer, Henry may not have been entirely comfortable speaking on a subject about which he would have known considerably less than many people in his audience. It was common to read the Bible every day, and some of his audience would therefore know many passages by heart. Some would also be knowledgeable about theological differences between the various Christian denominations, which was an important issue in this period when anti–Catholicism in particular remained a consistent theme. A carelessly uttered sentence might suggest he agreed with a doctrine that some of his listeners regarded as heretical but others did not, provoking arguments. He could speak with more knowledge and conviction about slavery because that had been a larger part of his experience for longer.

The Indian Mutiny

At the beginning of March 1858 Henry announced that he would be revisiting Jersey, a place where he had been extremely successful. The local paper welcomed his forthcoming return, saying this would be "A Treat for Easter-Week" in April. It might be expected that the Holy Land would be a good choice of subject for the date, but it was another, more topical, subject that was unveiled. What became known as the Indian Mutiny had been taking up more newspaper columns since its outbreak in March 1857. At this time, the East India Company (EIC) had a monopoly of British trade in the Indian subcontinent and Asia. In India it was based in four centers, called presidencies: Madras, Bengal, Bombay, and the North-Western Provinces. The French, Portuguese, Dutch, and Danish were also well established and competing in other regions. The East India Company had been set up by Royal Charter in 1600 and from the mid–18th century effectively ruled parts of the subcontinent, theoretically jointly with the native rulers, who played off the various European nations against each other to support their own interests. The EIC still had its own army, although by this time it no longer had a navy.

The rebellion began as a mutiny among sepoys, Indian soldiers of the EIC's Bengal army, in Meerut. New powder cartridges issued to the army were covered in paper that had to be torn off with the teeth before being loaded into guns. Muslims believed the paper was greased with pig fat and Hindus with cow fat, which offended both communities' religious sensibilities, and when ordered to use them they rebelled. Those who refused were imprisoned for ten years and put in chains, which for the Hindus especially was a public humiliation because they were from an elite warrior caste in the social hierarchy of India. On May 10 a sympathetic Sikh opened the prison gates and all the military prisoners there escaped. This was the spark that ignited long-standing resentment of colonial rule. The Indian soldiers killed local officers and marched on Delhi, the ancient Mughal capital. There was no garrison there and they killed many Europeans and Indian Christians. The news spread to other regions, setting off revolts, and there were massacres on both sides.

In Jersey, their advertisement in the local paper stated that Mr. and Mrs. Box Brown, Proprietors of the Panorama of the War in India, had spared neither trouble nor expense in procuring the "most truthful and thrilling information respecting the all-engrossing topic of the day." The "celebrated" Mr. Mills of London had produced the pictures. An artist called Edward Mills first surfaces in 1882, when an exhibition of his works was held in London. He painted a number of pictures of locations overseas, including Egypt and Italy.[17] The Box Browns might well have spotted a talented youngster at the start of his career, or it may be that "celebrated" was hype. Whoever created the images, the audiences would have known about these scenes, as newspapers carried detailed reports about a month after the events themselves. The panorama depicts the most dramatic events, which were listed in the Box Browns' advertisement to show how exciting this presentation was. The audience would have identified with what was happening in India, which became known as the "Jewel in the Crown" of Britain's empire. Their sympathies would have been with the British, so this was the main emphasis, but the Box Browns included early a scene that reminded their audiences that the British also behaved cruelly. This, however, may have been received with a "serves them right" response by chauvinists. They would have also been able to tell the story of William Edward Hall, born in Nova Scotia, Canada, the son of American ex-slaves, who became the first black man to be awarded the Victoria Cross, the highest award for bravery in the British armed forces, at the Relief of Lucknow.[18]

The Indian Mutiny

Most of the views are self-explanatory but I have added notes on some of the events in the scenes.

Part I

The Commencement of the Indian Revolt at Meerut.
The Fearful Massacre at Cawnpore.

The settlement at Cawnpore was besieged by rebels, and after three weeks an agreement was reached that the British could be evacuated. They went to boats waiting to take then to Allahabad. On the way some British officers and loyalist sepoys were killed; then at the river the others were fired on and their boats set alight when the crews fled. Survivors were rounded up. The men were killed on the spot. The women and children were held hostage and later massacred in Bibighar. Only four men managed to escape.

Repulse of the Sortie from Delhi on July 14, 1857.
Indians Blown from the Guns at Peshawar.

It was not just the rebels who behaved dishonorably. At the Peshawar garrison, British junior officers were intercepting the sepoys' mail and discovered some of them were planning to rebel. They were executed by being tied to the mouth of cannon that were fired. Bodies were blown to pieces and scattered over a wide area. Originally a Mughal method of execution, this had been used before the rebellion and remained in use on a number of occasions during the Mutiny and after.

General View of the City of Delhi before the Siege.

Destruction of the City of Delhi and the Explosion of the Cashmore
    Gate.
The Slaughter inside the City of Delhi.
Fight in the Lines before Delhi.
Engagement with the Mutineers at Badulee-Serai.

     Badulee Ke-Serai was on a ridge above Delhi. On July 12, 1857, it was seized by the British. In a supplement to the official publication, the London Gazette *on October 13, 1857, carried detailed reports from the commanding officer.*[19]

Rout of the Mutineers at Allahabad by Colonel Neill.

Part II

The Revolted Sepoys Driven from a Walled Village near Guzneede Nugger by
    the 60th Rifles.

     On April 21, 1858, an estimated 6000 rebels were attacked by British soldiers at Nageenah (today's Nagina). It was a celebrated victory by combined forces, not just the 60th Rifles.

The City of Calcutta, at Fort William, with the Arrival of Reinforce-
    ments.
A Splendid View of the City of Lucknow.
The Boomee Durwara Gate and severe Battle at Lucknow.
The Relief of Lucknow by the Scotch Highlanders, and the Screamings of
    Jessie Brown.

     Lucknow was an important center of British settlement. It was besieged by rebels but well defended by combined British and Indian forces until, after a long period, reinforcements arrived and the residents could be safely evacuated in November 1857. Jessie Brown (or maybe Cameron or MacPherson, sources differ) was a Highland soldier's wife who was reported to have fallen asleep and woken, screaming that she had heard the sound of the bagpipes of the relieving force, long before they were audible to anyone else among the besieged. The popular and prolific dramatist Dion Boucicault wrote Jessie Brown or the Relief of Lucknow *immediately after the event and it remained popular for the next twenty or so years. Doubt was not cast upon this highly dramatic episode until 1890, following a correspondence in* The Times.[20]

The Mahomedan Festival of the Muhaurrim.

     Muharram is the first month of the Islamic calendar. It is a month of remembrance and mourning. This suggests the Box Browns were not ignoring the sufferings of Indians.

Concluding with an Exquisite Display and Illumination of Indian Fireworks
    at Moorshedabad [Murshidabad].

The Indian mutiny presentation is the first time Jane is mentioned in connection with Henry's work, and she is shown as an equal partner. She was doing more than being co-owner of the diorama. Before the visit to Jersey, Mrs. H.B. Brown made her debut as a public speaker. On March 15 and the following four evenings she described the scenes and explained the situation in India to an audience in Greenwich. Her education and background as a schoolteacher were invaluable. She had learned how to marshal information to hold the attention of bored and hungry children, but now she could revel in adults who chose to be there, were interested, and wanted to be told things. At a time when a woman as high profile as Harriet Beecher Stowe did not speak publicly, this was daring, but Jane could appear in her schoolteacher role, explaining events rather than directly imparting her opinions on current affairs, which was what men mainly condemned. Reporting the Greenwich event in advance of their visit, the *Jersey Telegraph* said that there had been crowded houses for *Mr.* Box Brown's Panorama of the War in India. The editor probably thought there had been a misprint in the original report. It looks as if the presentation in Greenwich, a well-to-do suburb of London where many women were active in charitable works, was a trial run to see how audiences responded to the sight of a woman talking about current events with authority. Plainly, she was successful. Although Henry made the opening address and was "greeted with a hearty welcome," it was Jane who launched the Box Browns' season in Jersey, and her descriptive part was "ably conducted by Mrs. Box Brown." In the second week, Henry presented American Slavery and The Holy Land.[21] By the end of the fortnight the Box Browns had finished their presentations in Jersey, where they had proved they were a winning couple. Jane was an accomplished and confident woman and Henry was an accomplished and confident man, not intimidated by her abilities. From this point on, their newspaper advertisements usually stated that Mr. and Mrs. Box Brown were the joint proprietors of the shows.

Initiated as a Freemason

Jersey welcomed Henry in another way; on the island he joined the Freemasons. He was initiated in the Royal Sussex Lodge in St. Helier on April 20, 1858. Despite apparently not paying any dues after 1858 (although some records appear to be missing), he was passed a year later on March 2, 1859; raised on April 5, 1860; and his certificate of full membership was sent out by the Grand Lodge in London on June 6, 1862. He claimed to be 36—actually he was 43—and his occupation is given as theatrical.[22] How he came to join is not known, but he liked the camaraderie of societies, being a member of the Odd Fellows and also of the Ancient Order of Foresters. He may have thought the Freemasons were another Friendly Society but although their aims were similar, to help members professionally and if they fell on hard times, it was more of a networking organization, which was better suited to those living in one place and regularly attending meetings. Henry's itinerant life made it impossible to maintain contact with his Lodge, although, as will be seen, he later made contact with other Freemasons in mainland England.

Beyond the benefits and support of membership of an organization, becoming a Freemason was another opportunity for Henry to become part of British society. Although they had never discriminated on the basis of color or race, Freemasons were supposed to be freeborn, which should have ruled Henry out; as he had never been formally manumitted, he was still technically a slave in the United States. This ruling had been softened in the British colonies after the abolition of slavery, and in mainland Britain there had never been any discrimination, so he was able to join. Because neither color nor ethnicity is noted in the Freemason records, it is difficult to recover how many were initiated, but there is evidence of black members from the mid–18th century onward. In the United States white Freemasons refused to accept black members of their Lodges, even if they were free or freeborn. Black Americans petitioned the Grand Lodges in the United Kingdom for permission to found Lodges, which was often granted. The first was founded in 1784 by Prince Hall, who had been rejected by a white Lodge in Boston, and was followed by many others.[23]

The Box Browns revisited Guernsey in May. Henry advertised that all three of their presentations would be given on each of the three days they were booked to appear, but there is no account in the press of how they were received. By June they had returned to the mainland and were appearing in Basingstoke, Hampshire, where they replaced Gompertz's panorama of the Indian War, which had remained in London beyond the original intended dates because of its success, an indication of how popular this subject was. They returned in July to Woolwich, where Mr. Box Brown's Brass Band was again mentioned in advertisements. Music had always been a strong part of his entertainments, and he probably paraded through the street with them to advertise his presence. Samuel Fielden described such a visit to Todmorden, Lancashire, in 1861 in his autobiography:

> There had appeared in my native town at different times, several colored lecturers who spoke on the slavery question in America. I went frequently to hear them describe the inhumanity of that horrible system, sometimes with my father, and at other times with my sister. One of these gentlemen called himself Henry Box Brown; this gentlemen brought with him a panorama, by means of which he described places and incidents in his slave life, and also the means of his escape. He used to march through the streets in front of a brass band, clad in a highly-colored and fantastic garb, with an immense drawn sword in his hand.... He was a very good speaker and his entertainment was very interesting.[24]

By October the couple were in Deal, a seaside town in Kent, where there was a spat with someone else publicizing a rival show, possibly on the topical War in India. It ended up at the local petty sessions, a meeting of Justices of the Peace where minor cases were heard. Henry was always ready to defend his interests, and he accused Richard Friend of posting over his advertising posters with his own. Friend alleged the same against Henry. This was a common practice; perhaps one or the other overstepped the bounds of what was regarded as acceptable. After a few minutes of deliberation, the JPs agreed: "It was no doubt very annoying to have one's bills posted over or destroyed, but they were not aware it was an offence."[25]

Throughout October other presentations of the war were taking place in Glasgow, Belfast, and Stafford. Hainault's *Moving Diorama of the Indian Rebellion* went to Nottingham and Leicester, and Gompertz's *Panorama of the Indian Rebellion* went to Winchester and Brighton. In Devon a moving panorama was to be sold or lent.[26] This was during just one month, an indication of how topical and popular the subject was. Despite the generally enthusiastic welcome the Box Browns received, there were still places where only a limited number of people were willing to attend their presentations. In Lewes, Sussex, in November there were "tolerably large audiences" for the first two nights but the third did not come off because there were so few people present. In response they announced their intention to stay on another week, which may have been a mistake. In their next stop, at Gosport, audiences were also small, but when they returned to the Isle of Wight, they had more success, which would have helped to recoup any losses. The couple had spent time here after their marriage, so it must have held happy memories. Their new panorama of the Indian Mutiny, along with the old favorite American Slavery, was well received in Ryde and Ventnor. The local paper said, "Mr. Brown is the best Negro speaker of the English language we have ever heard, and he has mastered the subject of his lecture exceedingly well." The report added that the entertainment was "at once pleasing and instructive, especially to juveniles."[27] There is no mention of Jane's contribution to the evening, but it may be her influence that placed emphasis on the appeal to children.

Back on the mainland at the end of January 1859 they visited Petersfield, a market town some 17 miles (27 km) north of Portsmouth. They were there for three days, delivered all three presentations, and received a rapturous review in the local paper:

> The Panoramas exhibited by Mr. and Mrs. H.B. Brown were very successful. The scenes brought before our notice caused many a circular drop to flow and none but those whose hearts were scared could behold such ... distressing incidents without experiencing a thrilling and sympathising spirit towards those poor degraded Negroes. At the same time our very heart's blood seemed to wax

cold, and again became heated to a revengeful inclination against the perpetra-
tors of such atrocious barbarities; but while passing through these different sentiments our minds were calmed in a certain measure by the sweet melodies from
the harp. Great credit is due to this performer. After Mr. Box Brown had graph-
ically and ably described the African and American slaveries, he gave place,
amid shouts of applause, to Mrs. H. Brown, who undertook the sacred depart-
ment, viz., scenes in the Holy Land. To hear a lady in a fluent and eloquent manner describe the most important incidents relative to the holy place, Jerusalem,
and the chief events in the history of Jesus could not fail to enlist the attention
and admiration of her numerous and respectable hearers. The last evening we
had presented to our view a representation of the war in India, and the circum-
stance attending them. Once more English blood became warm and our feelings
were animated, first, at the cruelties of the demonical Sepoys, &c., and secondly,
hearing of the heroism of our brave men not forgetting "The Bonny Scotch
Highlanders," who relieved the distressed at Lucknow.[28]

Experimentation

In Brentford, Middlesex, a suburb of West London, Henry experimented
with a new kind of presentation, which would not reemerge for some time.
At some point, possibly in early 1851 when both were touring in Lancashire
and Yorkshire, he had met Richard Sheldon Chadwick, a mesmerist, who in
the late 1850s was also appearing in and around West London. Although he
is sometimes described as an American, Chadwick was born in Manchester
and seems never to have left Britain.

> Mr. Brown together with Professor Chadwick (who was engaged expressly for
> the occasion) introduced several experiments on mesmerism, human magnetism
> and electro-biology, which proved most successful, and afforded the crowded
> audience much pleasure and amusement. The mesmerism and biology by Mr.
> Brown, being his first experiments in public, was [sic] excellent and very suc-
> cessful, as was [sic] also many experiments by Professor Chadwick.[29]

Daphne Brooks finds that these three presentations and this experiment
in mesmerism created a "maddening elixir of panoramic grandeur, abolitionist visual display, anti-imperialist propaganda, spiritualist and magic
spectacle show" resulting in "excess and overload."[30] As advertisements and
other reports make clear, these were three separate presentations, often delivered on different days, and it seems that only on this one evening did Henry
show a panorama at the same time as he gave a display (with Chadwick) of
mesmerism. Presumably there was an interval after the panorama, probably
musical, then the mesmerism demonstration. Victorian audiences found it
easy to focus their attention and switch interest from one subject to another.
In 1853 in Chelmsford, Essex, a Mr. Montague had advertised that his show

would consist of "Pictorial Illustration of Uncle Tom's Cabin, an Exposition of Legerdemain and Clairvoyance, and a talented Troupe of Dogs and Monkeys, which will go through the most astonishing performances. Mrs. Montague will preside at the piano forte."[31] Today's television watchers are able to spend an evening taking in a quiz, a news bulletin, and a sit-com, finishing with a documentary program or drama, without becoming maddened or overloaded. Although this was to become a much more important factor in Henry's career, this very early experiment with mesmerism would not be repeated for some time, so will be discussed at that point.

During this visit to West London, on March 5, 1859, Henry was passed in the Freemasons' hierarchy in the Zetland Lodge in Kensington.[32] The couple then had a hit in the Surrey Assize Courts, not with a legal case but with three presentations of their panoramas on successive evenings. Whether this was in Guildford, Kingston-upon-Thames, or Croydon, all of which held Assizes, is not stated. It was most likely Kingston, as the Box Browns were due next week in nearby Richmond. Then they crossed the Thames to appear in Hammersmith for five days.

Like any modern celebrity, Henry did occasional charity gigs and appearances. On March 16, 1859, the Ancient Order of Foresters inaugurated a new Court. The local committee staged an impressive parade from the Windsor Castle Tavern in Hammersmith, where another Court met, to the Old Pack Horse public house two miles away on Turnham Green, which would be the meeting place of the new Court. The parade was led by three members of the Order on horseback and the band of the local militia and was followed by, according to the local newspaper, some one thousand people. Nothing like it had been seen before in this London suburb. Henry was unable to take part in the parade itself because he was giving a presentation but afterward came to the Old Pack Horse and, in his African robes, spoke last as the guest of honor, saying that he observed with much pleasure the blessing that shines upon the Order, and congratulated them on the opening of a New Court. He hoped they might meet every fortnight; that the Brothers would do good; and after saying that he had worked 16 hours a day for six years, expressed his gladness at being Member of the Order, concluding, "May God smile upon it, and may we do our duty to support it."[33] It is the kind of speech regularly delivered on similar occasions, including a reminder of the speaker's skills and importance.

Like the Freemasons, the Foresters did not discriminate on the basis of color, and the society's rules clearly stated that any man could be a Forester if accepted by a court. In the later 19th century the Foresters established a Subsidiary High Court in the United States, where there were thousands of members. This new body banned black members and would not back down. The British Society took the decision to sever ties with any court that did not

The Old Pack Horse public house in Turnham Green, West London, where Henry made a celebrity appearance in 1859 to inaugurate a new Court of the Ancient Order of Foresters. By circa 1880, when this photograph was taken, it had become rather dilapidated, and it was therefore restored to its former state and redecorated. The public house is still owned and run by a local brewery company, Fullers.

accept this element of the rules. While some courts did continue to follow the AOF rules, and some are still in existence, the majority split off to form their own American version of the society.

Diminishing Interest

The couple moved on to Uxbridge, and to Windsor, where, at the beginning of April, they were so successful that they prolonged their stay for three days. Reviews of Henry's Slavery presentation were all complimentary, although the *South Bucks Free Press* did say, of the Uxbridge visit, that the subject was "not a very novel one." People were beginning to show signs of diminishing interest. In Maidenhead in Berkshire in mid–April at both presentations the audience was not large, and in Wallingford in Oxfordshire in early May it was "smaller than anticipated." In Abingdon, 10 miles away, the audience was "liberal," which may have been a reference to their political leanings or to what the writer regarded as an overly generous reception of the show.[34]

Only Henry's own advertisements about appearances in nearby Banbury and in Leamington Spa in Warwickshire in June appeared in newspapers, so how well the couple were received in these places is not known. When they went to Coventry also in Warwickshire at the beginning of July, an act was appearing at Coventry Fair that may have given Henry other ideas for the future besides mesmerism. The Chinese magicians Arr Hee and Arr Samm were astonishing audiences with their feats, producing cups from table covers, and apparently devouring burning paper and then pulling out long rolls of undamaged paper from their throats. Arr Hee also juggled three knives and used his partner in a knife-throwing act. Arr Hee and Arr Samm are first mentioned as part of a troupe of Chinese jugglers and magicians on a provincial tour who were performing in Manchester and in Bradford in 1855, when Arr Hee, an acrobat, was said to be ten years old. Arr Samm performed magic tricks and also played the banjo. Later in their career the pair were joined by Arr Yau.[35] Although Arr Hee and Arr Samm may have been Chinese performers who decided to stay on after the rest of their troupe moved on, Arr Yau was almost certainly of British origin.

The Great Exhibition at Crystal Palace in 1851 had increased interest in the outside world, reinforced by the growing emphasis on the British Empire as a force for spreading values now regarded as white Eurocentric but then as civilizing. Many British entertainers on the Victorian stage exploited this, and performers from supposedly exotic cultures were often of European or American ancestry, like one of the Chinese clowns in Pablo Fanque's circus who was an Irishman. Arr Hee, whatever his true name and identity, seems to have been influential in the history of magic. Later, an American of pure Scottish descent named William Robinson (1861–1918) performed under the stage name of Chung Ling Soo. Before assuming a Chinese identity, Robinson had experimented with another exotic persona, beginning his career performing as Achmed Ben Ali. At times he claimed to have been an orphan taken in by Arr Hee, and at other times said he learned ancient Chinese magic in South America under the tutelage of an Asian mystic.[36]

Seeing the response of the visitors to the two Chinese performers' act may have planted a seed in Henry's mind. Just as to be a genuine black person performing in a minstrel show was an attraction, someone from a glamorous ethnicity performing tricks was a selling point. The mesmerism he had experimented with in Brentford was also in his thoughts. Now, however, it was still the panoramas that preoccupied him. In Rugby he seems to have presented both Slavery and the Holy Land, but whether he delivered the Indian Mutiny as well is not clear, because the paper just added that the Indian Mutiny had been listened to "with the greatest attention." When they mentioned her, newspapers were always respectful of Jane's lectures, but no one ever said she had the engaging and vivid manner of her husband, so it is probable that she delivered this presentation. She gave the factual talks, while Henry had a more emotional and dramatic style. They spoke in the Town Hall, where, in the room below, the local Temperance Society was listening to a stern lecture on the evils and dangers of alcohol, which received more prominence than the Box Browns did in the other local newspaper's report. When they went on to Staffordshire, speaking in Atherstone, Stafford, and Newport, it was Henry's name alone that was given in reports.[37]

In Wellington a note of mild hostility appeared: "Mr. Brown represents himself as a fugitive slave," as if this were some kind of false identity. It was also the first, and so far the only, time that I have found Jane's color mentioned in any report, and this may reflect a degree of racial prejudice. Although the reviewer said that "the scenes in the Holy Land were good, especially the dissolving views," it concluded "the attendance was not so numerous as might have been expected." Another newspaper was kinder, attributing the lack of numbers to the unfavorable weather and saying, "Mrs. Brown gave a very good explanation of the scenery of the Holy Land." The audience increased on the last two days, either in response to better weather or through word-of-mouth praise, and at their next stop in Dawley in the neighboring county of Shropshire they "met with good success." After four days in Bridgnorth, the Box Browns arrived in Shrewsbury. As it was the biggest and most important town in the region, they were prepared to spend more on advertising here, and the local papers carried a detailed listing of the contents of the Slavery presentation. There was also a note designed to flatter Henry's potential audience:

> But not able to breathe the pure air of Freedom in the so called Free States of America he was compelled to seek the shores of Great Britain, where he has for the last seven years travelled with his Entertainment of African and American slavery with the utmost success.[38]

The county record office for Shropshire holds what is so far a unique copy of a poster used by the Box Browns to advertise their entertainment. Henry, in his dress as a "Native Prince," was to present the *Grand Moving Mirror of Africa & America* and also the *Diorama of the Holy Land*. Some scenes from the original panorama, like tarring and feathering in South Carolina, are not listed and may have been cut from the presentation because they were specifically American. Jane is given second billing to appear with the Indian War diorama, but its contents are not listed. Music also formed part of the program. At this time Shrewsbury was not a garrison town and did not have a barracks, but Henry emphasized the appeal his presentation had to soldiers, listing all the places where he and Jane had performed for

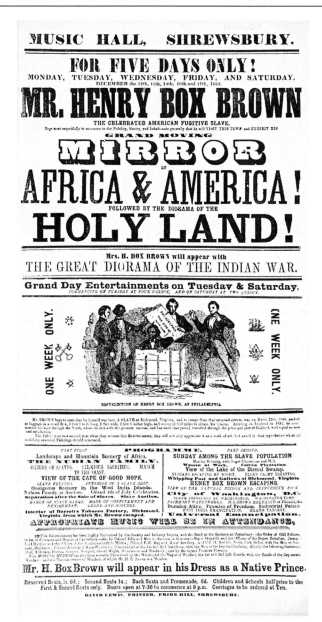

Poster from Shropshire Archives, Ref: 655/4/367—Entertainments Bill: Henry Box Brown showing a Mirror of Africa and America at the Music Hall. Discovered in 2008 by student Shukar Bibi, cited in Price, Alan, *Creating Memorials, Building Identities: the Politics of Memory in the Black Atlantic* (Liverpool University Press, 2011), p. 79, n24.

various regiments. This may simply have been because he had used the same advertisement in previous places where there was a strong military presence or perhaps it was because of the events in India. Henry added, as further endorsement,

> this *MOVING MIRROR* has recently been Patronised by the Worshipful the Mayor of Windsor, the 1st and 2nd Life Guards, with band of the Regiments Windsor: and also the Masonic Order of Windsor of which Mr H.B. Brown is a Member.

Henry had been in Windsor earlier in the year but there is no record in the Lodge's minute book of him attending a meeting there, although the Mayor and fellow Masons were the patrons of this show.[39] Perhaps he had been entertained by them in their meeting place at the Windsor Hotel opposite the castle and thought it was a regular meeting. This indicates, however, that he still regarded himself as a member and looked for support for his entertainment from other Freemasons.

The Box Browns moved on to Staffordshire, performing in Newcastle-under-Lyme, Stoke, Hanley, and Longton, where they arrived in February 1860. Here, having learned a lesson in Wellington, they decided not to risk losing audience numbers through inclement weather—they emphasized that the theater would be heated with stoves. They also announced an afternoon performance for schools, as they had done in other towns.[40] Jane's teaching experience was proving a hit with reviewers:

> We must, in justice to Mrs. Henry Box Brown, say that, throughout, the concise and truthful discussion of events, and also the explanation of the views were given in a superior style, and elicited the applause of the audience.... Mr. H. Box Brown has added a special feature of attraction to his panorama by the scenes given of the Indian Mutiny, coupled with historical events connected therewith, and so elegantly explained by Mrs. Brown.[41]

They were still including a musical element ("The band too played in masterly style the Hallelujah Chorus, and other selections") but at their appearance in Burslem in February they introduced a new element: the distribution of articles like books or silver watches, which resulted in "very crowded and highly appreciative" audiences.

This visit was mentioned in a meeting of the Burslem Board of Health, when the committee debated the pros and cons of reducing their charge for the use of the Town Hall. The standard fee was £3 3s for the first night, reduced thereafter. The committee had found that the Box Browns had used slightly more gas—17s worth—than the usual 14s or 15s. It concluded this was because this entertainment occupied the hall for a longer period than public meetings or concerts.[42] The Box Browns were giving value for money, but it was not just the cost of hiring the venue. The couple needed to think about how successful the distribution of prizes had been and whether it would be worth making prizes a regular part of the show. Even the cheapest articles were a cost factor.

They returned to Newcastle-under-Lyme at the end of February. Here and in Congleton in March, in Hyde in early April (where he was under the patronage of the local Masonic Lodge and where he was raised in the hierarchy of the Freemasons, the last stage in becoming accepted as a full member), and in Bury in May there was no mention of prizes.[43] The couple then stopped touring, and a few months later their first known child arrived.

A New Family

Possibly there had been miscarriages or the early deaths of babies, but on August 25, 1860, Agnes Jane Floyd Brown was born at 4 Cale Green, Stockport, on the Cheshire-Lancashire border. Henry felt comfortable in this region, where he was well-received and where audiences responded to him. Now part of Greater Manchester, in the mid–19th century Stockport was a separate town. It had been a place for textile manufacture for some time, initially silk in the 18th century, and by the 19th cotton had become the major product. It was also one of the country's premier hat-making centers and the Box Browns were lodging with a hatter, George Shatwell. When Henry registered the birth he gave his occupation as "tobacco manufacturer." He may have been trying to impress a snooty local official, accustomed to recording events in local businessmen's lives, but this is an indication of the uncertainty he still felt about his status and that he was again, as he had done at his marriage in Falmouth, upgrading his enslaved background. Just as he turned his father's occupation of field hand or smallholder into farmer when he married Jane, he now upgraded his work in the tobacco factory in Richmond, Virginia, to being a manufacturer when he registered the birth of their daughter. There had been other times when Henry had dropped out of public sight for extended periods. He was earning well and, as his youth in America shows, he had the habit of saving to provide for his first family. This responsible attitude to his earnings meant that he could afford to take time off before and after his daughter's birth and enjoy this new child, who was baptized on October 5 in St. Mary, Stockport, when Henry again gave his occupation as tobacco manufacturer. He could have supplemented his income by singing locally with touring groups or even undertaken singing engagements in private homes if necessary. It was not until November 1860 that he went back to performing, this time presenting only his original panorama in Manchester, where the whole family were staying. At Christmas he was in Huddersfield, some 21 miles (34 km) away in Yorkshire. He then may have taken a break of a few months, but it seems more likely there were other unrecorded shows.[44]

At the end of 1860, on December 20, South Carolina became the first state to secede from the Union of the United States. Henry may have noted this a few weeks later when news reached Britain, but he could not have realized how significant this would become—his mind must have been on closer and more mundane events, not least providing for his wife and newborn daughter. But in the first months of 1861 as more and more states began to secede, he cannot have been unaware of the gathering storm. At the census on April 7, 1861, the couple and baby Agnes were still in Yorkshire, staying in North Street, Keighley. At this time they did not have a settled home, so Jane and his daughter accompanied him, both for company and to save money. It is likely Henry was doing solo shows, but Jane could also have appeared, and if both her parents were performing then Agnes, as was usual then, would have been left sleeping in a trunk backstage. No records of appearances in Keighley or the surrounding area have yet been found. The family is recorded as a separate household, so the Box Browns were renting self-contained accommodation rather than lodging with others, suggesting they were using this address as a base.[45]

At the end of April they were in Burnley in Lancashire. Before his marriage Henry had been enthusiastically received here and elsewhere in the county, and he now put on a show for the locals by parading through the street dressed as an African chief to announce his arrival and by distributing presents at the end of the stay. Jane was back to presenting. She did the Indian Mutiny and the Holy Land, while her husband delivered Negro Life in America.[46] The Mutiny itself had been suppressed in 1859, primarily because the various rebel factions were not unified. Some Muslims called for *jihad*, a holy war, but some supported the British, and there were divisions between Shias and Sunnis, who feared each other. Sikhs dreaded the return of Mughal rule, and there were other political fissures in the Indian population. The major effect of the Mutiny was that in 1858 the EIC was dissolved and the British government assumed direct rule as the British Raj. This was astounding to a population who, like their parents, grandparents, and previous generations, had grown up with John Company, as it was familiarly known. Established in 1600, the EIC had been an apparently permanent and important feature of British life, but had now just disappeared. The mutiny was not the only reason, but it was a contributory factor, and there was still interest in it. Jane, like many of her audience, had personal knowledge of its reach into aspects of local life, not just the cotton cloth imported from India that was made into the clothes they wore every day, but the exports on which industries depended. Copper and tin mined in Cornwall were a large export to India, something that must have been well known to a schoolteacher, and the EIC had a monopoly of trade with Asia. As an American, Henry must have regarded the whole concept of a monarchy and an empire as completely alien and so been happy to leave this presentation and fielding questions about it to his wife.

The change of title for the presentation and Henry's dressing up as an African chief, as he had been doing for a while now, might be regarded as him discovering his African heritage, but that is perhaps to impose a 21st-century concern about ethnic minorities' personal identity on a 19th-century businessman. Africa was becoming a subject of growing public awareness in Britain. What became known as the Scramble for Africa, the division of the continent between the European powers, had not yet started, but the explorations of Richard Burton, John Speke, and James Grant along the great rivers were arousing increasing interest in the so-called Dark Continent. Missionaries had a long history in the coastal areas to which European traders were confined, and some now ventured further inland, sometimes with unhappy results. The memoirs and talks by those who had returned were popular. No one has left any detailed description or a picture of Henry in his robes at this time, so it is not clear on what he based them, but he was, as ever, keeping up with political events and fashions and using them in his own way for his own ends. At this moment, however, it was his American background that would come to the fore.

The American Civil War

Civil war in America finally erupted on April 12, 1861, when Confederate forces fired on Fort Sumter in Charleston, South Carolina. Virginia decided to secede and join the Confederacy. Shortly afterward, 48 counties in the northwest of the state split off and joined the Union as West Virginia. Its position between the northern and southern states and its division between the Confederacy and the Union meant that Virginia became a key battleground in the war. More battles were fought here than anywhere else, among them Bull's Run, an important early conflict, and Appomattox Courthouse, the penultimate battle of the entire war. The Virginian general Robert E. Lee played a major role, eventually becoming overall commander of the Confederate forces. Richmond, Virginia, chosen as the Confederacy's capital, became a particular target, partly due to its symbolic role but mainly because of its geographic and strategic position. It was a seaport and five railways terminated in the city. It was also one of the few places in the South with iron works capable of manufacturing artillery. Had Nancy and their children not been sold, Henry might still have been living there with them, still working in the tobacco factory, so he must have followed the news in his homeland keenly.

A cable to carry telegraphs had been laid from Dover to Calais as early as 1851 but although there had been attempts to lay a transoceanic cable, it was not until 1866, after the war had ended, that Britain and America were connected. Until then, it took about two weeks for news to cross the Atlantic by ship. Members of Henry's audience must have asked his opinion and assessment of the events and would have expected him to incorporate current developments into his original presentation on American slavery, which now had fresh contemporary relevance. The couple commissioned a new panorama on the American Civil War, but in the meantime they had to do the best with what they had.

June 1861 did not start well. The Box Browns had not realized the significance of arriving in Bacup in Yorkshire on Whit Friday, a gala day, when factories closed and many people had left the town on excursions. As there were so many other entertainments on offer, some of them free, the Box Browns did not draw large audiences. To add to their woes, the editor of the *Accrington Guardian* sued Henry for 7s 6d over an advertisement placed in his newspaper in connection with his appearance in Burnley two months earlier. According to Henry, he had agreed to pay 3s 6d rather than the usual 2s 6d charged by the *Preston Guardian* for an advertisement, and his evidence was corroborated by his two employees who had been in the public house with him when the verbal agreement was made. The verdict went in his favor and he was also awarded the costs of traveling with his two witnesses from Stockport to attend the hearing. He was back in Accrington in November, speaking about the war in America and slavery.[47] This may have been with a new panorama, but he did not place an advertisement with the newspaper that had sued him and the no-doubt-disgruntled editor ignored his visit, so what this presentation contained and how it was received are unknown.

When he revisited Manchester at the end of November, Charles Dickens was also appearing in the city, reading from *David Copperfield*, his favorite among his novels. In the face of this fierce competition, Henry offered presents as well as a band of musicians. From this point on, gifts became a regular feature of his entertainment and appeared in Leigh, Atherton, and Bolton in January 1862. His advertisement for his appearance in Leigh lists songs he will be singing. In addition to his standard numbers, "Freedom's Song" and "Mr. Henry Box Brown's Escape," he gave the "Song of the Nubian Family by the North Star."[48]

Henry was always a big name in the north of England. In March 1862, when the blockade of the Southern ports because of the American Civil War caused unemployment among British textile workers, a newspaper in Wigan, Lancashire, carried an impassioned editorial headed WE MUST HAVE COTTON! In a long account of the effects, the writer said, "We may, perhaps, be induced to join the crusade against the evils of negro servitude, and endeavour to work out the emancipation of Quashee in the mode suggested by Messrs. Lloyd Garrison, Box Brown, Benson, and other platform notabilities of the New and Old World."[49] Here, Henry was being bracketed with William Lloyd Garrison, the editor of *The Liberator* and for the British the face of American abolition, and probably George Benson, Garrison's brother-in-law, a Quaker abolitionist. It is an indication of his fame that these were the three best known Americans connected with abolitionism that a journalist in Lancashire in the 1860s would expect his readers to recognize.

Return to Jersey and a New Subject

Four years after their second visit the Box Browns returned to Jersey. With the need to support his family, Henry was becoming increasingly reluctant to go to new and untried places, sticking to regions where he had been successful before. He was so much a star in Jersey that his arrival was announced in the list of Passengers Arrived from Southampton on April 17, 1862. Only the more socially prestigious appeared in these lists and among them is "[Mr.] Box Brown and family." He went back to his usual venue, bringing the new, topical panorama of the America War. This may have been the first time that it was unveiled.

The American Civil War became the first conflict to be extensively photographed, but at the time it was not possible to incorporate photographs into newspapers. Nor, because of the long exposure times required, was it possible to capture battles in progress. That is why it is mainly portraits, posed re-creations, and battlefields in the aftermath that represent the Civil War pictorially. In the 1850s and 1860s wood engravings based on photographs could be used, but it was a laborious and expensive process, confined to periodicals like the weekly magazine *The Illustrated London News*. A process called photogravure was used to reproduce photographs in books and as prints from the 1850s onward, but it was not yet possible to produce them on the scale and size needed for a presentation, so the Box Browns had to use old technology.

The paintings in Part I are fairly general and some could probably have been adapted from battle scenes that had been used in other panoramas. Where the images on which the panorama paintings were based came from is not known, but they may have been photographs. The Battle of Bull's Run and the Battle of Rich Mountain had both taken place five months before, in July 1861 in Virginia, and the Battle of Springfield took place in Missouri in October 1861. The Confederates had been victorious at the first two battles but the Union forces triumphed in the third. The emphasis on Virginia may have been prompted by Henry's knowledge of his home state, but unfortunately the Union forces did not do well there in the early period of the war. It was necessary to counterbalance this with a Union victory, like the important

The American Civil War Panorama

Part I

Distant View of New York.

New York Broadway.

Departure of the Troops by Land from New York.

City of Washington.

Camp Ground near Washington City.

Soldiers leaving the Camp for the Seat of War.

Heights of Maryland Fortified by the Rebels within Sight of the Camp Ground.

London Bridge across the Potomac.

March of 15,000 Northern Troops to the Great Battle of Bull's Run.

Part II

The Great Battle at Bull's Run—commencing at Fairfax Court-house with Masked Batteries.

Prominent View.

The Southern Commander Jeff[erson] Davis with His Two Generals, Johnson and Beauregard.

Russell the English Reporter of the London Times, to be seen in the Distance on the Hill, Taking his Sketches for the English Mail.

The Grand Retreat from Bull's Run.

The Great Battle at Richmountain.

The Cotton Valley at Richmountain with the Growth and Cultivation of Cotton.

The Great Battle of Springfield Missouri between the Federalists and Confederates, Assisted by Half Bred Cherokee Indians.

Concluding with the

GRAND NAVAL ENGAGEMENT

OF

THE MONITOR AND MERRIMAC

AND

ILLUMINATION OF RICHMOND CITY

sea battle fought between the *Monitor* and the *Merrimac* on March 8 and 9, 1862. The local paper noted that the Box Browns had recently added a new view of this naval battle, and it was Jane who described it "in an exceedingly lucid manner."

The *Merrimac* (sometimes spelled *Merrimack*) was a steamship that had been in the Norfolk Navy Yard in Virginia when Fort Sumter was burned. On the day Virginia seceded, in order to prevent her falling into Confederate hands, she was burned to the waterline and sunk, but her engines remained intact. So desperate for ships was the Confederacy that she was raised and plated with iron manufactured in Richmond. She was relaunched as the CSS *Virginia* in February 1862 to break the blockade of the James River, on which Richmond stands, and initially did well against wooden sailing ships. The USS *Monitor* had been recently built by the Union. She was an iron-hulled steamship, the most technologically advanced of the time, and took on the *Merrimac* in the Battle of Hampton Roads. The result was inconclusive; neither ship was irreparably damaged and the blockade continued, but this could be represented as a Union victory. This was a significant event because it was the first battle between ironclad warships. The painting produced would have needed to be specific, rather than simply using a standard battle-at-sea view. Then, as now, there were people in the audience who would know the difference between one kind of vessel and another. The images must have been supplemented with up-to-date information drawn from newspapers.

In the second week Henry also presented American Slavery and the Holy Land. The Civil War panorama was not the only novelty that the audiences were offered, and it looks as if the couple were trying out new elements in their joint enterprise. The two weeks of the Box Browns' planned stay in Jersey were extended by two more. In the initial additional period they offered prizes. The first prize, the advertisement stated, would be worth £5, with the others in proportion. Then one more week was added to the stay, with more new elements: Henry would be presenting three silver cups to the winners of a donkey race. So popular was this donkey race that a prisoner in the local jail, John Gabeldu, was able to take advantage of the crowds to escape from an officer while he and another convict were moving timber to a sawmill. Henry also offered "Roars of Laughter at the Extraordinary Sayings and Doings of the Mesmeric Subjects!,"[50] an element that had briefly figured over a year ago in Brentford, West London, but did not become a regular part of his act until later, although he must have been considering and practicing this new subject for some months.

Honesty Questioned

Back in England, only the panorama of African and American Slavery was presented in Plymouth in July and in the suburb of Stonehouse in September. In Plymouth was the great naval base and in Stonehouse the Royal Marine barracks and a naval hospital. Henry was probably wary of presenting his Civil War panorama to an audience of experts in armed combat, or maybe he thought they would not want to be reminded of their day jobs when out for an evening's entertainment, but he retained the presentation of articles to members of the audience. This provoked an exchange of letters in the columns of the *Western Daily Mercury*. On September 15 "Lover of Justice" wrote to the editor, saying that Henry had shown partiality in drawing for "prizes," claiming that on September 12 a young boy had been the winner of a timepiece but it had been presented to a person "who had no claim whatever." Henry replied immediately:

> Sir, I wish through the aid of your valuable columns to contradict the statement contained in a letter in your paper signed "Lover of Justice," concerning my entertainment now open at St George's Hall, Stonehouse. In the first place, he complains of partiality shown in the distribution of the tickets. That is certainly false, everyone who visits my entertainment gets ticket given him before he enters the hall. There is no distinction whatever made in the distribution of them. Secondly, I neither have the tickets drawn, neither I give away prizes, as was intimated in the paragraph in question, at the close entertainment. He next calls the attention the public to my advertisements. There never has in any way or any time been advertisement inserted in any of the papers here containing anything about "drawing," "prizes," or parties "winning" them at my entertainment; therefore I can clearly contradict the statement from beginning to end. At the close of my entertainment I freely give number of "presents," not "prizes," and whatever party holds the corresponding ticket with the one I should chance to call I immediately present that party with the article I called the ticket for. This was done Friday night, the very night in question, but by accident there were two tickets alike—whether from misprint or not, I cannot say ; but the first party that answered to the ticket I presented with the article I called the ticket for. I now leave the matter the opinion of the public generally whether the "presents" were honestly given away. I am, Sir, yours respectfully,
>
> H. B. BROWN.
> Sept. 16th 1862.

He was being a little disingenuous but he must have been aware of the law. It is still the case that although prizes may be given for competitions in which some skill is required (even if it is of the most basic kind of selecting between two alternatives), a license is necessary to hold a raffle or lottery in which tickets are bought and the awarding of prizes is random. The careful language of this letter, drawing a distinction between prize and present, suggests he needed to get expert legal advice, and it would have been a lawyer's clerk who actually wrote the letters to ensure they were correctly worded, so there is no clue here to his degree of literacy. Lover of Justice was not persuaded. He replied immediately:

> Sir,—A letter appeared in your columns of Tuesday, the inst., signed H.B. Brown, contradicting the assertion made respecting the distribution of tickets

at the above-named entertainment. I must again assert that consider the articles alluded to are "prizes" notwithstanding their possessing the appellation of "gifts" "presents", if they are not drawn for would enquire why each person should, entering the Hall, presented with ticket bearing particular number and colour. Mr. H. Brown, in intimating his ignorance of the cause of the mistake, suggests that it may have been on account of a "mis-print" in the ticket: admitting this, I should scarcely imagine that misprint would convert "pink" ticket into a "white." In concluding, I will remark that the "mistake" referred was not singular, as similar ones have been committed since the night in question. I am, Sir, yours very sincerely,

LOVER OF JUSTICE.
Sept. 17th, 1862.

Henry had a possible explanation:

Sir,—I again wish, through your columns, to contradict a statement, made by "A Lover of Justice," in your paper of yesterday, concerning the "presents" "given" at my entertainment. They are not prizes drawn for they are not prizes won by any particular party, but freely given by myself. He also says that the same mistake has occurred since "the" night in question. It has; but how? A young man who has never paid for admission to my entertainment, but has had several free tickets for admission, was dishonest enough pick up old tickets from the hall that were scattered about the audience when leaving the hall, and preserve them, until by chance I might call any number he had thus secured. Thus "the" ticket which has been the subject so much spoken of in your paper by the so-called "Lover of Justice" might have been secured the same way. I am, Sir, yours very respectfully.

H. B. BROWN.
Sept. 18th 1862

Nothing resulted from this exchange. It seems unlikely that Henry was running some kind of scam by giving prizes to people who would return them, although it would not be impossible to ensure that particular individuals had certain numbers. Given the quality of artificial lighting in public places at that time, both mistaking pale pink for white and misreading numbers are plausible. There were, however, no further claims of malpractice in future accounts of the distribution of gifts, so Henry must have learned a lesson, either to be more careful about reading numbers or not to fiddle the results. The last performance in Stonehouse was on September 20, and there was no reference to mesmerism in the week Henry and Jane were there.

Separation

After the success of their visits to Jersey and Stonehouse, the Box Browns took a couple of months off and probably spent them with Jane's family in

Cornwall to introduce their daughter, now two years old. It seems as if Henry alone went with the American Slavery and American War presentations to St. Austell, where he was well received, and then on to Redruth in November 1862. In Redruth there was competition from an American equestrian company, and because there had been a previous visit to the town, the panorama was only "slightly attended." Henry put on a free show for the Sunday School children and a month later at the beginning of January gave another presentation, donating the proceeds to the Widows & Orphans Fund of the Druids Lodge of the Odd Fellows Society. In the New Year he appeared in Falmouth and Truro; then in late March he returned to Newton Abbot, at Easter he was in Torquay in neighboring Devon, and in summer he traveled to Exmouth and Exeter before going to Bristol, Bath, and Cardiff, where he began an extended tour of Wales, which did not finish until he returned to Bristol in October 1864. During this time all presentations were by Henry of the slavery panorama and the American Civil War; there is no mention of Jane in any of the advertisements or notices, nor of the panoramas she had delivered. For a year Henry performed alone.[51]

There are a number of possible reasons for the couple's separation, although Henry could have visited her from time to time if, as seems likely, Jane was with her family. She might have been ill or had a miscarriage, exacerbated by exhaustion, or may have been needed at home. Her father John Floyd is missing from the 1861 census. Miners generally did not live to a great age; if they were lucky enough to escape accidents, their working conditions often led to ill health. The death of a John Floyd, aged 66, is registered in Penzance in the September quarter of 1859, and this is most likely her father. By 1862 his widow would have been 68, and if she were in need of help, Jane would be the one in the best position to stay with her for a while. And of course there is always the possibility that the couple fell out. Living and working with the same person 24/7 is a great strain and some idiosyncrasies and habits that in the first flush of love seem endearing become major irritants, so they may have wanted a break from each other. Given the couple's previous and subsequent history this seems unlikely but must still be considered. The donation Henry gave to the Odd Fellows in Redruth seems significant; the Box Browns would have benefited from support from the organization if Jane or another member of the family were ill. On balance, this seems the most likely explanation. Whatever the reason, Jane and Henry were back together by the end of January 1864, when she became pregnant and they were ready to embark on another momentous phase in their joint career.

ACT 3: MAGIC

Scene 6

Goodbye to Enslavement

Henry gave his last slavery presentation in Britain (that I can find evidence for) in Cardiff in November 1863.[1] With this behind him, he became completely free of the shackles of enslavement. For Americans this is still a heavy legacy, but the position in Victorian Britain was different. Although the British Empire profited massively from slavery, there had never been plantation or chattel slavery in the mother country. Even during the period of the British slave trade, c. 1660–1807, when there were thousands of black people, mainly servants and mariners, in England, they lived on equal terms with their white counterparts, whom they often married and got pregnant (although not always in that order) without any major problems. Ports like London, Liverpool, and Bristol had long-standing quarters where black and white lived together; there were no ghettos. Of course there must have been prejudice and discrimination, as there still are in all societies, but in Britain these were aimed at other minorities as well, most notably the Irish and Jews. The only legal discrimination during the period of the British slave trade had been on grounds of religion. Those who could not swear an oath to uphold the Anglican church, like nonconformists, Catholics, and Jews, were excluded from government and other posts and, until the mid–1850s, from university education at Oxford and Cambridge.

How far Henry had adjusted to this different environment, where religious affiliation was legally more important than ethnicity, must remain an unanswered question. Frederick Douglass, William Wells Brown, David Dorr, and others were fundamentally changed by the much shorter time they spent away from the United States, and they returned there, heartened, in order to continue to fight for rights, or, like Dorr, to free himself. Although Henry had now been in Britain for 14 years, all his formative years and a long period of his adult life had been spent in enslavement. Initially his living had come from rehearsing again and again this period of his life. With the introduction of new lecture subjects he had been moving away from enslavement for some time, but this was still part of the program, especially with the Civil War presentation as it had been with *Uncle Tom's Cabin*. Some of his attempts to diversify, like the ventures into straight acting, where he had also played slaves, had failed. Henry and Jane had introduced other newer and more topical subjects—the Indian Mutiny, the Holy Land, and the American Civil War—but now the Indian Mutiny was over, slavery had turned into an old story, and this type of illustrated lecture was becoming literally yesterday's news. Although he must have continued to follow events in America, Henry would have sensed they were not of immediate personal interest to the majority of the British public. It was also dragging on too long; even in the 19th century, the news cycle was relatively short.

What W.E.B. Du Bois called the double consciousness of looking at one's self through the eyes of a white, racist society that regarded black people with contempt put Henry in a position where he was enacting this role in another society, but where in almost all places he himself was not treated with contempt; rather, he was admired, applauded, and accepted with enthusiasm. There was a third dimension, the consciousness of his professional abilities in presenting his enslaved self, and a fourth, off stage, dealing as a businessman with the managers of premises and newspapers, as well as with his employees. Privately, he was a husband and father, whose wife also had a significant input into their joint professional life. At times he must have felt as if he were holding up a mirror to his mirror image, seeing an infinity of representations. This was the moment to let go of his past and relaunch himself, unencumbered by enslavement. As Lee Jackson has detailed, mass entertainment began to burgeon in the 1860s,[2] so it was a good moment to move into pure entertainment. At the end of 1863, Henry reinvented himself as mesmerist or electro biologist.

Mesmerism

Franz Anton Mesmer (1734–1815) was a German doctor. Working in the 18th century, he developed a theory that there was an invisible fluid permeating human and celestial bodies, a natural transference of energy between all animate and inanimate objects. He called this animal magnetism and believed that an understanding of this force could be used therapeutically to treat both physical and mental illness. The practices that developed from this were called mesmerism, after him. A scientific commission set up by Louis XVI of France in 1784 proved that animal magnetism had no existence; cures had been made through suggestibility. This did not deter a number of practitioners, and in the late 18th century many made a very profitable living in Britain, mainly in London, from the credulity of the fashionable and well-to-do. Even the rational intellectual Harriet Martineau believed mesmerism had cured her of a malaise that had afflicted her for some five years, although her brother-in-law, a surgeon, disputed this. By 1812 some of the medical profession were claiming that mesmerism was completely debunked, but others remained uncertain.[3] In 1843 the Scottish physician James Braid gave the term "hypnosis" to a technique derived from Mesmer's theories that he used to treat the sick. Increasingly, rather than being used for strictly medical purposes, the techniques Mesmer advocated and Braid had developed, putting people into trances and giving them instructions, were employed as a parlor game and in stage acts for entertainment purposes, where it was known as "electro-biology," as electricity was seen as a kind of spirit in the body.

Henry was not the first black man to use mesmerism on stage in Britain. H[enry] E[dward] Lewis, sometimes called "the Negro Mesmerist," hypnotized strangers; he made them fall asleep and then act on his suggestions. He arrived from New York and first appeared in Liverpool in April 1850. Henry could not have seen him there, as by November Lewis had left on a tour of Britain. Lewis seems to have genuinely believed this was a valid medical treatment, but the first entertainer to present mesmerism in Britain as an amusement, rather than a subject of scientific interest, was another American, G.W. Stone, who arrived with the medium Maria Hayden in 1850. While Henry and Smith were making their first appearances, he was also performing in Liverpool and placed an advertisement in a local paper:

> Mr. G.W. STONE begs to announce that he may be seen at No. 56, Duke-street, every MONDAY, between the hours of Nine and One o'clock, for the purpose of giving Instructions to those who desire to learn this wonderful Science; and will guarantee that everyone receiving instructions from him shall be able to produce all the results which he himself produces. N.B. One lesson only required.

The fact that everyone could learn this skill in only one lesson, lasting about four hours, suggests it was not a scientific technique that was taught but how to entertain the public with tricks. Stone also appeared in other Lancashire towns while Henry and James Smith were touring the area.[4] To say that in 1850 this might have given Henry ideas for his future is too far-fetched, but he may have attended a performance and it is an indication of how early the craze for electro-biology had arrived.

Zamoiski, a Polish man from Warsaw, was another of the early exponents of electro-biology and was first mentioned in the British press in 1852, when he gave lectures in Leeds. He apparently relieved the rheumatism of a member of his audience at his first appearance. Although initially presenting himself as treating illness, he moved into entertainment and many successful tours followed, but there were those who were not impressed. When he appeared on the Isle of Wight in 1858, the local paper was not taken in:

A person named Mons. ZAMOISKI, has given three entertainments at the Victoria-rooms during the week, upon what is called mesmerism. We have yet to learn of what, besides humbug, this "science" consists; and the absurd puffing used on the occasion has certainly not raised it in our estimation.[5]

He too was later to be exposed as a fraud.

Undoubtedly there were and are individuals who are more or less susceptible to suggestion and can be made to behave in unnatural ways, but most, possibly all, of the many stage electro-biologists at this time recruited people who for a fee pretended to be in a trance and to obey commands. Advertisements for professional subjects appeared in the *Era*, carefully coded. Had these been genuine enquiries for medical subjects, the advertisements would not have appeared in the trade journal for the entertainment industry:

WANTED, immediately, a YOUNG LADY, a good Mesmeric Patient; also, a Young Man that is a good Patient. Address, General Manager, 30, Prince-street, Bristol.

WANTED, immediately, a LECTURER and EXPERIMENTER in the Science of MESMERISM and PHRENOLOGY. Likewise, a good MESMERIC SUBJECT. Address, Mr Truton, Post-office, Liverpool.

MESMERISM

WANTED, immediately, a good MALE and FEMALE MESMERIC and BIOLOGICAL PATIENT, to travel. Address, Mr. Henry, Post-office, Newport, Monmouthshire.[6]

The Performing Self

Henry's unsuccessful forays into acting would have been of some use as he now played a different part. He knew his personality and presentation style attracted people; they liked him and wanted to listen to him. This consideration of how Henry represented himself to and how he was seen by audiences raises the question of identity, which is very much a contemporary concern. There are now those who regard Henry's changes of career in terms of reinventing himself, a voyage of self-discovery, a quest for identity. As Martha J. Cutter writes:

I have come to the conclusion that Brown manipulated alter-egos throughout his life, including (but not limited to) such sobriquets as "The King of All Mesmerists," "The African Chief," and "Dr. Henry Brown, Professor of Electro-Biology." He created a trickster-like presence and an ever-changing, innovative performance art that melded theater, street shows, magic, painting, singing, print culture, visual imagery, acting, mesmerism, and even medical treatments. Brown's multi-media art attempted to move beyond the flat and stereotypical representation of African Americans present in the phenomenally popular trans-atlantic performance mode of the nineteenth-century minstrel show. Ever the escape artist, Brown sought to evade nineteenth-century culture's prescriptions for appropriate African American behavior, as well as for the representation of Blacks within art.

To some extent this is true. In his career Henry presented himself in different ways, appropriating a kaleidoscope of methods, but I would argue this is more to do with the nature of employment in his profession than with a consciously or unconsciously personal or political stance. What he was doing was not projecting his personal identity but a persona, an aspect of his personality that he presented to his public; it was part of his act. As the showbiz joke has it, "If you can fake sincerity, you can fake anything." Most, if not all, performers do this. Some are much the same on- and off-stage, others are very different, but all project some part of their true personality. To see the performative face or faces Henry presented to his public as his true self is to misunderstand the nature of his profession. He seems to have been agreeable, well liked, and popular but there is no firsthand account of his personality from anyone who met him privately.

Even a cursory look through the *Era* shows that most specialist performers used distinctive sobriquets, which changed in line with new directions in their careers or in response to current events and fashions. Tom Gordon, a mixed-race singer (probably British), called himself "the Gem'blam of Colour" in the early part of his career when his signature tune "Old Bob Ridley" came from American minstrelsy. Toward the end of his long period in show business, he seems to have stopped singing and moved into comedy, calling himself the "Black Jester."[7] His color (though not always mentioned in reviews) was part of his performative persona; how far he saw it as part of his personal identity is currently unknowable.

Henry's new direction would move people around the stage instead of showing static pictures. Cutter also sees Henry's reinvention of himself in contemporary terms of identity and trauma:

> My suspicion is that Brown increasingly turned in the later part of his life to magic and mesmerism because these performative modes offered him a stronger means to symbolically take control of the traumatic legacy of slavery.

She might have added that not only was he symbolically taking control of a legacy, but mesmerism allowed him to control other, white, people by telling them what to do, to become the master, as Britt Rusert does.[8] These positions seem to me somewhat over-intellectualized and seem to detach him from his professional and family responsibilities. Undoubtedly, Henry's choice of mesmerism appealed to an aspect of his character and experiences. He had always shown himself to have an independent turn of mind, determined to be autonomous and in thrall to no one, but he was not the only performer to see the opportunity to cash in on a fashion that was sweeping the country, and it is extremely unlikely that all of them were taking control of a trauma rather than jumping on a bandwagon. The *Era* carried advertisements for performers as well as subjects:

TO LADIES, LECTURERS, &c.
WANTED, a LADY, competent to Lecture on, and give Experiments in, MESMERISM. Good appearance essential.
Address, William Henery, Post-office, Leicester.[9]

Had genuine scientific qualifications been required, a different publication would have been chosen to advertise for this job as well, nor would the gender (and appearance) of a lecturer have been specified. As attractiveness was as important as ability for this show, entertainment must have been the primary aim, not scientific inquiry, and a woman would be a novelty. Miss Montague, "the Lady Lecturer on Mesmerism and Electro-biology," Madam Gilliland Card, "the Renowned Electro-Biologist, Illusionist and Mesmerist," and Miss Poole, "the Celebrated Star Mesmeric Performer of the World," took advantage of this.[10] At this time, women would not have had the opportunity to study science in any formal way, so they must have been performers.

Experiments in Wales

After his trial runs in Brentford in 1859 and then in Jersey in 1862, Henry had gone back to presenting the panoramas, but he must have been working on a new act until, at the end of 1863, he decided to try it out in Wales, where audiences had generally been receptive to his performances, although the press was less admiring. The *Merthyr Telegraph* was disparaging about Henry's mesmerism act in Merthyr Tydfil at the end of December 1863, but it did not go as far as the prejudice H.E. Lewis had experienced earlier in Scotland, partly on the grounds of his color but also because of his actions. The Scottish press found this cast a section of its population in a bad light:

Mesmerism and Superstition in the North.—Mr. Lewis, a man of colour, has for some time past been engaged in a tour the north delivering lectures on mesmerism. Among other places he had visited Invergordon, where (says the correspondent of the *Inverness Courier*) "some of our enlightened townsmen" suppose and say that Mr. Lewis, because of his sable colour, and because does extraordinary things, is an emissary of the evil one. We could scarcely have believed that such gross superstition existed amongst us, yet such is the fact, and the worthy managers, determined to "intermit no watch against a wakeful foe," refused to give the use of the room. One of the elders of the Free Church says that the house has been made a den of thieves, and if he can at all avoid entering it he will do so. It is also reported that some of the parents of the children attending the Free school, influenced no doubt by the conduct of the managers, are to take their children from it because Mr Lewis lectured in it.[11]

The *Merthyr Telegraph* did not connect Henry with the devil but called him "Dis colo'd g'emman," representing in stereotyped nigger minstrel parlance the speech that English journalists had called the best Negro speaker of the English language. The *Western Daily Press* was not impressed either:

> Every evening last week a "darkey" calling himself "Henry Box Brown" has been giving a mesmeric entertainment. The scene in the Temperance Hall on Thursday evening was ludicrous in the extreme, numbers obeying Sambo's wonderful attractive power, and exhibiting themselves on the platform in a variety of characters.[12]

This might be seized on as evidence of latent, or indeed overt, prejudice in Britain, but it must be seen in the wider context. The Welsh have a long history of being (and still are) mocked by the English. They were at this time stereotyped as liars and thieves. An old nursery rhyme starts:

> Taffy was a Welshman,
> Taffy was a thief.
> Taffy came to my house
> And stole a side of beef.

The Welsh in retaliation tend to regard everything that comes from England as culturally inferior. Henry did not bother to sue either newspaper because, whatever journalists thought of his act, the local inhabitants loved him and he now had an established reputation that no provincial journalist could damage. He was still in Merthyr at the beginning of March and the *Cardiff Times* said he had given a "grand entertainment." Before his performance he had paraded through the street "in the character of an African king, richly dressed and accompanied by a footman."[13] All this had to be paid for—plainly Henry was doing well and sections of the press, as so often, were out of step with the public.

In Aberdare the proceedings gave "the most complete satisfaction to all present." Gifts were distributed, and when he moved on to Pontypool he was warmly applauded. He astounded the locals by his "wonderful feats of mesmerism and electro-biology, the cleverest that have ever been witnessed by a Pontypool audience." He drew large audiences when he moved on to Blaenarvon, but here one of the local papers, the *Monmouthshire Merlin*, disparaged his working-class spectators:

> Mr. H. Box Brown is making a lengthened stay in this town, and succeeds in attracting crowded houses nightly. In the working classes of Blaenavon he has discovered a gullible public, and he prides himself upon this fact and the pecuniary result.

He was in Pontypridd in August but here "the mystery and fun of mesmerism" was "not so much patronised as might have been expected." His change of direction was so extreme that some did not believe he was truly the fugitive slave. When he appeared at Newport in April, a reporter described him as the "tall, brawny and good-tempered-looking son of the sable race whose cognomen is Box Brown, derived from the legend that he is the identical Brown who escaped from slavery in a box." The gift of prizes to the audience was mentioned and on the last evening this was to be an "educated donkey."[14]

Donkeys played a part in some of Henry's previous shows and he, like others, may have used the phenomenon now known as Clever Hans. In 1907 a German named William van Osten had a horse called Hans, which he claimed could solve puzzles. It would, for example, tap its hoof to indicate the answer to a sum. After long investigation and experimentation, it was discovered that the horse was responding to its owner's body language. When the correct number had been tapped out, van Osten made, either consciously or unconsciously, a small movement that indicated to the animal to stop. Dogs can be taught to bark an answer to a mathematical question as well, as long as the master knows the correct answer, so entertainers must have been able to train animals to do similar feats for a long time; it was a scientific investigation that revealed the trick behind Clever Hans. A donkey was a valuable animal and would take some time to train. If Henry had traveled with a donkey, this would have been observed and commented on. Perhaps he made enquiries about gifted beasts in the locale and came to an agreement with their owners to transport them to the venue. This is a mystery about his act that may never be solved.

In August the editor of the *Merthyr Telegraph*, who was always contemptuous of Henry, encouraged his readers to support a temperance campaigner instead:

> MESMERIC DEMONSTRATIONS.—The celebrated Captain Hudson is actually doing wonders at our Temperance Hall every evening. He addressed audiences last Sabbath in the Circle at five o'clock, and at our Temperance Hall at half-past eight, his subject being Temperance. The good Captain has not yet been appreciated by the public of this town. Shall it be said that Box Brown met with every encouragement at Tredegar, but Captain Hudson was not patronized at all? If so it will be an eclipse on our character. Friends! forbid it should be the case.

For some reason, and it is easy to attribute it to racism, the editor of this newspaper really disliked Henry, but it may have been because they did not get on personally or because Henry failed to advertise in this newspaper or was not a temperance campaigner. A few weeks later the editor reported that Roderick Jones, one of those who had been mesmerized by Henry, was behaving oddly:

> One of the pupils of Box Brown went to the lodge of the works on Monday evening last, with his best clothes on, and saturated with wet, as if he had just come out of a pond. He made no particular remark, and the next morning his working suit was found under the hedge by Dr. Sloper's gardener, and have been claimed by him. He says he was going on the tramp.[15]

But this personal campaign of animosity seems to have had no effect on audiences.

Mind-Reading and New Tricks

In October Henry was back in England, in Bristol, where he had presented the slavery panorama in 1855 before he met his wife. Jane was with him, and their son Edward Henry, named after Henry's father and himself, was born on October 28, 1864, at 25 Cumberland Street in Bristol.[16] Jane had been so prominent in their joint enterprises that her absence from advertisements and reports of performances even after she had rejoined him by the beginning of 1864 is significant. She had been the imparter of sober facts, and this change of direction was entirely based on fantasy, so she had no place in Henry's new act.

In Bristol Henry gave only his mesmerism show in the Broadmead Rooms, and coverage of the events shows that he did the performance in his African robes. These were not, as one newspaper noted, a "very primitive costume," but "a handsome, Othello sort of dress, tunic robe and turban, with a comely pair of boots on his nether extremities." He also introduced a new element, Miss Pauline, "the second-sighted Sybil." Theatrical mind-reading is now a well-known trick. With the assistant blindfolded on the stage, the performer moves among the audience, takes an object from one of them and asks the blindfolded one to say what she or he is holding up. The trick is accomplished by the use of code words to describe the article, but to prolong the act and tantalize the audience requires some acting ability. Henry already had a great deal of experience in holding attention, and Miss Pauline was probably an actress who could learn a script. She was with Henry when they moved on to Cheltenham in November. Here, calling himself Professor, Henry boasted to a local journalist that he was an African and American traveler who had attained "worldwide celebrity." At this time the word "professor" did not solely suggest the holder of a university post; it simply meant someone with some specialist skill. He also advertised lessons in magic; teaching basic tricks would be a welcome supplement to his income.[17] Illusion was a standard feature of the Victorian stage. As reviews of Christmas pantomimes show, transformations of scenes and people were expected, and undoubtedly there were conjuring and sleight-of-hand tricks in many people's acts. A number of books, some aimed at boys, showing how to do card and coin tricks, cup and ball, and the like, had been published since the 18th century. Henry could have seen these or may have already worked out how to copy some of the simpler tricks and entertained Jane and Agnes with them. Now he was adding them to his repertoire, mixing them with mesmerism and visual illusions drawn from spiritualist séances.

Spiritualism

Mesmerism became linked with spiritualism, the practice of speaking to spirits of the dead, because both had a common belief in an unseen electric force permeating the universe. A number of people in Britain had always claimed to be able to communicate with ghosts. In 1846 Queen Victoria took part in a séance and remained a firm believer in communion with the dead and in clairvoyance. Modern spiritualism came to Britain in 1852 at the same time as mesmerism for entertainment purposes, when the American Maria B. Hayden arrived with mesmerist G.W. Stone. She offered séances involving table-rapping, as well as messages from spirits. A number of people then found that they too possessed this lucrative skill (Hayden charged 1 guinea per person), but the next practitioner from America offered even more exciting phenomena. Daniel Home (1833–1886) was born in Scotland but his family emigrated when he was a child. He came from a family that claimed to have second sight and at the age of 18 began to hold séances, which, as well as speaking to the dead, involved table-turning, phosphorescent lights, and other physical manifestations. Some observers were skeptical; others were convinced by the phenomena he produced. In 1855 he came to England, where he added levitation to his repertoire. Some of the events and illusions at his séances could be reproduced by professional magicians; others could not at the time be explained, but have now been debunked. Home, and others, were caught out in frauds, but such was the desire to believe that speaking to the dead was possible that spiritualism retained a strong following in Victorian England, and still has some believers today.

Ira and William Davenport were American brothers who claimed they were producing genuinely paranormal phenomena. After their bodies were thoroughly searched for any aids, the young men were tied down in seats inside a cupboard in which there were some musical instruments. A moment later, a trumpet was thrown out of an aperture in the cupboard door. The doors were swiftly opened to reveal the men still tied up. Members of the audience were allowed to place the instruments where they liked, even under the seat of one of the brothers, but just as quickly the feat was repeated. Then the musical instruments in the cupboard were heard playing inside. A local judge entered the cupboard with the men and felt unseen hands place the instruments on his body, but the men were still tied up. The act concluded with a standard séance, with objects flying around and spirit rapping.[18]

When the Davenports arrived in Britain in 1864 they repeated their act in a private performance at the home of the playwright Dion Boucicault, who specialized in melodramas and what was called the "sensation drama." The event was reported in a letter to the London *Evening Standard*. They tried to give the impression their effects were genuinely produced by spirits, but John Nevil Maskelyne, regarded as the most important of the early magicians in Britain, stated he could create the same effects by illusion. He had trained as a watchmaker so had mechanical ability and constructed instruments to perform his tricks. He and his long-term partner, George Alfred Cooke, who was a cabinetmaker, built a cabinet similar to that of the Davenport brothers and in Cheltenham in August 1865 demonstrated how they achieved their effects, exposing the fraudulent claims of supernatural forces. A few years later, in April 1867, while performing at Brighton Pavilion, Maskelyne was assaulted by two drunken youths. His evidence against his assailants revealed some of his methods. In the course of giving a private performance of what he described as "a dark séance à la Davenport brothers," Maskelyne was tied to a chair and, as well as producing raps on the table, sent phosphoresced objects flying around the room about the room, using apparatus that the drunks had damaged. In another contretemps, he noted that he allowed members of the audience to inspect his apparatus. Others also proved the brothers' assertions unfounded but this seems not to have damaged their popularity.[19] It was not until the publication of *Our Magic* in 1911, co-written by Maskelyne's son Nevil and his last collaborator, David Devant, that many of Maskelyne's original tricks were revealed.

The First Magician of Color on the British Stage?

Henry started to introduce conjuring tricks and elements drawn from spiritualism into his act at about the time the Davenports were attracting so much publicity. He was really keeping up with fashions, but even before Maskelyne had exposed the brothers' fakery, Henry never pretended he was not doing tricks. Reproducing the kind of effects produced in séances, he would have used objects painted with phosphorous to make them glow in the dark and, importantly, to hide wires or cords. He probably did not have the mechanical ability to construct elaborate equipment, nor, with his growing family and other financial commitments, the money to buy in the necessary expertise.

He was not the first professional magician of African descent. That crown is held by Richard Potter (1783–1835), who was the first professional American magician, hypnotist, and ventriloquist of any color. He was born in Hopkinton, Massachusetts, the son of a slave of the Frankland family named Dinah. That much seems certain, but like many socially insecure children of slaves he upgraded his ancestry. He let it be assumed (at the very least) that his father was Sir Charles Henry Frankland, but since Frankland retired to England and died there in 1768, this is impossible. Another candidate was Frankland's illegitimate son, Henry Cromwell. Cromwell was a naval captain who was fighting in the British Channel at the time of Potter's conception, so this is unlikely. At the age of 10 Potter is said to have traveled to England, either as a cabin boy or accompanying a Captain Skinner. Here he met John Rannie, a Scottish magician and ventriloquist, and became his assistant. They toured Europe; then, in 1800, Rannie relocated to America with Potter.[20]

This is the standard story, but very little can be relied on. It is not just the claims of an illustrious father that are in doubt. The reason Rannie moved to America was not solely in search of professional advancement but because in 1800 he was banished for seven years from Scotland for stealing oatmeal.[21] Unlike the English, the frugal Scots did not go to the expense and trouble of transporting wrongdoers to penal colonies. They simply banished them, leaving them at liberty in other countries. Saying he and Potter had toured Europe was probably also an exaggeration for publicity purposes. Undoubtedly, the two met somewhere and possibly performed in Scotland, but for Americans Europe was an exotic and glamorous location, which gave a borrowed class to their act when they performed. There is no evidence that Rannie and Potter had traveled in England, but it is possible. What is certain is that in 1811, with his period of banishment expired, Rannie alone returned from America to Scotland, leaving Potter to become a star in his own right in the United States.

Potter may have appeared on the English stage at some point when he was Rannie's assistant, but there is so far no documented evidence of this. There may also have been other black entertainers who executed a simple trick in the course of a pantomime or some other theatrical performance. I am always cautious about claiming "the first" for any black person, but I can find no other black performer regularly (or even occasionally) doing magic tricks on the Victorian stage. Henry must therefore currently be acclaimed as the first *known* performer of African descent to present a full magic act in Britain, which no one seems to have recognized. The reason he did not emphasize this in his advertisements and the handbills distributed to publicize his act is simply because this was not a selling point in Victorian England. No reviewer mentioned this, either; his race was not then an issue. If he had known of his pioneering status Henry might have made this part of his publicity, but by this point it was what he did rather than what he was that drew people to his performances. He had left behind the lectures on slavery where his color and experience were integral elements; now it was his talent alone that counted.

Performing Magic

Skills Henry had learned while lecturing could be, with judicious tweaking, transferred to conjuring. The actual technical ability to perform tricks is only a small part of the whole show in the way that the words a skillful lecturer speaks are in some ways the least important part of the whole experience. Conjuring, like lecturing, requires the audience to go on a journey, to follow a story, which must engage the audience's attention so they want to know what happens next, whether it is the development of an argument; the unfolding of a fairy tale or the progress of a trick. Telling any story is composed of a number of elements: the words used, the tone of voice, facial expression and body language which combine to put across the message. Henry had long experience of successfully using these elements to hold attention in his lectures and he was good at manipulating emotions; people at his presentations had both laughed and cried. Now he needed to add skills specific to conjuring.

Distraction is a core skill. The spectators' attention must be directed to the element that the magician wishes them to focus on, like the playing card held up, not the swift movement that flicks another one up a sleeve. This can be done by words or gestures. A puff of smoke or flash of light will also divert the audience's gaze or hide something, and an assistant can be a distraction or a core feature of a trick, sometimes both. A conjurer will lead an audience to expect one outcome but then produce another. Although in real life people are usually angered by deception, if it is done as part of a show and without malice or the intent to defraud, it produces amusement and pleasurable surprise at the gap between what people thought they perceived and what they actually noticed. It is not essential, but it is an advantage (as in so many areas of life) if the audience actually likes the performer. Being deceived by a genial person is nicer than being hoodwinked by an unpleasant one; also, people are more trusting of an amiable character. And Henry was well liked.

The tricks Henry performed in Britain were not detailed. The audience needed to be surprised at the outcome, not forewarned what would happen. Jim Magus, whose book was published in 1995, included various stories, handed down orally and told to him by Fetaque Sanders (1915–92), who had heard them from Leon Long (born 1891). Long was the first president of the United States' first black magician society in 1921 and the source of much oral history about magicians of African heritage. In 1995 there was no easy way of verifying the stories about Henry's act that Magus included in his book, but with today's digitized newspapers, it can be deduced that they seem to have been heavily embroidered in their transmission from one person to another. For example, the attack on Henry in Providence, Rhode Island, became far more dramatic in the oral tradition. Magus was told that a gun had been pointed at Brown; James Smith called out, "For the next five minutes, people are welcome to enter the panorama free of charge! Free admission now!" and people swarmed in, allowing Henry to duck under the canvas in the confusion. He rode away to the house of the abolitionist who had sponsored the panorama.[22] In the newspaper reports of the event Smith is not mentioned, nor that the panorama was being shown; Henry was simply—and boringly—out walking, not the behavior of a daring hero.

Magus also heard that Henry had learned his skills as a child slave from another slave called Tricky Sam. Nor is this tenable. Had he arrived in Britain as a practiced magician, why did he wait 14 years to reveal this? In the 1850s such skills would have been considerably rarer and better rewarded than he had been as an antislavery lecturer. Also, as British reviewers said (but this was not easily accessible until recently), the tricks he performed, though well executed, were not new. In 1864 he was still learning his trade as a magician, and in Gloucester he received a lukewarm reception and the audience was not numerous. Although the tricks were successful, they were not novel, "many of which we have seen before."[23] The ones later mentioned are the standard European tricks, or variants on them, using European artifacts like playing cards and watches. Although these might have been substituted for with objects of African origin, there is no credible evidence of this. I must admit I have not done extensive research, but the only indigenous tradition of African magic in the New World seems to be hoodoo (and variants), or, as it was also called in the West Indies, obeah. These practices were not to entertain the general public but were linked to the performance of religious rites. They have parallels in all religions and cultures where apparently paranormal effects along with threats of divine retribution were, and still are, produced to reinforce the power of a priest, a shaman, or some other person claiming divine authority.

In Gloucester there was no mention of Miss Pauline, so Henry seems to have done a purely magic act. The reviewer added, "Mr. Box Brown, himself a coloured gentleman, was a curiosity, by reason of his extraordinary professional costume," which did mark him out from others. Here he was allowed to use the Corn Exchange for only one performance, and he hired a solicitor to write a letter to the local council requesting compensation for potential lost earnings. The Town Council's Finance Committee simply laughed and wrote back saying there was nothing they could do. By then, Henry was back in Bristol for the baptism of Edward Henry in the church of St. James on December 7, 1864.[24]

Although his persistence, self-belief, and willingness to challenge authority, as shown by the letter to Gloucester Town Council and on other occasions, must be admired, the event itself in the town was a disappointment. In the larger towns and cities a variety of entertainments was on offer, so audiences would be more sophisticated in their response. Henry's new act was most successful in rural venues where there was little competition. At the beginning of 1865 he was back in Wales in a small town, Brynmey. Here there was a large attendance, probably swelled by the distribution of gifts. Henry also spoke about being a slave and the escape that had given him his name, perhaps thinking he might not be known by repute, but he was already a household name for some people here.

In 1865, letter writers to the *Merthyr Telegraph* were in a grumpy mood about the lack of culture in the area. In correspondence on the subject of penny readings, QST deplored the difficulties people had faced in establishing them in Tredegar. He contrasted the excitements of Box Brown and the theatrical representations of Jack Shepperd (an 18th-century criminal whose dramatized exploits were still drawing audiences) with the quietness necessary at readings. He and XYZ, another letter writer, attributed the final successful introduction of readings to the presence of a "superiority of class" at these readings, which set a good example to the lower orders. By implication, Henry's performances did not appeal to the educated classes, but he was not denigrated; it was accepted that this was legitimate entertainment, but inferior.

On another occasion, a meeting about political reform in Cwmbran, in a mining and industrial area, was poorly attended. As one of those present was reported to have remarked, "If Box Brown had been here, charging threepence a piece, th' room would have been full long ago, this in a tone savoring somewhat of contemptuousness." At a quarter past eight, the audience numbered about 30. Eventually about 100 people attended, in a room that could take 300, which gives an idea of how many Henry could expect to attract in these smaller venues as well as how much more popular he was than a political meeting.[25] In both Tredegar and Cwmbran, Henry's was the first name that came to mind when popular entertainment was discussed, an indication of how well known he was.

Challenged by a Rival in the West Country

Next Henry moved on to Somerset, where Miss Pauline was again part of the act in Taunton in March. Henry, "a very fair magician," had added some new tricks to his repertoire: "Many of his feats are new and the old ones are performed with great skill." She also appeared in Exeter, where Henry mentions in his advertisement the "performing drum, table, bell, etc," as well as her clairvoyance. These new elements seem to have been drawn from spiritualists' séances, blurring the boundaries between hypnosis and the spirits of the dead. He called himself the King of Mesmerists and again appeared dressed in his African chief costume. Henry was also performing standard conjuring tricks; his sleight of hand had caused "roars of amusement" in Taunton.[26] Having given up the lectures and presentations relating to slavery, Henry was competing on equal terms with all the other mesmerists and conjurers in show business. He dressed in exotic robes, partly because that had long been his trademark, the gimmick that distinguished him from others, but also because the British liked their magicians to be of foreign origins, and these robes offered additional benefits—somewhere to conceal props and create a potential distraction.

In Taunton another fugitive slave, the herbalist John Brown, the "Black Doctor," was offering a rival entertainment. Two local papers carried the same article, noting the coincidence with arch amusement: "The name of the proprietor of each was Brown, and yet both being 'brown' by name these gentlemen were black by nature, as both were men of colour, and said to be escaped slaves." They added that Henry was the more attractive, offering tricks in magic and prizes ranging from cooked beefsteaks to a live donkey, while his rival was lecturing on why the Englishman has a white skin while the slave has a black. John Brown also challenged Henry or any other black man to show white feet like his. Although undoubtedly out of the ordinary, his feet could hardly compete with an evening of magic and mesmerism with added prizes. The newspaper report added that John Brown's account of his escape from slavery was very interesting and that he claimed to have been instrumental in suppressing recent riots in Dorchester, where he lived and now claimed urgent business was preventing him extending his stay in Taunton. He used this reason to withdraw from the fray with as much dignity as he could muster, leaving Henry the winner of the encounter.[27]

In June Henry appeared for a few days in Penrhyn near Falmouth in Cornwall,[28] but the rest of the year seems to have been another period when little is known about his activities; no press reports have yet been found. Jane and the children must have been with Henry, probably touring small venues in Cornwall or in the West Country of England and advertising their events only with handbills.

Back to Wales

In 1866 they returned to Wales, and it is likely that at this point the Box Browns hired a young girl called Hannah Watts of Pontypridd to travel with the family. The ex-slave was now employing a servant. Although they had help, Jane does not seem to have taken part in the shows. Despite the derision of some local papers, Henry seems to have been welcomed in Wales, but a Cardiff newspaper and a Welsh language one supported superior Welsh culture by comparing Henry's "empty bombast" to a local man, Professor Morgan, one of the "upper class of professors of mesmerism."[29]

It seems that Henry continued touring in Wales at the beginning of 1866 without his appearances being reported in the press. The only indication comes from a court case in April in Neath. When Henry appeared in Ystalyfera, a small town in the Tawe valley, about 13 miles from Swansea, he lost his umbrella and boots in the local hotel and attempted to sue the landlord for their value, 19s and 17s, respectively. He lost the case. The items may have been part of his professional costume and would have been expensive for a local agricultural laborer, who was earning about 11s 6d per week at this time. The article stated that he had recently lost another similar case in Cardiff, but there seems to have been no report in the press about it, so it must have been a very minor matter.[30]

He returned to Neath, where he gave an entertainment in October 1866. As always, the *Monmouthshire Merlin* was sour: "The Hall was full, but the performance did not give entire satisfaction." The editor was an embittered man, frequently pouring scorn on other local events and people. He was less sarcastic when a couple of months later, in December 1866, he reported a resumed coroner's inquest into the death of George Kelly, Lord Tredegar's gamekeeper, in Bassaleg near Risca on the outskirts of Newport. Kelly was found shot on November 19 and three men were apprehended nearby. One of them, Abraham Brimble, claimed he had been at Henry's entertainment, then had been in the company of various people, including his co-accused Charles Bull and another man Joseph Marsh, on the way back to his lodgings. The coroner's jury returned a verdict of willful murder against Brimble and Bull. Marsh had been brought before magistrates but freed.[31] It was not necessary to call Henry to give evidence, but this sensational case was widely reported and it must have given him a moment's reflection—had the young man (Brimble was 20) really been at his entertainment? Had he played any part?

The distribution of gifts now seems to have become a permanent feature, even in small places like the village of Treherbert in January 1867, where there was unlikely to be much competition so no extra inducement to attend was needed. But Henry had now raised expectations, and if presents were not offered people might stay away out of pique: Why were they not being offered the same benefits as their neighbors? Although there is no mention of this, presents must have been a feature of his visits in January 1867 to Cymmer and Dinas, the last places on this long Welsh tour.[32]

There was then another of the periodic gaps that punctuated Henry's professional life. It may be he found his schedule punishing and needed to recuperate, although others were equally busy. Although the Box Browns no longer had to arrange for the transportation of the cumbersome panoramas, dioramas, and associated paraphernalia, which must have required considerable care, there were still stage props used in the tricks to maintain. Henry was now a one-man show, carrying the entire responsibility and refining his act, which was a never-ending process. He was already trying out new elements with a growing emphasis on paranormal effects, and a period without performing allowed a reevaluation of the components of his act, as well as developing and practicing new tricks. During this lull, Henry must have heard the end of the story of Brimble and Bull, who went to trial at the Assizes in April 1867, following the coroner's inquest. Brimble again mentioned that he had been at Henry's performance until about 10 p.m. and then on his way home he met the other men and two girls. The pair were acquitted.[33] Perhaps Henry wondered whether to include the story in his act, which incorporated effects used in séances. But his performances always came down on the side of laughter, and there is not much fun to be got out of an unsolved murder.

Back on the Road

In May 1867 Henry appeared in Weston-super-Mare in Somerset. By now the critical note that had been such a feature of the Welsh newspapers was beginning to creep into the English press. Although the *Era* reported that his magic and mesmerism had attracted fair audiences, it added unkindly, "There is a lack of sterling entertainment here, which is to be lamented." A few months later, in August in Faringdon, Oxfordshire, the local paper reported Henry's fine figure and fine voice (so he was still including singing in his act) as well as the ten youths and adults he had "brought under subjugation causing them by a word or a touch to do things more or less absurd or ludicrous." It then reported a local inhabitant allegedly saying in the broad local accent, "There's allers summat to dra' the money awoy vrom the town'd."[34]

A member of the audience went beyond disparagement in nearby Abingdon, where Henry was described by the local paper as a "stalwart Indian," suggesting either that he had retained a turban as part of his stage costume or was now appearing as a Native American. At the end of his first appearance on October 3 a man rose from the body of the audience and denounced Henry as an imposter, saying that he was the only person who could mesmerize and that Brown by his imposition had nearly ruined him. The heckler's wife joined in. Henry denied the accusations, saying they had gained free admittance under false pretenses, and the audience turned on the couple, hissing them and demanding they be ejected, applauding when this was done. The two were seen a few days later at a stall in the town, demonstrating their powers to an audience of between 15 and 20 people. A drunk enlivened Henry's act on the last night by singing, but a policeman who was present saw him out.[35] None of this did him any harm. The audience was on his side and always found it good fun when something went wrong, as long as it did not result in humiliation to the performer or injury to anyone. And Henry, quick-witted as he was, had much practice in dealing with disruptions.

Another long gap followed before the next report in the press of a performance. It must be assumed that Henry was making other appearances in small towns and villages, but he and his act were now literally unremarkable and not worth advertising in the local press because there was nothing else in competition. Instead he was putting up posters, as he had done in Shrewsbury, and one caught the eye of a Freemason. In November 1867 the *Freemasons Magazine and Masonic Mirror* carried a letter signed "Z" and headlined "Quality not Quantity." The writer had recently seen and objected to Henry's use of Masonic symbols on a poster but he was also appalled that an ex-slave had been admitted to the brotherhood. Z had learned Henry had been initiated in Jersey and demanded to know who had allowed "an unknown man" to join. He thought this was "disgraceful" and an example of initiating someone just for the fees. He called on the Grand Lodge to instigate an inquiry. In the next issue "H.H.," a previous inhabitant of Jersey and well known in Masonic circles there, responded. He listed the eight Lodges on the island and was confident this initiation had not happened in the three with which he was connected. He supported Z's call for an inquiry, adding that "the case of Box Brown is by no means the worst which would be laid before such a commission" and ending by promising to contact someone on the island. Correspondence followed until February 1868. Although the Royal Sussex Lodge was identified by H.H. after a number of enquiries, its Worshipful Master refused him access to the Minutes so the names of Henry's proposer and seconder were never revealed. The matter ended there; no inquiry was undertaken.[36]

Henry had settled into a pattern that suited him and his audiences. He knew his market. In his early days on the abolitionist circuit in Britain he had never appeared at the high-profile events and places where William Wells Brown and his like spoke, and now he was drawing crowds not in the big cities but in provincial towns and villages. When he had appeared in the fashionable spa towns of Cheltenham and Bath his performances had attracted no press coverage. As far as can be determined, he never visited the other fashionable resorts of Harrogate, Buxton, or Tunbridge Wells and did not test himself in the big London venues. Britt Rusert sees this as a conscious political decision:

Ultimately, Brown's eccentric and wildly popular experiments with an Africanist, supernaturally inflected popular science onstage helped to link the plight of African Americans to a radical abolitionism: a shared alliance forged not between former slaves and upper-class British abolitionists, but between black Americans and the British proletariat.[37]

This may well have been an element in his choice of venues, but it was also a practical recognition that these were people like him. He was not, like Douglass and Wells Brown, an erudite autodidact, and his earthy humor, boasting about how he had got his own back on the newspaper editor and locksmith, mocking authority figures like clergymen and detailing how he enjoyed himself, would not go down well with the more genteel, but the working classes experienced these same resentments and pleasures, especially at getting revenge on those who belittled them. Even in his early days on the lecture circuit, when he was still part of the abolitionist movement, he was regarded as too showy by Wells Brown and his like. Undoubtedly there were political aspects to his acts, but these were indirectly presented. He was showing that black people were not some alien, inferior race but shared the same concerns and sense of humor as a white audience. Nor was there any indication that he made any current political points; only in his early days did reviewers mention his satires on American slaveholders and preachers and a presidential candidate, but now they reported just his standard tricks and illusions. On the abolition circuit his experience had brought home to people the realities of enslavement; now he was showing that someone with African ancestry was as capable of learning and performing the same dazzling feats of mesmerism and magic as any other entertainer.

Daphne Brooks, Britt Rusert, Martha J. Cutter, and Audrey A. Fisch call Henry a popular scientist,[38] but the idea that he and the numerous other stage mesmerists who appeared in the pages of the *Era* were presenting real scientific experiments is highly unlikely. He was not making displays in a way that made the underlying principles understandable to the lay mind, as, for example, John Henry Pepper did in his lectures and books. The consensus in the medical field is that though some people are susceptible to hypnosis, mesmerizing a large number of people simultaneously is impossible. Henry was recorded as having up to 18 people performing absurd actions at the same time on stage. There was, admittedly, an element of carnival excess in the early days of mesmerism in a medical setting, as Wendy Moore explores in *The Mesmerist*. Dr. John Ellisson, a believer in mesmerism, was appointed Professor of the Theory and Practice of Medicine at University College Hospital in 1831. In 1838 he met the Okey sisters, who made spectacular displays when apparently mesmerized, and made them perform before both students and invited guests. Later, as their antics became more and more outrageous, they were discredited.[39] It seems only to have been on the stage that more than one or two people were mesmerized at the same time.

There is a more prosaic and practical reason why Henry and his fellow mesmerists, like "Professor" Chadwick, claimed they were doing experiments. Of course, it was partly because this made them sound respectable and educative, but mainly because of the 1824 Vagrancy Act, a catch-all piece of legislation aimed at itinerants of all kinds, from those who were like Henry gainfully employed to beggars. He and others presenting this kind of show needed to keep on the right side of the law. Mesmerism, or hypnotism as it was later named, was not specifically regulated until the 1952 Hypnotism Act, but the 1824 legislation (still in force) covers people carrying out a wide range of potentially undesirable activities, including "every Person pretending or professing to tell Fortunes, or using any subtle Craft, Means, or Device, by Palmistry or otherwise, to deceive and impose on any of His Majesty's Subjects." This act was so loosely worded that it enabled every stern-minded or spiteful official to bring to court anyone of whose behavior in public they disapproved, and an argument could certainly be made that the subjects Henry supposedly brought under his control had been deceived and were being imposed on by taking away their free will. If he were taken to court, he would either have to admit that he was faking it (which would be widely reported) or face the prospect of one month's imprisonment. Presumably, Chadwick had warned him of the need to be careful when describing what he was doing, to say he was giving lectures and carrying out experiments, which, as the pages of the *Era* demonstrate, all stage mesmerists did.

In March 1868 Henry appeared in Kennington, then a suburb of south London. There were some salubrious, middle-class quarters here, but it was generally a place of industry, where working-class people lived. He started his act with some sleight of hand, which a reviewer found "old and commonplace, though done neatly." What the reviewer did find astounding was the mesmerism, which was described in detail:

> Some sixteen or eighteen youths and young men among the audience volunteered to be the subjects of his experiment and were made to do a number of most ludicrous things at the bidding of the operation. First they were seated round the platform with their heads bent forward and after Mr. Brown had made a few motions with his hand, they successively dropped off their seats in a profound sleep. Having been awakened by the mesmeriser, they were in succession given a fit of sneezing, a horrible fit of the toothache; made to march, dance, sing, frantically whirl their arms around, chase and catch imaginary insects, fancy themselves in the cold regions and commence skating and sliding in all directions across the platform, and, as a climax, to imagine themselves converted into sheep, going down on all-fours, imitating the peculiar noise of those animals and devouring with great avidity greens and cabbage cast to them. The disgust and indignation manifested by the "subjects" on regaining possession

of their proper faculties, after the last named "amusement," may be more easily imagined that described.

Now, of course, we know this must have been staged, with Henry employing the subjects. Only people who as yet had little experience of such acts and were fairly unsophisticated (as the reviewer seems to have been) would have enjoyed this so wholeheartedly. The reviewer concluded, "Should Mr. Brown give his entertainment in South London again, which he probably will do, we can safely recommend it to those of our readers who wish to 'laugh and grow fat.'"[40]

In April Henry was back in Uxbridge in Middlesex. The reporter here noted that his girth made him an imposing figure and that he took snuff. By now Henry had replaced the turban he had worn as part of his representation of African robes with "a prodigious head dress of feathers, so that he looked a most mysterious incarnate wizard." Following the 1862 Homestead Act, land in the Midwest, previously occupied by Native Americans, was opened up to settlers. This led to an interest in the natives' cultures, and images of Native Americans, then called Red Indians or Redskins, in their traditional dress were being produced. Here is another indication of how carefully Henry followed current affairs and introduced novelties into his act to keep himself in fashion. The reviewer continued that he claimed to have

> wrought a wonderful cure upon a rheumatic lady, to whom he entreated the dubious to write, that their doubts might be dispelled, giving the fair patient's name and address, and leaving it implied that that gentlewoman, in return for the cure effected, would have deemed it delightful to answer the queries of any number of inquisitive skeptics.

Unfortunately, the skeptical journalist did not include her details. Henry's mesmerized subjects amused a large audience by "catching imaginary butterflies in an empty atmosphere, eating turnip-tops with indescribable relish … and executing a variety of other absurd freaks."[41]

Phrenology

In June Henry was in Braintree, Essex, repeating his act and affording merriment with "some of the youth portion of the audience."[42] It required a degree of acting ability, familiarity with performance, and above all rehearsal to achieve the kind of choreographed act Henry's young men carried out, so these may have been the same supposed volunteers who had appeared in other places. They may have gone on to Bury St. Edmonds in Suffolk, but here for the first time in more than two years Madame Brown is billed to appear, and another new element has been added to the show: phrenology.

Like mesmerism, phrenology was a late–18th century German pseudo-science that was taken up in the early 19th century. In 1796 Franz Joseph Gall claimed that the sizes of areas of the skull reflected the strength or weakness of different aspects of the mind. He identified 27, associated with such qualities as benevolence, religious feeling, pride, and even murderous instincts. There were medical practitioners who believed that this could help to diagnose and cure mental illness, like John Ellisson, mentioned earlier. The Edinburgh Phrenological Society was established in 1820, but by about 1840 this theory was no longer regarded as a credible. However, phrenology retained great popular appeal and having one's bumps read continued to be a fashionable pastime. Among the famous, Charles Dickens, Charlotte Bronte, Mary Ann Evans (whose pen name was George Eliot), and Ralph Waldo Emerson succumbed even after it was scientifically disproved.

The actual content of the phrenology element was not described, but if he was taking people from the audience and feeling their skulls to determine their character, Henry was probably employing the psychological trick of using the kind of generalities that seem specific to an individual but that no one can absolutely deny: "you are friendly and sociable, but sometimes you need to be alone," "you may seem very confident, but sometimes you doubt your own abilities," and similar one-size-fits-all statements found everywhere from self-help gurus to astrological profiles. Henry could make a quick general assessment of the subject's degree of sociability or self-confidence, as well as other qualities, in a preliminary chat while introducing him or her to the audience. This phrenology demonstration may have been Jane's new role, but that is less likely—no man would risk a woman revealing his character in public. Whatever they did, the *Cambridge Independent* was not impressed: "The performances were of the ordinary stamp and the audiences far from numerous." When in September they moved on to Norwich, the county town of Norfolk, neither Jane nor phrenology was mentioned, but Henry was very enthusiastically received.

> Mr. Box Brown, a gentleman of colour, is giving a series of entertainments … comprising magic, sleight of hand, and experiments in mesmerism and electro-biology. Mr. Brown is certainly very clever and the exhibition of his skills drew great applause every night from crowded audiences. Those who are interested in the marvellous will find in Mr. Brown a successful rival to some of the "Professors" who have come before the public with far greater pretensions.

Norwich was then something of a backwater, another place with a relatively unsophisticated population. Henry's appeal to ordinary people is confirmed by a letter to a local paper, shortly after his appearance, in which the writer called for less third-rate and more educated music, saying that popular taste was well catered for in the town, citing Henry among those who provided it but not denigrating his act. Again, his was the first name that came to mind when discussing popular entertainment. Henry next appeared in Great Yarmouth, a seaside resort in Norfolk, at the end of October, where he delivered magic using sleight of hand and "experiments in mesmerism and electro-biology, which are practiced upon persons taken indiscriminately from the audience."[43]

Exposed!

When the Box Browns started a tour of Kent by appearing in Chatham in November 1868, Jane was appearing with her husband but what she was doing was not recorded. Despite the claims that he was performing experiments, Henry was delivering nothing more than entertainment, and Jane needed to learn how to do this. Their roles were now reversed. Once the teacher who had introduced serious subjects, like the Holy Land and the Indian Mutiny, and who no doubt gave her husband useful feedback on lecturing to a British audience, Jane was now the pupil, being taught how to deliver pure amusement with minimal didactic content.

In February 1869, when the couple appeared in Ramsgate, phrenology was back on the bill. They were so popular—"the entertainment is one of the liveliest we have seen for some time in Ramsgate"—that the initial five-night run was extended by another four in the following week.[44] The week after, they were in Margate, a few miles along the coast, where there was a shock:

> During the past week Mr. Box Brown has been giving his entertainment at the Assembly rooms to crowded audiences, who testify by their applause their approbation of his performances. Tuesday night, however, considerable amusement was manifested on Athelstan Boys, Esq., going on the platform to test Mr. Brown's mesmeric powers. Some lads of the town were operated on with some success, or least a show of it, for they tumbled about in most absurd manner. But the operator could make nothing of Mr. Boys, who, after being subjected to various mesmeric passes, got up and left the platform, laughing heartily and denouncing the whole affair as humbug, intimating that the boys had been paid for their trouble. Mr. Brown loudly exclaimed against this, as did his wife, who appeared at the door and gave Mr. Boys a specimen of female eloquence.[45]

The lad was probably not one of the group Henry had recruited to pretend to be mesmerized but got up with them and then disrupted the act. It must have been a heart-stopping moment, but neither he nor Jane had thought about how to manage such an eventuality, although it was predictable. They simply railed against the young man, instead of making light of it. As was normal practice, but is rarely observed, there was no ethnic stereotyping in the newspaper report, no suggestion that this deception was linked to any racially determined moral deficit, nor even a mention of Henry's color. The reporter was very careful to say that Boys had only suggested that the other young men had been paid; this reporter could have laid his publisher open to a libel case had he claimed they had been, and Boys too could have been sued for slander.[46]

If word had spread to the next venue, it did not seem to damage attendance; a "good audience" saw them when they appeared in March in Dover, further to the southeast along the coast. Henry's advertisements in the local newspaper here laid a new emphasis on America. Since the end of the Civil War, papers had been full of the efforts to rebuild the United States, so it was a topical subject and, as ever, Henry was keeping up with current events. He now described himself as from Richmond, U.S. America. Among the elements in his act he listed the great American Tea Party and the New York Barber's Shop. He also promised to introduce the American Electric Drum and Bell, "with other feats of magic." Reports do not detail what tricks he was performing, simply referring to "sleight of hand," and although his advertisements sometimes named his tricks, Henry did not, of course, describe them to retain an element of surprise. He was not the first to demonstrate the drum and bell trick. An English magician, Professor Jacobs, sometimes called Wizard Jacobs, had performed this while touring Australia and New Zealand in 1865, and it was described in an Australian newspaper in 1873, when another magician, Professor Louis Haselmayer (1839–85), appeared in Kilmore, Victoria:

> Amongst his many other tricks, his wonderful drum may be described as the greatest. This article, placed in the midst of the audience, is made to tell precisely, by strokes, the card or cards those amongst the audience may draw from the pack, and also the number of figures that may be written on a piece or pieces of paper. A transparent bell was made to perform the same work on the second evening, as the professor remarked many imagined that a monkey or something was hidden in the drum the evening previous to do the striking.[47]

Calling it "electric" and "American" made it seem modern and glamorous, and Henry's emphasis on his American background continued in future advertisements.

Successful New Features

After a couple of days in Folkestone at the end of March, in April the couple were in Maidstone, where the advertised bill was much more detailed than in Dover. Now it was phreno-mesmerism, not just mesmerism and phrenology, that was to be demonstrated. This involved not just feeling the head to determine the character of the individual but putting the subject into a trance and then touching the part of the skull corresponding to the underlying attribute to activate it. An Edinburgh clergyman claimed to have demonstrated this with his daughter:

> Benevolence being excited, she put out both her hands, and with a kind expression of countenance, seemed to wish to shake hands with every one. Tune—she immediately began to hum…. Time being touched, she beat with her feet…. Veneration—she immediately put her hands together in the attitude of prayer…. Destructiveness, she pulled at and tore her dress.[48]

Stage phreno-mesmerism was another trick that needed one or more stooges planted in the audience. In Maidstone some boys and, as a novelty, two young ladies apparently became hypnotized, performing feats similar to those in Kennington, and there was no mention of the Margate incident, perhaps because Henry had advertised so heavily in the local newspaper. His advertisements also listed some of the phenomena to be produced: "Producing the Magnetic Apple Trees, Butterflies, and Infuriated Swarm of Bees, Catching the Magnetic Fish, the Great Ghost Illusion, Shower of Frogs, &c."[49] The distinction between calling a performance an entertainment, which Henry always did, and a séance was another legal nicety. Actually contacting the spirits of the dead for money could be classed as an offense (those who conducted private séances requested "donations" or "gifts"), but if accompanied by a supposed lecture, this kind of entertainment was on the right side of the legal divide. Although he never claimed to be conducting séances, Henry was using some of the mediums' tricks.

The Great Ghost Illusion was the paranormal effect known as Pepper's Ghost, a trick using mirrors that was developed in 1862 by John Henry Pepper from a method of producing apparently disembodied objects pioneered by Henry Dircks. It was being demonstrated by Pepper in Bristol when Henry was speaking there in 1863, so he may have seen it at that time.[50] Ghostly images were made to fade in and out of visibility, and it was often employed in séances for a supernatural effect. There are other ways of making objects seem to materialize and vanish using phosphorus, mirrors, gauze, and lighting, which were regularly used in theaters, and Henry must have employed them to produce his other effects.

The Box Browns had found a winning formula. They took it on to Landpoint and Southsea in Hampshire. Henry was no longer getting the bored dismissals of his performance that he received in Wales, Cambridge, and Oxfordshire. In Southsea a reviewer said, "His feats in magic, &c., are very good, many of the tricks being quite new and far above the average." The audience here, although provincial, would have included mariners who had experience of international entertainment and magic tricks. Henry could tour the same factual lecture for a long time with only small adjustments and updates, but with magic tricks entertaining a fickle public, always seeking something new, required a great deal more effort. He must have used much of his down time going behind the scenes at other entertainers' performances, picking up new tricks, working out how to incorporate them into his routine, and practicing them on Jane and the children. The Box Browns crossed the Solent to a previous popular venue, the Isle of Wight, at the end of September, where they appeared in Ryde, Ventnor, Newport, and Cowes. The audiences welcomed his transformation from lecturer on slavery to mesmeric enter-tainer and also the gifts that ended each performance. The couple were giving value for money; their shows lasted about two hours, which is tiring. Current solo acts are about 50 minutes long, and although he and Jane were both per-forming, sharing the load, and there was probably a musical element as there had been previously, Henry took the starring role, carrying greater respon-sibility.[51] He was now 54. Although this is not a great age, he was probably tiring of being constantly on the move and his growing family needed stability. It was time to settle down.

Scene 7

A Home in Manchester

About this time the couple decided to find a home, to settle down rather than being itinerant. Their children Agnes and Edward were nine and five, respectively, and another child was due in early 1870. In theory everybody loves a rebel, like the maverick cop, the outsider, the challenger of the establishment, and so on, because rebels are much more interesting than those who conform. In his younger days Henry was an innovator who introduced new ways to present his message, cut himself off from the abolitionist movement's hierarchy, and went his own way on his own terms. So far, so rebellious, but from the beginning he was not a political operator. Although he made some political points in the slavery presentation, these were more satires on attitudes than proposals on how to change the system. In Britain he became a solid, respectable citizen, belonging to organizations that did not challenge the status quo, like Friendly Societies and the Freemasons, and he was married and had children with no scandals about his private life. He worked hard to support his family and carried out occasional charitable appearances. His panoramas on the Holy Land and the Indian Mutiny seem to have been conventional enough, but encouraging his wife to deliver them (and the American Civil War one) was unusual. The switch to mesmerism and magic was surprising but can be seen as a continuation of his career as an entertainer. Now he was to become that most conventional of Victorian figures, a householder and paterfamilias in a prosperous middle-class area.

The Box Browns chose to settle in Manchester, where they would spend the rest of their time in Britain. This might seem an odd choice because there were numerous other places where Henry had been successful. He had been a star on the Isle of Wight and on Jersey, and in other parts of the kingdom with a much better climate and environment than Manchester, but audiences in the northern towns were of the kind with whom Henry felt at home— hard-working men and women who liked a good laugh. He had long been well established in Lancashire. A letter writer on the subject of slavery to *Soulby's*

Ulverston Advertiser and General Intelligencer had criticized the representation of black Americans' speech and, as so often, Henry was the first of those he expected his readers to recognize from his name alone:

> It is well known that the English is the principal language in use in the United States, and Box Brown, Moses Roper, Joseph [*sic*] Aldridge, and a host of others of the negro race, have visited the North of England, and spoken the language without ever betraying such expressions as "tousand dollars" and, "Ize neber sick," &c.[1]

White Slavery

Manchester was, however, notoriously unhealthy. In 1781 the first steam-driven textile mill had been built in the town. Ninety years later, in 1871, the mechanization this introduced had turned Manchester into the biggest manufacturing center in the world, producing almost one-third of global cotton textile production. As in all industrialized cities, most of the workers lived in crowded, unsanitary houses and were poorly fed; diseases were rife, with epidemics of cholera caused by inadequate water supplies and drainage; and open sewers ran through the streets and flooded basements. Families lived more than one to a room, and in places the child mortality rate was as high as 20 percent. Foreigners were struck both by the city's prosperity and by the price that purchased it, like the Frenchman Alexis de Tocqueville, who described conditions in 1835:

> These vast structures keep air and light out of the human habitations which they dominate; they envelop them in perpetual fog; here is the slave, there the master; there the wealth of some, here the poverty of most; there the organized effort of thousands produce, to the profit of one man, ... one-story houses whose ill-fitting planks and broken windows show them up, even from a distance, as the last refuge a man might find between poverty and death. None-the-less the wretched people reduced to living in them can still inspire jealousy of their fellow beings. Below some of their miserable dwellings is a row of cellars to which a sunken corridor leads. Twelve to fifteen human beings are crowded pell-mell into each of these damp, repulsive holes. The fetid, muddy waters, stained with a thousand colours by the factories they pass, of one of the streams I mentioned before, wander slowly round this refuge of poverty.... A sort of black smoke covers the city. The sun seen through it is a disc without rays. Under this half daylight 300,000 human beings are ceaselessly at work.[2]

Slave owners in America often claimed that their slaves lived better than agricultural workers in Britain. During the American Civil War the English visitor Anthony Trollope was shown slaves' quarters in Kentucky and found them "preferable in size, furniture, and all material comforts to the dwellings of our own agricultural laborers." William Wells Brown (and others) tried to expose this myth. He describes examining "an English peasant's cot" near Aylesbury in Buckinghamshire, and finding it "as fine a picture of neatness, order and comfort, as the most fastidious taste could wish to see."[3]

Harriet Jacobs wrote a more nuanced description of the comparative conditions of English rural inhabitants, who would not have been pleased to be described as "peasants," as both she and Wells Brown patronizingly did:

> We next went to Steventon, in Berkshire. It was a small town, said to be the poorest in the county. I saw men working in the fields for six shillings, and seven shillings, a week, and women for sixpence, and sevenpence, a day, out of which they boarded themselves. Of course they lived in the most primitive manner; it could not be otherwise, where a woman's wages for an entire day were not sufficient to buy a pound of meat. They paid very low rents, and their clothes were made of the cheapest fabrics, though much better than could have been procured in the United States for the same money. I had heard much about the oppression of the poor in Europe. The people I saw around me were, many of them, among the poorest poor. But when I visited them in their little thatched cottages, I felt that the condition of even the meanest and most ignorant among them was vastly superior to the condition of the most favored slaves in America. They labored hard; but they were not ordered out to toil while the stars were in the sky, and driven and slashed by an overseer, through heat and cold, till the stars shone out again. Their homes were very humble; but they were protected by law … the most destitute of these peasants was a thousand fold better off than the most pampered American slave.[4]

Other studies, however, found agricultural workers living in crowded, squalid conditions. The two residences shown to these American visitors must have been as carefully selected as the model slave quarters shown to Trollope and others in the United States. Neither Wells Brown nor Jacobs seems to have visited an industrial slum, where they would have found a very different state of affairs. De Tocqueville was not the only person to call the workers here slaves, nor was it only Americans who, with some justice, did so as well. British writers also compared the conditions of their industrial workers, not agricultural workers, to slavery. The differences from the position of slave in the United States were that British workers were not chattels who could be bought and sold and the law did prevent flogging and other excessive punishments, although there are reports of workers being beaten and children being chained to the machines they minded. Orphaned children were sent by parish authorities to work in the mills. They were preferred because they were cheaper and because they were able to crawl more easily under moving machinery to remove loose cotton that could block operation. Their smaller fingers, like those of women, were more suited to delicate tasks and they were cheaper than adult men. As inquest records show, many, both adults and children, died in industrial accidents, but the coroners' juries, made up of factory owners and other businessmen, rarely found employers blameworthy, except in cases of the most blatant breaches of health and safety or criminal negligence. A series of early 19th-century acts did improve conditions, especially for children, but it was not until 1878 that it was forbidden to employ children under the age of 10. The appointment of Manchester's first Medical Officer of Health in 1868 saw the start of improvements in the city's living conditions with the removal of cellar dwelling and the construction of proper sewers, but it was a long process, only partially achieved by the beginning of the 20th century. Rickets, caused by lack of vitamin D and lack of exposure to sunshine, remained common in poor children in British cities until after World War I.

The Box Browns chose 89 Moreton Street in the northern part of the city in the area known as Cheetham, Cheetham Hill, or Strangeways. Even though the northern suburbs of towns in Britain are generally the healthiest places because of the prevailing winds, the buildings here were thickly furred in grime from air pollution caused by the coal that fired the factories, which de Tocqueville and others had noticed decades earlier. Erecting taller chimneys had just spread grime and acid rain over a wider area. Louis Hayes recalled that the nearby cathedral was black with soot and had such a thick coating of accumulated deposits that it had "quite a velvety appearance."[5] Moreton Street ran north from New Bridge Street, parallel to Great Ducie Street. It has disappeared under redevelopment and the site is now occupied by a block of wholesalers. The southern end of the street was close to Victoria Station, which had local and regional railway services so would have been convenient for travel. To the east side of Great Ducie Street was a printer's shop, handy for advertising material. To the north was the new prison of Strangeways, opened in 1868, to the east the workhouse, and to the south the hospital and cathedral. It was a good, middle-class locale.

The owner of the Box Browns' house, and the others from numbers 79 to 93 (odd numbers), was a J. Miller. Henry appears in the ratebooks from 1870. Rates were a method of local taxation based on the notional rental value of the house, which was not the same as the actual sum charged. Every year the authorities estimated how much they would need to run various services, like caring for the poor and sick, maintaining streets, and so on, and then set the rates, at so many shillings to the value of the house, expressed in pounds. In both 1870 and 1871 Henry paid £1 15s 4d poor rate, equivalent to £997.00 ($1262) for an average earner today.

The intellectual environment may have appealed to the Box Browns. Support for abolition had always been strong in Manchester. An abolitionist committee was formed there in 1787, and between 1787 and 1788 about two-thirds of the city's adult males signed a petition in support of the cause, despite the reliance by the industries there on slave-produced goods. As mentioned earlier, in 1862 during the American Civil War cotton mill workers here and throughout Lancashire refused to process raw cotton picked by American slaves. By describing their experiences, Henry and the other fugitives who had lectured here must have contributed to this principled stand. The blockade of the southern ports in America that prevented the export of cotton meant that many people in Britain became unemployed and the workers were encouraged to drop their embargo. They refused.[6] In early 1867 Manchester had formed the first society in Britain to campaign for women's suffrage. These historic reasons would not have been a major factor in the Box Browns' choice of residence, but it shows the kind of intellectual atmosphere where they felt at home. Both were aware of the need to keep abreast of current affairs, whether in world events or fashions in entertainment, and there were many ways to do this in the lively city, with its numerous ways to support, educate, and entertain working men.

Manchester's industrial importance gave it a leading role in the political and economic reform of 19th-century Britain. Nonconformity was strong here, too. Those who could not or would not swear to the 39 Articles of the Anglican faith had been until recently excluded from many powerful professions and government posts, as well as the only two universities in England. This left trade and commerce as the main fields where a bright, dynamic, and ambitious man could advance in the world, and nonconformists were strongly represented in Manchester's business community. Although the theory of the Protestant work ethic, proposed by Max Weber in 1905, is not regarded as a complete explanation for the growth of capitalism and for Britain's early industrial revolution, there were religious factors that contributed to its success. The Protestant emphasis on personal autonomy and not accepting traditional practices led to many innovations and discoveries. The most successful businessmen, though excluded from government posts, had become politically influential because of their financial muscle. The Quakers, whose banking expertise and personal integrity gave them considerable political clout in Britain from the 18th century onward, were represented in Manchester. It was also a multicultural city. From the 1780s Sephardic Jews had been moving in from London and from the Middle East. Germans, among them Friedrich Engels, the patron of Karl Marx, had also settled here, although Engels moved to London in 1870. There were also Greeks and Turks whose trading links extended to Egypt and India. Politically the city was a bastion of free trade. As Louis Hayes said, "Manchester makes no distinction as to creed or race. She opens her portals and offers an equal chance to all those who wish to settle here and get gain."[7] This last certainly applied to Henry. His neighbors must have approved of his work ethic.

On Trial in Rochdale

Henry performed in Hulme, a suburb of Manchester, at the beginning of December. Jane was at home with the children, awaiting the birth of their next child. In the event, it was twins. Annie Amelia Helena and Mary Emma Martha arrived on January 15, 1870, when Henry was performing in Heywood, 12 miles away. It was not the fashion then for fathers to be present at the births of their children, but he was able to spend time with his growing family until a booking in Rochdale, next to Heywood, on February 2. Before his appearance in Burnley at the end of February, there was one other show he had to put on. He was summonsed to appear in Rochdale Magistrates' Court on February 9 to answer a charge of running an illegal lottery. A detective named Marshall had paid 1s for a ticket to his entertainment. In evidence, he said that after the first two parts of the show, magic and mesmerism, Henry sold song sheets, costing one penny, on which there was a number. After the sing-song, numbers were called and a prize was given to the person with that number on their song sheet. As an added inducement, Henry had said that silver-plated articles would be distributed at his next show. In answer to questioning, Marshall said he had seen a placard and gone into the show. He had not informed Henry that his proposed activity was illegal or improper, as he did not think it was his duty. He considered that Henry did know it was wrong, as he had been summonsed for the same thing at Newark. Questioned further, he admitted that the entertainment contained nothing objectionable and was respectably conducted. Henry's counsel told the bench that "Mr. Brown was a person of good character, and was very well known in the town." After mentioning his antislavery lectures and recent move into magic and mesmerism, he added that he was not one of the ordinary itinerant performers but was a resident householder in Manchester and a man of respectability, so should not be punished as a "rogue and vagabond," the catch-all phrase used in the 1824 Vagrancy Act. Henry had assured his counsel he had never been accused of a similar offense in Newark (although he kept silent about the questions that had been raised in Stonehouse in 1862). As a final clincher, counsel said that in Newport Henry's entertainment had been patronized by the mayor, who had seen nothing wrong. Perhaps playing on some private knowledge about the relationship between the magistrates in attendance and other factions in the town, he added that the case had been brought because there were "stricter moralists" in Rochdale with "more astute" lawyers. He asked for his client to be let off if he promised not to repeat the offense. The magistrates dismissed the case. Henry thanked them and left the court, unpunished, although he would have paid his legal costs.[8]

His next (theatrical) performance in Burnley was warmly received. In his advertisement he called himself the King of Biology and Animal Magnetism and Professor of Magic. He also emphasized America, saying he was from Richmond in the United States, and listed among the features of his act the American drum and bell trick, the Great American Tea Party, the New York Barbers' Shop (probably a musical element) and the African Prince's Drawing Room. The review in the local paper, calling him "the eminent magician," reported that he had been performing to "crowded and delighted audiences" in Manchester and the surrounding districts.[9]

Here in Lancashire, Henry had found a place where he fitted in and was appreciated. Rochdale, however, may not have forgiven him for his victory over their local moralists. When he appeared at the Odd Fellows Hall in nearby Todmorden in March, the local paper called him the "pseudo-mesmerist." It reported that his entertainment had been below par but the prize system and the sale of jewelry had created considerable interest, so he had found a loophole in the law. Jane joined him for an engagement in Bradford, and then packed houses greeted him in Manchester in April and in Oldham at the end of May.[10]

A Bereavement

During this tour the Box Browns suffered the death of one of the twins. The pair had not been baptized until April 6, 1870, perhaps because of Henry's schedule. In accordance with Jane's Anglican faith they were christened in Manchester Cathedral, which sounds very grand but was their nearest church.[11] As he stood in the vast space, recently restored in fashionable Gothic style, watching as his daughters were welcomed into the established Church of England, Henry must have reflected with understandable satisfaction that all his hard work had been rewarded.

Two months later, aged five months, Mary Emma Martha died on June 13 and Henry reported the death. The cause is given primarily as marasmus, undernourishment causing a child's weight to be significantly low for its age. The secondary cause was diarrhea, which may have accounted for the weight loss.[12] Breast-feeding two babies is a struggle, requiring the mother to be well nourished and healthy, and the baby bottles then available were not easy to clean and could harbor harmful bacteria. Jane seems to have had a robust constitution, but at this time it was quite rare for twins to survive long after birth, so they were lucky Annie lived.

After a month, Henry went back on the road, appearing in Congleton, Leek, and Leigh in Staffordshire. He was maintaining contact with the Freemasons, as he next appeared in the Masonic Rooms in Warrington, then went on to Hyde, where he had been raised as a Mason in 1859. There was a less enthusiastic reception in Ashton-under-Lyne in September, but this may

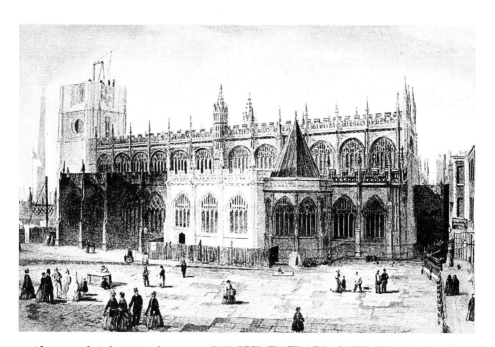

Above and right: Manchester Cathedral, where three of Henry and Jane's children were baptized. This engraving was made when the building was being renovated.

have been due to inadequate publicity; Henry's return visit to the area in January 1871 was a great success.[13] Whether Jane was with him in all these venues is not clear; by now he was so well known in this part of the Midlands that his advertisements were minimal, usually stating only venues and dates, and the newspapers simply noted he had appeared.

In Ashton-under-Lyne in September 1870 he performed legerdemain and ventriloquism. He may have been trying out a new skill, but it probably did not succeed, as ventriloquism is never mentioned again. As Henry was so well known he did not need to pay for advertisements in the press, and there is a break in reports of his appearances until November, when he was in Bolton. In January 1871 he made a triumphant return to Droylsden, two miles from Ashton-under-Lyne, both now in the Greater Manchester area. Here his main appeal was to the very old. Henry (who must have been the same age as many of his audience) boasted of how much he could eat, drink, and smoke, showing he was still enjoying his life and his material success. In March he appeared in Rawtenstall where the local newspaper called him "our American cousin," indicating he was still emphasizing this facet of his act.[14]

Home Life in Manchester

At the time of the census on April 2, 1871, the whole family was at home at 89 Moreton Street. Henry gave his occupation as public lecturer, another example of his need to represent himself as respectable because in reality he was a full-time entertainer. The three surviving children were ages 10, six, and one, and there was a domestic servant, Surrey-born Susan Smith, aged 21. The Box Browns seem first to have hired a servant after the birth of Edward when they were on the road, but Jane would still have needed help after they decided to settle down. At the time, with the lack of laborsaving devices, it was customary for even the lower middle classes to have a very young maid of all work, earning about £6 per year but being given her food, accommodation, and sometimes a contribution toward the cost of clothing. Susan Smith would have been paid slightly more because she was older. The pollution produced by coal fires both inside the house and by the factories of Manchester meant that keeping the house, the family's clothes, and the bedding clean was a never-ending job. As well as a live-in servant, they would have sent out their laundry to be done and hired a specialist charwoman to give the house a thorough cleaning at regular intervals. It must have been a source of satisfaction to the ex-slave to employ a house servant himself, and Henry would also have reflected on how his first wife, Nancy, had been forced to do the laundry of her master, as well as general domestic tasks to prevent her being sold. He had come a long way since then, not just geographically but socially. His immediate neighbors were respectable, lower-middle-class or skilled working-class people: a bookkeeper, an accountant, a cotton machine maker, and a plumber, glazier, and gas fitter (who also had a servant). Others in just this one street show how cosmopolitan Manchester was. Although most of the birthplaces given are local and there are people from Scotland, Ireland, Wales, and other locations in the United Kingdom, there is an international presence: a Russian; Germans; a Frenchman; people from Prussia,

Syria, and Moldavia. The Poles may have been, from their names, Jewish, and one had an Austrian-born lodger.[15] The Box Browns were not exceptional here.

By now the public was beginning to become aware of how at least some of Henry's illusions were achieved. There had been the incident in Margate, the local paper in Rochdale had called him a pseudo-mesmerist, and other mesmerists were also being exposed. Zamoiski, one of the earliest and most successful, had been revealed as a fake in Ipswich in 1859 when boys he had coached to pretend to be blind, deaf, and dumb confessed the deception. Four years later when Zamoiski appeared in Blaenarvon the *Monmouthshire Merlin*, disparaging as ever, reported, "As the Blaenavon public had been recently 'sold' with an entertainment of a similar character, they were very chary about parting with their money, and the consequence was, that M. Zamoiski was but poorly patronised."[16] Word was already spreading that those who were supposedly mesmerized were acting, but people were not deterred by this and similar exposés and went on paying to attend performances. Even if they were aware of the deception, they must have enjoyed the spectacle of people behaving ridiculously, appreciated the skill with which it was done, and felt themselves superior because they knew what was happening.

At the end of April 1871 the *Ipswich Journal* reported the appearance of a Mr. and Mrs. Matthews in Woodbridge, Suffolk, where they performed an act including palmistry and clairvoyance. The newspaper reporter praised the way this had been achieved, "the key words being well concealed," but regretted the introduction of the couple's "stale and exploded trick" of electro-biology, adding, "We have seen and known the exposure of 'Zamoiski,' 'Box Brown,' and others, and heard from the lips of those who were their 'subjects' the history of their whole course of training." There were many other people doing similar acts, yet by 1871 only Henry was being coupled with Zamoiski, one of the earliest and apparently best known nonscientists who was a proponent of electro-biology. It is a tribute to Henry's self-publicity skills and fame that his was the name that readily sprang to mind and would be the one the journalist expected his readers to recognize, as it had previously been on the other side of the country in Wales, in the middle county of Oxfordshire, and in Lancashire in the North.

Further Bereavements

In August Henry appeared in Glossop, only 13 miles from Manchester, where he won "loud applause" and then returned to Leigh later in the same month. Jane was again pregnant, and on October 26, 1871, John Floyd Brown, named after his maternal grandfather, was born. Henry performed in New

Mills and Audenshaw, small towns in Derbyshire, before registering his son's birth on December 7, giving his occupation as a public lecturer. He was baptized in Manchester Cathedral on January 1, 1872, where Henry promoted himself to "gentleman," which was entered in the cathedral's baptism register with, it appears, no questions or reservations.[17]

On June 2, 1872, at age seven months, the baby boy died of bronchitis and convulsions, according to the death certificate. Henry must have been away from home at the time, appearing somewhere not mentioned in the press, and Jane was ill, because two days later it was Agnes who registered the death. This seems an onerous task to lay on a 12-year-old girl, but her parents may simply not have been available to do this. He was buried on June 6, 1872, in Ardwick Cemetery, where the records gave the cause of death as whooping cough. Henry was 57, and Jane was 38. They were to have no more children, or at least none that survived.[18]

Throughout the rest of 1872 Henry took his act around local venues. He was very enthusiastically received on his return to Heywood. The local newspaper's account of his appearance shows that he retained some elements of the lecture, but it was primarily an amusement and neither his color nor his ethnicity was any longer relevant.

> Mr. Box Brown … [is] now one of the best known and most accomplished of mesmerists, phrenologists, and magicians.… His feats of legerdemain are many of them of startling excellence, marvels of patient study and skill. They evoked frequent bursts of applause from the admiring audience His expositions of phrenology were clear and concise, and very interesting. His mesmeric illustrations of that science were display of the most masterly skill, his perfect influence over the persons operated being only equalled by the unique tact with which he directs it, making them by a few rapid touches, exhibit the feelings of cold, heat, hunger, &c., as easily as the keys of a piano would flow forth music at the touch of an accomplished pianist. The comical pranks he evoked from his mesmerised guests elicited a continued roar of laughter from the large audience which crowded the hall on Wednesday evening.

"A distribution of handsome presents" concluded each entertainment, so he was still able to afford this element of the act.[19] Henry must also have been employing stooges here. Although there may be some dispute about how far hypnotism can be practiced instantaneously on strangers, phrenology has been completely discredited, and to mix it with mesmerism, as he did here, was pure showmanship, not science.

So far no records of appearances in 1873 have been found, except for one performance given to the inmates of Manchester workhouse on May 8 for which he would not have been paid, but he needed to keep working to support his family. He was no longer news or even doing an exceptional act, so his standard appearances would not have been reported. By 1874 he was being referred to as "this veteran coloured entertainer," with veteran being code for old-fashioned but still regarded with affection, like an elderly uncle who does the same old trick every year at family gatherings, long after everyone but the youngest knows how it is done.[20]

On October 20, 1874, the Box Browns' eldest child died. Agnes was 14 and the cause of her death was Bright's disease, which covers a wide range of conditions causing nephritis, inflammation of the kidneys. Whether this was an acute attack as the result of an infection or the outcome of a long-standing illness is not known. She joined her siblings in Ardwick Cemetery on October 23.[21]

Goodbye to Britain

In early 1875 Henry was in his 60th year and had been on the road in Britain for 25 years. The decline in his popularity—audiences by now were moderate and mainly the very young, who did not remember him in his heyday, or the old, who were nostalgic—would have been one of the factors that made him think of returning to America. People rarely make momentous decisions for a single reason, so other considerations would have played a part. An economic depression in Britain had been triggered by a crash on the New York Stock Market in September 1873. This particularly affected the United Kingdom, reducing its industrial lead over mainland Europe, and lasted until 1879. The effects locally can be seen in the rates that Henry paid to support the poor of Manchester. Even before the crash there were economic problems, and in 1872 the rates had been increased by almost 50 percent, going up by £1 to £2 15s 4d, then in 1873 increased again to £3 1s 10d. Until 1874 Henry had no trouble paying his rates (unlike some of his neighbors) and paid promptly and in full. That year he paid in three installments, one in arrears.[22] Although the full sum was paid off eventually, for a man now styling himself a "gentleman" and with a comfortable lifestyle to maintain this was worrying. Working-class people, who formed the bulk of Henry's audiences, were those most affected by the economic downturn. They needed to make savings and entertainment would be the most disposable item in the family budget.

He had lost at least three children in England, and perhaps he thought of being reunited with the children of his first marriage, who by now might have children themselves, or with some of his siblings. He had apparently shown little interest in them while he was working to build his career and his new marriage and family in Britain, but at 60 the future is shorter and the past longer. The American Civil War had been over for 10 years and the enslaved had been freed, so he probably believed his situation would be better.

A combination of factors—declining audiences and income, the knowledge that there was a whole new public who had not seen his act and, perhaps, thoughts of reuniting with his first family—must have sown ideas of returning to America, which was, despite the crash, managing far better economically than Europe.

On March 1, 1875, U.S. Congress passed the Civil Rights Act, prohibiting racial discrimination in public accommodations and in jury duty. By now the Box Brown family must have decided to relocate to the United States, but this would have seemed confirmation that they were making the right decision. Henry's last known appearances in England are, fittingly, recorded in the *Era*. The "very popular coloured entertainer" appeared in Rochdale, a place with good memories for him, on January 30 and February 1 and 2. Then in March he performed his sleight of hand act at the Odd Fellows Hall in Stockport, where he received "fair houses." On Saturday July 3, 1875, he, Jane, Edward, and Annie set off from Liverpool on the *Algeria*, taking the iconic box with them. They landed in New York on July 14.[23]

Epilogue

In his 25 years in Britain, Henry had become a celebrated, respected figure. He had joined well-established societies, become a householder, and had several brushes with the British legal system, sometimes as plaintiff, sometimes as defendant. He had received damages for libel and for breaches of contract, but had lost other, mainly trivial, cases. He had traveled first class while the men who worked for him went in second. Some of his neighbors in Manchester had not employed a servant, as he was able to do. In the latter part of his career, his was the first name that often came to mind when popular entertainment was discussed. Newspapers reported his doings, occasionally without reference to his color, and usually praised him. Did he believe that with the Civil War over and, theoretically, full equality being granted to ex-slaves, the situation would be the same in the United States? If so, he was about to be grievously disillusioned. Although the Civil Rights Acts in 1866 and 1875 made black people legally equal, attitudes internalized over centuries are not swept away overnight. Even in the North, attitudes rooted in the era of slavery continued to militate against equality of opportunity. In the South the Jim Crow laws, so called after a character in minstrel shows, were passed from 1877 onward, two years after Henry's return to the United States, but these were not new; they simply legalized established practice. Legal segregation and discrimination in the South were not seriously challenged until the 1950s, and remnants remain today.[1]

Practices and soon laws in the South mandated separate seating for black people on public transport and in theaters, libraries, and train stations. There were different facilities for black and white citizens in lavatories, swimming pools, and other services, where those for blacks were always inferior. In restaurants without separate seating areas black people could order only take-away food, so Jane could enter, sit, and eat, while her husband and children had to stay outside with their food on their laps. They could not travel in the same railroad car. Even more seriously, in terms of the family's professional life, sports matches, musical performances, and other entertainments were segregated by color, which prevented the Box Browns from performing their family act in the South from where Henry came and where they may have visited, as will be seen. Although it must have been wearily familiar to him, the situation would have come as a great shock to his wife and children. Jane, Edward, and Annie were used to being accepted as a variant on the standard, respectable, lower middle-class British family, but this was not going to happen in the 19th-century United States. Although Henry and Jane could perform together in the North, they were in danger of being shunned by audiences and abused in the street by racists who thought there should be no association between black men and white women, let alone marriage. Frederick Douglass's marriage in 1884 to Helen Pitts, a white woman, was opposed by both their families, condemned by both white and black contemporaries, and in public the couple attracted much unwelcome attention, even though, or perhaps because, he held a respected, prominent position.[2]

Billing himself as "Prof. H. Box Brown," Henry continued to perform as a magician. In England he had played on his American origins (although he also billed himself as an African Prince) to emphasize his modernity, in America he highlighted his English experience to stress how classy his act was, calling it a "drawing room entertainment" when he appeared at the Broadway Hall in Boston in 1876. It is not stated whether Jane and the children performed with him. By the following year, Annie, then aged seven, was part of the act. When he returned to Portland, Maine, in January 1877, Henry found he was well remembered:

> This genius, who gave entertainments in the Old City Hall twenty-six years ago, appeared at Mechanics Hall last evening in his novel entertainment. There were but few present but the tricks were very cleverly done. This evening he will give the history of his escape from slavery in 1849 in a box; and he carries the box with him and has it on stage. His little daughter will also assist and perform several feats of sleight of hand.[3]

Henry must have reflected on the changes since his previous visit. He was no longer a star and his magic act was not enough to draw crowds, so he needed to revisit his escape from slavery and to show the box in which this had been effected. This element had been absent from his act in Britain for many years, but he had preserved this memento of his past—or had he had it recreated? Whatever its origins, the box, with his recent experiences in mind and his audience's memories of his past, had renewed resonance for him. Although those who came to his performances enjoyed themselves, in general America did not welcome these. Later in the year, in September, they were in Montpelier, Vermont. The local paper, the *Argus and Patriot*, reported:

> While Prof. H. Box Brown, a *gentleman of color*, was in town recently, some of the people wondered a little to see him and the Judge walking up street arm in arm. They afterwards learned that "Uncle Joe" had so strongly recommended him to the Judge's patronage, that the matter is no longer one of merriment [italics in the original].

Uncle Joe was Joseph Lewis, an Irishman, then 76, connected with the local mining industry and a long-time subscriber to the newspaper, which described him as a staunch Democrat who was "respected by all for his honesty and good nature." How he came to know Henry is a matter for conjecture, but if the ex-slave had hoped to attract people to his show by this display of approval he was to be disappointed. When Henry gave his entertainment at Barron's Hall there was only a small audience, although "those in attendance were well pleased."[4]

The family moved on to Massachusetts, and in November Henry appeared in Leominster in Worcester County, where his escape from slavery was mentioned but where he seems to have performed just "mirth, magic and mystery" on two nights. The Box Browns were still in Massachusetts at the beginning of 1878 when they performed in Milbury. In May they were in Boston, and here at Gothic Hall Henry gave an exposé of spiritualism together with an account of his escape from slavery in 1849.[5] How this exposé was done may have been preserved in one of the accounts Jim Magus heard. According to his informant, in a trick called the Spirit Cabinet Henry was tied hand and foot by a member of the audience, then placed behind a curtain with a bell and tambourine on a tray, as the Davenport Brothers had done many years before. The sounds of the instruments would be heard, and then the curtain would open to reveal him still tied up. It seems that a trick he exposed became, when handed down orally, a trick he performed. This seems to have become a regular part of his act in other places. They were again attracting juvenile audiences, as a ticket from a show indicates:

> Scholar's Ticket / Mr. H. Box Brown's World-Renowned Performance And Lecture, Entitled The African Prince's Drawing-Room Entertainment / Admission For Scholars … 6 Cents…. Little Annie Brown will Perform the Wonderful Sack Trick…. All the Schools from Boston, Lynn, Salem, Marblehead … have recently attended this Entertainment in large numbers…. Admission 10 cts./ Reserved Seats 25 cts.[6]

Annie would step into a sack at the center of the stage. Henry would pull up the sack to cover her and tie the top. After suitable patter, he revealed that the sack was empty. Suddenly Annie would appear at the back of the hall, presumably having concealed herself in Jane's skirts or behind a backcloth and, while Henry distracted the audience, slipped off stage. It was advertised as "such as was never performed by any child." Jim Magus was told that one of *Henry's* tricks was to escape from a canvas sack, after being tied up and having a chain wrapped round the sack and padlocked. Henry freed himself in less than five minutes.[7] This appears to be a conflation of Annie's role and the exploits that escapologists like Houdini performed. Nowhere is there any recorded account of Henry performing such a feat and it is extremely unlikely that he did this. As an 1899 photograph shows, Houdini was 25, slim and muscular, and wore few clothes so the audience could see he was not concealing anything like a knife or tool that he could use. An elderly, fat man in minimal clothing struggling inside a sack is a comedy routine, not something that would captivate an audience as a fit young man or a winsome child would.

An extant handbill announces an appearance at Brookline not far from Boston, Massachusetts, on May 9, 1878.[8] This handbill says that in Brookline Henry will perform and make an exposé of spiritualism. There were probably other appearances in small towns, as the scholar's ticket suggests, where it was not worth the expense of advertising in local papers and he was not of enough interest to merit a review.

The Box Browns were back in Vermont in 1879, where Henry (and perhaps his family) appeared in Island Pond, Essex County, then an important railroad center on the line between Montreal, in Quebec, and Portland in Maine. The local paper noted: "Not a very large audience attended the entertainment given by Box Brown in Association Hall last week. Our people seem to want something better and of a higher nature than shows of this kind, and we are glad to note the fact."[9]

Soon after this, they were back in Montpelier at Union Hall, but there is no indication of how Henry's show was received. The following year, in March, he gave a sleight-of-hand performance and lecture at School House Hall in Proctorsville, Vermont. Two months later, in May 1880, they were back in Montpelier:

> The Brown family gave entertainments at the Village Hall, Montpelier, last Saturday and again Monday evening. The head of the family, H. Box Brown, is a colored gentleman of courtly manners, debonair deportment, and *distingue* appearance, while the other members conducted themselves all as good citizens should, and gave a show that had merit in it[10] [italics in the original].

Although the press gave a warm welcome, only a small audience attended; five months was too soon to give a repeat performance. The minimum period between appearances for this kind of act is generally accepted to be a year, and by now the family must have recognized it had come to the end of the road in the United States. By 1881 the family had relocated to Ontario, Canada, where they must have hoped that they would receive more appreciation of their skills.

Black Communities in Canada

Since the first French settlers arrived in what became Canada, there had been slavery but, because of the nature of the land and the settlements, there was less of it. The crops grown and goods produced in this new territory did not require the intensive labor that tropical crops, like rice, cotton, and sugar, needed, so slaves were mainly personal servants brought by Loyalists or other settlers moving from the United States, but some were enslaved indigenous people. In 1791 Upper Canada (today the southern part of Ontario) was established as a separate British colony. Two years after that, the lieutenant governor, John Graves Simcoe, ordered the legislature to prohibit the import of slaves and to provide for the gradual emancipation of children of those already enslaved in the colony, but *de facto* slavery continued into the early 19th century.[11] In the 1812–1814 war against America, many black men volunteered to fight on the British side. News of "black men in red coats" who were free in Canada was carried back to the United States, which led to the beginnings of the Underground Railroad, and fugitive slaves from America started to arrive in numbers from 1814.

In 1830 the Wilberforce Settlement, named in honor of the British Member of Parliament who had driven the bill to abolish slavery in the British Empire through Parliament, was established in the area that became Ontario. It was not primarily for freed slaves but for a number of free black people who had relocated from Cincinnati, fearing the enforcement of repressive discrimination there.

Amherstburg was the Canadian town at the end of the Underground Railroad where many fugitives arrived. Some stayed, and others dispersed to other settlements, either those nearby like Chatham, Buxton, Dawn (now called Dresden), and Colchester or places further afield, like London, Ingersoll, Norwich, St. Catherines, Hamilton, and Toronto. The Canadian census of 1851 required just the place of birth, like the census in Britain, so it is not easy to know how many black people there were in Canada at this time. Henry Bibb, publisher of *Voice of the Fugitive*, estimated there were 35,000. He said that before the Fugitive Slave Act there had been about 30,000, of whom 20,000 were fugitive slaves. Samuel Ward put the number higher, at 40,000. Even some who had been manumitted decided they would be safer in Canada. There were enough to establish an independent black press, but neither of the publications, the *Voice of the Fugitive* (1851–54) or the *Provincial Freeman* (1854–59), was long-lived. Although the fugitives welcomed their freedom here, there was prejudice and discrimination, as editorial comments in both the black press and the local white-owned newspapers showed, especially following the influx after 1850. Between 1850 and 1860, an estimated 15,000 to 20,000 African Americans settled in Canada, increasing the population to about 60,000. Before the American Civil War about 35,000 people of African descent were living in Ontario. Censuses of 1871 and 1881 required origin/ethnicity. Sometimes this is given as American, which probably indicated white people, as the classifications African and Negro were also used. This question was dropped in 1891. Although some black people had returned to the United States from Canada following the end of the Civil War, there were some 800 in London, Ontario, when the Box Browns were first mentioned in July 1881, although they did not themselves appear in any of the returns for the recent census in the province of Ontario.[12]

Schools were often segregated, not legally but at the demand of white residents, and some private schools, funded by religious bodies, were also intended solely for black people. There was also an attempt by the white community in Colchester to prevent the black residents, then about one-third of the inhabitants, from exercising their legal right to vote for the local authorities. The chairman of the meeting was heavily fined, but the white inhabitants collected money to cover this. Black men were not summoned for jury duty in some places, and discrimination on boats and in taverns was experienced,[13] but these were scattered and sporadic events. By the time the Box Browns arrived, the usual panic and overreaction that any migrant wave causes had somewhat abated.

Life in Ontario

Ontario been the destination of many thousands of fugitives, and this was where the Box Brown family settled. It was a very different environment from their previous home. In 1881 the population of the whole of Ontario was 1,923,228; back in England, the city of Manchester alone had a population of 1,866,649, with many more in the nearby towns and villages. Toronto, then the second largest city in Canada, had 86,415 inhabitants; London had a population of just 19,746 and nearby Kingston had 14,091.[14] Most nonconformists (and there were many here) shunned Henry's type of entertainment in which he flirted with the supernatural; indeed, they avoided public amusements of all but the most religiously inspired kind, so his possible audiences were further reduced. In the whole of the province there was not enough of a potential market to sustain a career as a traveling magician. The small population was scattered in settlements some way from each other and not easily accessible off the main rail routes. To make even an annual visit to towns across the whole of the region, where there would be enough people to make a journey worthwhile, would have been both expensive and physically demanding. Henry and Jane seem to have operated in a very small part of the southwest corner of the state where there was an extensive railroad network. Even so, the distances were long; London was some 50 miles from Brantford and more than 100 miles from Toronto. In Britain Henry had rarely traveled more than 20 miles between locations when touring an area, so he must have been spending a lot of time (and money) assessing possible venues and making arrangements.

It seems likely that Henry, ever resourceful, became more of an impresario, putting together a full program of entertainment, which sometimes included his family act. He had always used musicians in his performances and in some places, like Jersey in the Channel Islands, had presented prizes for races so this would just be an extension of this practice. In July 1881 Henry organized an entertainment in Tecumseh Park, a baseball ground in the suburbs of London, and awarded the victor of a three-mile walking race a six-dollar cup. The event was not advertised; presumably, handbills and word of mouth were enough in what was then a relatively small city with little competition for audiences, but it was mentioned in the local press.[15] He and his family could have done their magic act in a marquee, and there must have been a musical element.

He was working solo when he crossed the border into the United States in February 1882 to appear in Cheybogan, a logging town in Michigan on Lake Huron, where his appearance in the Opera House (which doubled as the schoolhouse) was well patronized, perhaps because of the distribution of "very unique, if not valuable presents." The same edition of the newspaper that reported his performance noted there had been a six-inch fall of snow, welcomed by the lumber dealers, but it might have made traveling to his next venue, St. Ignace, some 25 miles further north and across a stretch of water, troublesome. Only Henry was mentioned; perhaps Jane and the children did not want to face the rigors of a northern winter. His fortitude, at the age of 67, must be admired, but to endure such a journey suggests that the family was in some need of funds. Henry seems to have remained in the area, perhaps using Cheybogan as a base, because in March, always keen to defend his legal rights, he lodged a complaint with the village council against a night watchman named O'Brien. His accusation (not detailed) was upheld and O'Brien was suspended, with another man appointed in his place.[16]

Back in Canada, he appeared again in London in November 1882 and the local paper reported:

> Professor Box Brown appeared in the Town Hall last night, and obtained leave to address the Council. He related the thrilling scenes and incidents connected with his escape from slavery, and how he was packed away in a box three feet one inch in length by two feet in width; that he wanted the use of the hall for one of these lectures, and if so granted would expose conjuring, give an exhibition of legerdemain, and would lecture on animal magnetism, biology, sociology, tricology, and micology. The use of the hall was granted, the Professor to pay all expenses.

These lectures and shows could be spread out over a long period to provide a regular income. In 1883 he again applied for the use of the city hall in London to give a lecture on mesmerism. As an added inducement, he offered the members of the council free invitations and proposed to mesmerize them individually or collectively, and permission was given.[17] He was taking a chance on their acceptance of his offer to hypnotize them because he must have planned to use stooges, but gambled that the councilors would be too conscious of their dignity to take part in the kind of entertainment he put on. It seems they declined his offer; there is no report of them being part of any show.

At the end of 1883 Henry, and possibly the rest of the family, went back to Cheybogan for what seems to have been his last appearance there. Previously Henry's magic act had been fairly well received, but now the tone of the local press was mocking when this was replaced with singing:

> The Au Sable Saturday Night thus sketches a familiar subject: A week ago Friday an antiquated antiquity in the shape of an aged "cullud" man struck town. He was accompanied by three younger members of the human family. Saturday and Sunday evenings they held forthat [sic] Opera Hall under the formidable name of "Professor" Box Brown's Troubadour Jubilee Singers.[18]

This was a massive miscalculation. Although Henry had had a good voice, he had apparently not performed in public for many years and singing had always been a secondary element in his shows. Jane, Edward, and Annie were never previously mentioned as singing in the various incarnations of the family act, and although it looks as though they were performing here, those who appeared with Henry are not called his own family, just "three younger members of the *human* family." Before recorded sound, every community had good amateur singers regularly performing in public and at social events, and this small group was probably nothing out of the ordinary. Henry learned his lesson. He never seems to have returned to Cheybogan, nor to have performed in a singing group again, although he did retain music in his future programs. But on his travels in Michigan, he may have met someone who was later to play an important part in his family's life.

Three year later in Kingston, some 150 miles (241 km) from Toronto, in May 1886 Henry performed his magic act for two nights, but a proposed lecture and concert did not go ahead because it failed to draw an audience. He also tried to get the City Hall in Kingston at reduced rates for a troupe of Jubilee singers. As an inducement he offered free seats to the mayor and council but there is no further information about the outcome.[19] Jubilee singers, black American choirs, were popular from 1871 when a group of students from Fisk University went on tour in America, Britain and Europe to raise funds. They were so successful that many others imitated them. This choir may have been a troupe Henry was now managing, using his extensive experience to work as their tour manager rather than being hired as a performer. Even nonconformists approved of Jubilee singers of spirituals and gospel-inspired music, so they were guaranteed an audience. If these singers were also performing in places of worship this would not have to be advertised; it could be announced from the pulpit and spread by word of mouth. This may indicate how Henry earned at least a part of his living. It must have been a fairly hand-to-mouth existence and Jane could have contributed to the family budget, perhaps by returning to teaching on a private basis. It is also possible that Henry performed at private functions, like children's parties, as before leaving Britain he had increasingly focused on young audiences.

By this time the family was living in Toronto. Martha Cutter's research has found Henry in street directories, legal documents from Toronto General Hospital, and the city of Toronto tax rolls from the 1880s and 1890s, showing the Box Browns lived there from 1886 to 1897. Sometimes he gives his occupation as "Professor of Animal Magnetism," "Lecturer," or "Traveler," and in 1891, tax rolls for the city of Toronto list his employment as "Concert Conductor," which suggests he had become an impresario, still involved in music, but Martha Cutter has as yet found no actual notices of performances.[20]

In February 1889 in Brantford, some 71 miles (115 km) from Toronto, Henry was invited to lecture on slavery. In Britain, music had usually been part of his act, and in 1889 in Brantford, singers were on also the program when he and his family gave one of their "unique" entertainments in the local YMCA, Wycliffe Hall. After delivering a lecture about slavery and relating his escape, Henry performed magic tricks. Music formed part of this act, and the evening ended with "the Company" singing plantation songs. This must have been a full-sized troupe: "the ladies were very good singers."[21] This is a further indication that, by now, he was an impresario.

Descendants

Henry lived to see the marriages of Edward and Annie. It has not yet been possible to find out much more about Edward with any certainty. His name is common and, as in Britain, Canada did not record color or race in most official records. The last Canadian census to request ethnicity was the 1881 version, in which the Box Browns do not, apparently, appear. An Edward H. Brown was married in Sault Ste. Marie, Michigan, on October 30, 1883, to Jane E. Price. His residence is given as London, Canada; his birthplace Bristol, England; and his occupation "Traveler." The age of both Edward and Jane was 21. There is no birth for an Edward H. Brown registered in Bristol between October 1861 and March 1863, although there is one Edward Brown.

Henry's son would have been 19 years and two days old, but, if this was him, which seems almost certain, he may have said 21 to claim he was not a minor who required permission to marry, chancing that no one would go to the trouble or expense of checking. No member of either family seems to have been present; the couple's marriage was by Alex. Dauskin, pastor of the Presbyterian church, and Mrs. H.L. Dauskin was one of their witnesses. The other was a Miss Jennie Johnston. Although the record required color to be given and other couples are annotated W or W & I, presumably White & Indian, there was no color given for Jane, and Edward was marked A, possibly for African. Jane's birthplace was Richmond, Virginia,[22] more than 700 miles away to the southeast; this seems an unlikely distance for a woman to have traveled in search of work. It is more likely that the Box Browns visited his old city so Henry could show his wife and children from where he had escaped, and they met Jane there. Could she have been a relative of some degree, if Henry had been able to contact any of his siblings? Or she may have been another person captivated by this attractive performer who decided to go on the road with them. These suppositions must remain tantalizingly unanswered, as nothing more is yet known about Edward and any of his possible descendants.

Much more is known with more certainty about what became of Annie, who seems to have become a musician. Her husband was Charles W. Jefferson, a barber. He was born in Michigan—perhaps they had met while Henry was on tour there and he was another person drawn to his personality and lifestyle. The Jeffersons married in 1890 and moved to Kane, Pennsylvania. This town, some 94 miles south of Lake Erie and next to the Allegheny Forest (later Allegheny National Forest), was founded in the early 1860s and named after General Thomas L. Kane, who had fought in the American Civil War. Its proximity to woodland meant that wood formed an important part of the town's economy, with lumber mills and the manufacture of goods such as brush handles, doors, and windows. There was also a large glassworks at the turn of the century. When the Jeffersons moved there it was just one generation away from its founding and probably still had a frontier-town atmosphere. It was a very different landscape from Annie's childhood in the towns of industrial Lancashire. Her husband was the owner of his own business and home. Their first son, Charles Henry, was born on November 29, 1890, and Manley Lawrence followed on April 27, 1892.[23]

Death of and Life After Henry

About the time of the birth of his second grandson in 1892, Henry unsuccessfully sued Toronto General Hospital (from which he had been renting a property since 1886) after he fell through some stairs it refused to repair. He died on June 15, 1897, and Annie arranged for his burial the following day in Toronto's Necropolis Cemetery. She gave his age as 67, the last in a long line of gentle untruths—actually he was 82. The cause of his death was locomotor ataxia, the inability to control the movements of his body due to spinal damage.[24] One cause of this condition is trauma, so this was most probably the result of his fall. It was an unlucky end for a man whose body had served him well in his escape and in the following decades when he so tirelessly toured and performed.

Henry's grave is marked with a small headstone. It seems to encapsulate Jane's raw grief. The most prominent feature is the word HUSBAND emblazoned across the top, the first word that any passerby sees. No occupation is given, just his name, omitting the Box that made him famous. The only other piece of information is the date he left her. Henry had been an uxorious man, working hard to look after and try to protect his first wife Nancy and their children. He had given his second wife Jane adventure, travel to places a provincial schoolmistress could never have hoped to see, and experiences she could not have expected. He treated her relatively equally—they were the joint owners of their panoramas—and he encouraged her to flourish and use her talents, which many other men of that time would have regarded as unthinkable. She must have been devastated to lose him after 42 years of partnership. Not only had they shared the births and deaths of children and other personal events and experiences, they had also known professional triumphs and disappointments. She could not then see him as the successful and moderately famous entertainer he had been to the world, just as what he had been to her personally.

Annie took her mother to live with her in Pennsylvania. Two years later, in 1899, Mae Gertrude Jefferson was born. At the 1900 census there were 2,944 inhabitants in Kane and the Jefferson family was living in Kane Borough in Ward 2 & 4 McKean. Both boys were at school. Ten years later the family was still at the same address. All the family members, including Jane, are recorded as "Black," which suggests the enumerator spoke only to Charles and made assumptions about the other members of the household. Their neighbors were white. The 1910 Kane Directory shows that

Henry Brown's gravestone in Toronto Necropolis. Photograph by Rupert Collister.

C.W. Jefferson was living in Moffitt Avenue and had his business at 35 Fraley. He was one of 12 barbers in the town, eight of whom had their salons on Fraley.[25] Being a barber was a common occupation among black men. Although Frederick Douglass encouraged men to learn other skills, barbering was relatively easy to learn and enabled a black man to be moderately successful because he was running a business that offered a personal service that in no way threatened white men.

After their long years of being on the move, Jane and Annie were now settled. This was to be their home for the future. Perhaps they welcomed the certainty and security; perhaps they felt stultified by the sameness but they had family events to welcome and share. Charles Henry, the eldest, was the first of the Jefferson children to marry. His wedding to Hazel Brooks, a domestic servant, took place in Portville, Cattaraugus County, New York, on January 16, 1911. She was 18, and he was 21. He gave his occupation as glassworker in Kane. Five years later, on February 1, 1916, his younger brother Manley married Bertha Wright, a 23-year-old hairdresser, in Jamestown, Chautauqua County, New York, and later in the year the marriage of the youngest Jefferson was announced in the *Kane Republican*:

> The marriage of Miss Mae Gertrude Jefferson, daughter of Mr. and Mrs. C.W. Jefferson, of 125 Moffitt Avenue, to William O. Holly, of Ashtabula, O., was solemnized at the A.M.E. [African Methodist Episcopal] parsonage, last evening, the Rev. Norris officiating. Mr and Mrs Holly will reside in Ashtabula.[26]

Charles Jefferson, his children, and their spouses had the kinds of occupations to which many black people were confined by American social stratification: barbers, factory workers, domestic servants, chauffeurs, even an entertainer. In Britain their choices might have been equally circumscribed, but there it would have been primarily education, determined by class, that ordained their occupations.

A year later, during World War I, Charles Junior's draft card shows that in 1917 he was living in Highland, Elk County, Pennsylvania, and employed by the Nanson Chemical Company as a carpenter. At that date he had four children. Elk County is south of McKean, so Charles was still near his parents. His brother Manley was living at this time at 17 Lockwood, Ashtabula, Ohio, possibly with his sister and brother-in-law. His draft registration records that he was working as a barber for Hiram Keyes. His height was "medium" and his build "stout," which suggests he took after his grandfather.[27]

By 1920 only the Jeffersons' daughter Mae Gertrude, at that point a musician in the theater and calling herself Gertrude Mae, and Jane were at home with Charles and Annie. Charles was still the proprietor of a barbershop. All three Jeffersons were recorded as Mulatto, while Jane was "white." Their neighbors were Italians. Only Mae Gertrude inherited the show-biz gene—

perhaps the stories her mother and grandmother had told her of life in the theater inspired her. She may have been fulfilling a local engagement, as her husband was back in Ashtabula, Ohio, lodging with Dan and Leah Williams in Precinct E. William Holly, like his father-in-law, was a barber. He was born in 1891 in Maryland and was classified as Black. The Williamses were both "Mu[latto]."

Manley Jefferson and his wife Bertha (born in New York) were also living in Ashtabula, in Ward 4, where he too had a barber's shop. In 1920, Charles Jefferson, Jr., was still in the township of Highland in Elk County, with his wife and children. Since 1917 two more had been born. The family now consisted of Charlotte (eight), Margarette (six), Edward (five), Dorothy (three), Josephine (two), and Charles (one). His occupation was given as laborer in a chemical works. The racial classification of the whole family was "Mu[latto]." All the children, except Edward, were born in Pennsylvania. Edward's birthplace was given as New York; presumably, Hazel was visiting her family there at the time, as that is given as her birthplace too.[28]

Life After Jane

Jane Box Brown died on June 1, 1924, following a fall, and was buried a week later. There is no obituary for her in the local paper. A few years later Mae married for the second time on April 15, 1929, after being divorced in 1923. She had given up the theater and was working as a hairdresser. Her spouse, Charles H. Maxfield, was a chauffeur, born in 1900 in Boston, Massachusetts. They lived at 158 W. 4th Street, Erie, Pennsylvania. By 1963 they had a daughter Patricia and were still living in Erie.[29]

Charles and Annie remained in Kane. At the 1930 census the value of his home, which he owned, was $3500, about average for the town. Their grandson Edward, Charles Junior's son, aged 15, was staying with them. Bizarrely, Edward's race was entered as "Indian" and his father's birthplace as Canada. Charles Junior, living in Erie, was also classified as Indian. Hazel, his wife, has now become "White," but all the children still at home were "Indian." I like to think that Henry's irreverent spirit was living on in his grandson's claim of ancestry that mocked both the American obsession with race and color and the inability or unwillingness of the enumerator to verify his assertion of Native American forebears. As entries from censuses and various other records show, classification of race in the United States was a highly unscientific process. Charles Junior was working as an auto mechanic in a foundry, and the eldest child at home, Charlotte, 18, was a waitress in a restaurant. Since the last census another daughter, Thelma, at this time three years old, had been born.

In 1940 only Charles Senior and Annie were at home in Kane. Charles was 74 and was working as a barber in a hotel. Son Charles Junior and his family had moved to Buffalo City, New York, about 85 miles north of Kane. He was working as a laborer in sewer construction and living in Ward 8 with his wife Hazel and children Charles, 21, Thelma, 13, Richard, six, and Dolores, four. Dolores was born in 1936 and seems to have been the last of what must have been at least nine children. His eldest son Charles was a porter in a shop. They are all classed as "White." Manley and his wife were living in Ward 2 of Jamestown City in New York. He was a chauffeur in a private family; she was a maid in a beauty shop. They seem to have had no children, or at least none that survived infancy.

On October 21, 1941, Margaret Jefferson married Edward W. Page in Erie, Pennsylvania. Both were described as "Black" and the addresses for both were recorded as Apartment 1A, 21 North Pine, Buffalo, New York. His occupation is given as a bottler but no occupation is given for either of his parents, James T. Page and Bessie Craff, both born in Virginia, who were deceased. Margaret's father's occupation is given as "Foreman."[30] Either Charles had been promoted since the 1940 census, or Margaret was following her great-grandfather's tradition of upgrading occupations.

World War II and After

The United States entered World War II in 1942. As his draft card shows, Charles Junior was now working for the Bell Aircraft Company at Niagara Falls. On his draft registration, his height is given as six feet one inch and his weight was 195 pounds. His address was 197 Sycamore Street. He was probably temporarily relocated while his wife remained at home in Buffalo. By 1942 Manley had moved to 56 Tenth Street, Jamestown, and was the owner of a business, a restaurant-tavern at 20 Harrison, Jamestown, New York. He called himself "African."[31]

Just before the end of World War II, on August 8, 1944, Charles Junior's daughter Dorothy Elaine Jefferson, a waitress, married in Rutland, Vermont. Her spouse was Charles Henry Mohler, born in Olean, New York, which was also given as her mother Hazel's birthplace, so she may have met him on a family visit. At this point, Dorothy was living in the state of New York in Nott Terrace, Schenectady. Both she and her husband were recorded as White.[32]

On September 16, 1963, the *Kane Republican* reported Charles Senior's funeral:

> Funeral services for Charles W. Jefferson, well-known Kane barber who died Saturday at the age of 88, were held Tuesday afternoon at 2:30 at the Cummings

funeral home; with the Rev. Clarke M. Cochrane of the First Congregational church officiating. Mrs. Joseph M.J. Harre, soloist, accompanied at the piano by Mrs. James McDade II, sang "Abide With Me." Pall bearers were Charles W. Jefferson and Richard Jefferson, grandsons of the deceased, Herbert Young, Henry Richardson, J.C. Chatmon, and J.R. Chatmon. Interment was in Forest Lawn cemetery. Out of town relatives and friends who attended the last rites were Mr. and Mrs. Charles H. Jefferson, Mr and Mrs Edward F. Jefferson and son, Edward, Jr., Mr. and Mrs. Edward Paige, Mrs. Thelma Miller and son, Jeffrey, Mrs Blanche Van der Graff, Mrs. Marie Bragg, Miss Delores Jefferson, and C. William Jefferson, Buffalo; Corp. Richard Jefferson, Camp LeJeune, N. C; Mr. Johnson, Washington, D. C; Mrs. Charlotte Porro, Mrs. Harry Gordon, Mt. Vernon, N. Y.; Mrs. Douglas Stone, Aliquippa; Mr. and Mrs. Charles Maxfield and daughter, Patricia, Erie; Mr. and Mrs. Manley L. Jefferson, Mr. and Mrs. Elious Flemister, Mrs. Charles Russell, Mrs. John Wharton, Mrs. Richard Lattimore, Mrs. Louis Roberts, Mrs. William Wharton and daughter, Nancy, Harold Farmer, and William Washington, Jamestown, N.Y.

They got his age wrong; he was probably 95. His wife Annie was executrix of his will.[33]

Thelma Miller and her son Jeffrey must be Charles Jr.'s daughter and his grandson. Camp Lejeune, where Corporal Richard Jefferson was stationed, is a Marine Corps base. It seems that no one from the Mohler branch of the family, now classified as white, attended.

Manley did not long survive his father. He also died in September 1963 and is buried in Lake View Cemetery, Jamestown, New York. Two years later, at the age of 95, Annie moved to Jamestown, presumably to live with her widowed daughter-in-law: "A Kane resident for three-quarters of a century leaves Kane today to make her home at Jamestown, N.Y. She is Mrs. Anna H. Jefferson, widow of the late Charles W. Jefferson, who conducted a barber shop here for about 60 years."[34]

In 1971, aged 101, Annie was living in Buffalo, with her son Charles, at 38 Dodge Street. Her death was reported in the *Kane Republican*, where she and her husband had been so well known:

Mrs. Annie Jefferson, Aged 101, Formerly of Kane, Dies at Buffalo

Mrs. Annie Helena Jefferson, aged 101, a former many-years resident of Kane and widow of Charles W. Jefferson, who operated a barber shop here for a half-century or more, succumbed last week at Buffalo, N.Y. Funeral services were held Friday at Buffalo at the Emmanuel Temple with interment in Forest Lawn Cemetery in Buffalo. Mrs. Jefferson was born Jan. 15, 1870 at Manchester, England. She came to Kane to reside when she was 12 years of age and was a member of the former Congregational Church here. She had been residing in Buffalo with her son Charles Henry Jefferson, at 38 Dodge Street. She leaves the one son, nine grandchildren, 13 great-grandchildren and eight great-great-grandchildren. Besides her husband she was preceded in death by a son Manley L. and a daughter.[35]

There appears to be discrepancy or a typo in the age recorded when she came to Kane; it is more likely that she was 22. Possibly it was her great age that prompted the newspaper to record the death of a previous resident, but it may be that Annie, with her show-biz background, used her personality to draw customers to her husband's business and became a memorable local figure in her own right. No mention was made of her father, either here or in the British press. Henry Box Brown was no longer a famous name, forgotten both in the land of his birth and in Britain, where he had experienced such a successful career.

Appendix: Timeline of Henry Box Brown's Life

This is not complete. I hope it will encourage local historians to investigate what was happening when Henry and Jane Box Brown were appearing in their locales.

Note that exact dates and venues were not always given. See the text for more precise references. In 1972 Britain's historic counties were reorganized, and I have given the modern county names to enable researchers better to trace tours. Symbols: > = before, < = after.

Date	Event	Source
	1815	
Unknown	Born on The Hermitage Plantation, Louisa County, Virginia	*Narrative*
	1830	
June 9	Death of John Barret: Henry becomes the property of his son William	*Narrative* *Families of Virginia, Vol. III, Barret*
	Sent to Richmond, Virginia, to work in William Barret's tobacco factory	*Narrative*
	1836–1848	
1834/5–1848	Marriage to Nancy	*Narrative*
Dates unknown	Births of three children	McKim papers, March 28, 1849, in Carl A. Kroch Library, Cornell University
August 1848	Sale of Nancy and the children	*Narrative*

201

Date	Event	Source
December 25, 1848	Resolution to free himself	*Narrative*

1849

Date	Event	Source
March 23	Mailed from Richmond, Virginia	
March 24	Arrival in Philadelphia, Pennsylvania, spent day with James and Lucretia Mott, then stayed with William Still.	Letter Lucretia Mott to Dugdales, May 26, 1849 Still, William, *Underground Railroad*
March 26/27	New York	Still, William, *Underground Railroad* *Narrative*
	Boston	*Narrative*
< April 29	New Bedford, Massachusetts	Letter Joseph Ricketson to Debra Weston, April 29, 1849
May 29 and 30	Melodeon Theatre and Faneuil Hall, Boston, Massachusetts New England Anti-Slavery Convention	*The Liberator,* June 8, 1849
July 4	Abingdon Grove, Boston, Massachusetts Mass meeting on Independence Day	*Brooklyn Evening Star,* July 9, 1849
August 3	Hospital Grove, Worcester, Massachusetts Celebration of emancipation in the West Indies	*The Liberator,* August 10, 1849
August 9	Henry's story reprinted in the British press from a newsletter circulated from Newcastle-upon-Tyne and from a Boston, Massachusetts, newspaper	*Bradford Observer,* August 9, 1849 *Cheltenham Chronicle,* August 16, 1849 And others
< September 7	Boston, Massachusetts Publication of the *Narrative of Henry Box Brown*	*The Liberator,* September 7, 1849 *Boston Emancipator and Republican,* September 13, 1849
September 9	Newburyport, Essex County, Massachusetts	*The Liberator,* September 7, 1849
September 10	Amesbury, Essex County, Massachusetts	*The Liberator* September 7, 1849

Date	Event	Source
September 11	Haverhill, Essex County, Massachusetts	*The Liberator* September 7, 1849
September 12	Methuen, Essex County, Massachusetts	*The Liberator* September 7, 1849
September 13	Lawrence, Essex County, Massachusetts	*The Liberator* September 7, 1849
September 14	Andover, Essex County, Massachusetts	*The Liberator* September 7, 1849
September 15	Swampscot, Essex County, Massachusetts	*The Liberator,* September 14, 1849
September 16	Lynn, Essex County, Massachusetts	*The Liberator* September 14, 1849
September 17	South Danvers, Essex County, Massachusetts	*The Liberator* September 14, 1849
September 18	Danvers, N. Mills, Essex County, Massachusetts	*The Liberator* September 14, 1849
September 19	Marblehead, Essex County, Massachusetts	*The Liberator* September 14, 1849
September 20	Gloucester Harbor, Essex County, Massachusetts	*The Liberator* September 14, 1849
September 21	Annisquam [suburb of Gloucester], Essex County, Massachusetts	*The Liberator* September 14, 1849
September 22	North Danvers, Essex County, Massachusetts	*The Liberator* September 14, 1849
September 23	West Gloucester (afternoon) Essex (evening) Essex County, Massachusetts	*The Liberator* September 14, 1849
September 24	Manchester, Essex County, Massachusetts	*The Liberator,* September 14, 1849
October 12	Norton, Bristol County, Massachusetts	*The Liberator,* October 12, 1849
October 13	Raynham, Bristol County, Massachusetts	*The Liberator,* October 12, 1849
October 14	Bridgewater, Plymouth County, Massachusetts	*The Liberator,* October 12, 1849
October 15	North Bridgewater, Plymouth County, Massachusetts	*The Liberator,* October 12, 1849

Date	Event	Source
October 16	Stoughton, Norfolk County, Massachusetts	*The Liberator,* October 12, 1849
October 17	Canton, Norfolk County, Massachusetts	*The Liberator,* October 12, 1849
October 18	Foxborough, Norfolk County, Massachusetts	*The Liberator,* October 12, 1849
October 19	Mansfield, Bristol County, Massachusetts	*The Liberator,* October 12, 1849
October 26	Uxbridge, Worcester County, Massachusetts	*The Liberator,* October 26, 1849
October 27	Mendon, Worcester County, Massachusetts	*The Liberator,* October 26, 1849
October 28	Milford, Worcester County, Massachusetts	*The Liberator,* October 26, 1849 *Practical Christian,* November 10, 1849
October 29	Holliston, Middlesex County, Massachusetts	*The Liberator,* October 26, 1849
October 30	Hopkinton, Middlesex County, Massachusetts	*The Liberator,* October 26, 1849
October 31	Southborough, Worcester County, Massachusetts	*The Liberator,* October 26, 1849
November 1	Marlboro, Middlesex County, Massachusetts	*The Liberator,* October 26, 1849
November 2	Feltonville [now Hudson], Middlesex County, Massachusetts	*The Liberator,* November 2, 1849
November 3	Berlin, Worcester County, Massachusetts	*The Liberator,* November 2, 1849
November 4	Bolton, Worcester County, Massachusetts	*The Liberator,* November 2, 1849
November 5	Lancaster, Worcester County, Massachusetts	*The Liberator,* November 2, 1849
November 6	Leominster, Worcester County, Massachusetts	*The Liberator,* November 2, 1849
November 7	Fitchburg, Worcester County, Massachusetts	*The Liberator,* November 2, 1849
November 8	Westminster, Worcester County, Massachusetts	*The Liberator,* November 2, 1849

Date	Event	Source
November 9	Ashburnham [Ashburton in *The Liberator*], Worcester County, Massachusetts	*The Liberator*, November 2, 1849
November 10	Gardner, Worcester County, Massachusetts	*The Liberator*, November 2, 1849
November 11	South Gardner, Worcester County, Massachusetts	*The Liberator*, November 2, 1849
< December	Arrival of James Smith in Boston to join HBB	Ruggles, p. 73
1850		
February 1	Boston Letter HBB	to Gerrit Smith
April 11	Washingtonian Hall, Bromfield Street, Boston, Massachusetts *Mirror of Slavery* panorama shown for the first time	*The Liberator*, April 5, 1850
April 27	Washingtonian Hall, Bromfield Street, Boston, Massachusetts	*The Liberator*, April 26, 1850
< May 3	Lynn, Essex County, Massachusetts	*The Liberator*, May 3, 1850
May 9	City Hall, Worcester, Worcester County, Massachusetts	*Massachusetts Spy*, May 8, 1849 *The Liberator*, May 31, 1850
May 22–25	Hampden Hall, Springfield, Hampden County, Massachusetts	*Springfield Republican*, May 22, 1850
< July 12	Dover, Strafford County, New Hampshire	
August 26	Fugitive Slave Act approved by the U.S. Senate	
August 30	Providence, Rhode Island Assaulted twice	*Boston Post* September 5, 1850, and other journals *The Liberator*, September 6, 1850
September 15	Springfield, Hampden County, Massachusetts	Letter HBB to Gerrit Smith, September 15, 1850
September 18	Fugitive Slave Act passed by the U.S. Congress	

Date	Event	Source
October 7	Departure from New York with James Smith on the *Constantine*	
November 1	Arrival in Liverpool	*Liverpool Mercury,* November 5, 1850
November 12, 13, 15, 16, and 22	Concert Hall, Lord Nelson Street, Liverpool, Lancashire	*Liverpool Mercury,* November 5, 8, and 12, 1850 *Liverpool Mail,* November 16, 1850 *Liverpool Mercury,* November 22, 1850 Story reprinted in newspapers all over Great Britain.
December 14– January 1, 1851	Mechanics Institute Manchester, Lancashire	*Manchester Guardian,* December 14 and 21, 1850

1851

Date	Event	Source
January 8	No venue given Blackburn, Lancashire	*Manchester Examiner & Times*
January 16, 17, 18	William Street Schoolroom Over Darwen, Lancashire	*Blackburn Standard,* January 22, 1851
January 24, 26, 28, 30, 31	Assembly Rooms, Corn Exchange, Preston, Lancashire	*Preston Chronicle,* January 25, 1851 *Preston Pilot & County Advertiser*
< February 4	No venue given Bolton, Lancashire	*Bolton Chronicle,* February 8, 1851
February 10, 11, 13, 14, 15	Temperance Hall, Little Bolton, Lancashire	*Bolton Chronicle,* February 8, 1851
March 22–23	Lecture Hall, Burnley Church of England Literary Institute, Burnley, Lancashire	*Blackburn Standard,* April 2 and 9, 1851 *Nottinghamshire Guardian,* May 11, 1854
March 28–29	Assembly Rooms, Padiham, Lancashire	*Blackburn Standard,* April 2, 1851
March 30	9 Curzon Street, Burnley, Lancashire	UK Census
3 days, last on April 28	Oddfellows Hall, Bingley, Lancashire	*Bradford Observer,* May 1, 1851 *Leeds Times,* May 3, 1851 *Leeds Intelligencer,* May 3, 1851

Date	Event	Source
April 29, 30, May 1, 2, 3	Mechanics Institute, Leeds Road, Bradford, Yorkshire	*Bradford Observer,* April 24, 1851
May 22	Travels in box from Bradford to Leeds, then appears at the Music Hall, Leeds, Yorkshire	*Leeds Times,* May 17, 1851 *Leeds Intelligencer,* May 24, 1851
> June 21	Philosophical Hall, Huddersfield, Yorkshire	*Huddersfield Chronicle,* June 21, 1851
June 26–28	Centenary Chapel, Dewsbury, Yorkshire	*Huddersfield Chronicle,* July 5, 1851
July 25	Partnership with James Smith officially dissolved	*London Gazette,* July 29, 1851
> August 16	Oddfellows Hall, Halifax, Yorkshire	*Huddersfield Chronicle,* August 16, 1851
> August 30 > September 30, October 1, 2	Public Hall, Baillie Street, Rochdale, Lancashire	*Manchester Guardian,* August 30 and October 8, 1851
> December 13	No venue given, Stockport, Lancashire	*Manchester Guardian,* January 7, 1852 *Manchester Times,* January 7, 1852
< December 13	No venue given, Hyde, Cheshire	*Manchester Guardian,* January 7, 1852 *Manchester Times,* January 7, 1852
1852		
March 17–24	Corn Exchange, Wolverhampton, Staffordshire	*Wolverhampton Chronicle and Staffordshire Advertiser,* March 24, 1852
> June 19	Whitehall Buildings, Kendal, Cumbria	*Westmorland Gazette,* June 19, 1852
July 28	Court No. 2, Old Shire Hall, Warwick, Warwickshire Libel case against *Wolverhampton Herald*	*Morning Chronicle,* July 30, 1852 Newspapers across Britain and Ireland.
August 17	Rose Street Chapel, Kirkcaldy, Fife	*Fife Herald,* August 19, 1852
> September 23	Waterloo Rooms, Edinburgh, Scotland	*Edinburgh Evening Courant,* September 7, 1852 *Greenock Advertiser,* September 7, 1852

Date	Event	Source
		Caledonian Mercury, September 23, 1852
October 4–22	Music Hall, Nelson Street, Newcastle-upon-Tyne, Tyne & Wear	*Newcastle Guardian and Tyne Mercury,* October 2, 1852 *Newcastle Courant,* October 8, 1852 *North & South Shields Gazette and Northumberland and Durham Advertiser,* October 15, 1852 *Newcastle Courant,* October 22, 1852
November 8	Central Hall, South Shields, Tyne & Wear	*North & South Shields Gazette and Northumberland and Durham Advertiser,* November 5, 1852
November 11	No venue given, North Shields, Tyne & Wear	*North & South Shields Gazette and Northumberland and Durham Advertiser,* November 5 and 12, 1852
November 19–21	Town Hall, Hartlepool, County Durham	*Durham County Advertiser,* November 26, 1852
> November 27	Central Hall, Darlington, County Durham	*Darlington & Stockton Times, Ripon & Richmond Chronicle,* November 27, 1852
> November 27	Letter to *Sunderland News* (not in newspaper archives)	Reported in *Bolton Chronicle,* November 27, 1852; *Morning Advertiser,* December 9, 1852; and other newspapers
December 6	Music Hall, Jarrett Street, Hull, Yorkshire	*Hull Packet,* November 26, 1852
> December 31	Lecture Hall, Goodramgate, York, Yorkshire	*York Herald,* January 1, 1853
1853		
February 28– March 5	Exchange Rooms, Lune Street, Preston, Lancashire	*Preston Chronicle,* February 26 and March 5, 1853
May 28–June 10	Adelphi Casino, Sheffield, Yorkshire Engagement to perform *Uncle Tom's Cabin*	*Sheffield Independent,* July 30, 1853

Date	Event	Source
July 28	Action for damages against Richard Scott of Adelphi Casino	*Sheffield Independent,* July 30, 1853
October 17	Public Hall, Baillie Street, Rochdale, Lancashire (with his *troupe* of Negro Harmonists)	*Manchester Times,* October 22, 1853
November 3–4	Huddersfield, Yorkshire	*Huddersfield Chronicle,* November 5, 1853

1854

Date	Event	Source
January 23, 24	Town Hall, Hanley, Staffordshire	*Staffordshire Sentinel and Commercial & General Advertiser,* January 21 and 28, 1854
No dates given	No venues given Tunstall, Staffordshire Burslem, Staffordshire	*Staffordshire Sentinel and Commercial & General Advertiser,* January 28, 1854
January 28–31	Town Hall, Newcastle-under-Lyme, Staffordshire	*Staffordshire Sentinel and Commercial & General Advertiser,* January 28, 1854
February 1–4	New Market Hall, Stoke, Staffordshire	*Staffordshire Sentinel and Commercial & General Advertiser,* January 28, 1854
> February 11	No venue given Longton, Staffordshire	*Staffordshire Sentinel and Commercial & General Advertiser,* February 11, 1854
March 27–April 10	Oddfellows Hall, Temple Street, Birmingham, Warwickshire	*Birmingham Journal,* March 18, 1854 *Aris's Birmingham Gazette,* March 20 and April 17, 1854
> April 26	Lecture Hall, Wardwick, Derby, Derbyshire	*Derby Mercury,* April 26, 1854
May 15–June 8	Exchange Rooms, Nottingham, Nottinghamshire	*Nottinghamshire Guardian,* May 11, 1854
> June 29 (4 nights)	Feoffees School Room, Church Gate, Loughborough, Leicestershire	*Nottinghamshire Guardian,* June 29, 1854 *Leicester Journal,* June 30, 1854
July 5 +	Temperance Hall, Leicester, Leicestershire	*Leicestershire Mercury,* July 1, 1854 *Leicester Journal,* July 7, 1854

Date	Event	Source
< September 18	Star Assembly Room, Oxford, Oxfordshire	*Oxford Journal,* September 16, 1854

1855

Date	Event	Source
> January 12–21	Bethany Chapel, Church Street, Cardiff, Wales	*Cardiff and Merthyr Guardian, Glamorgan, Monmouth, and Brecon Gazette,* January 12 and 19, 1855
> February 2	Town Hall, Newport, Gwent	*Monmouthshire Merlin,* February 2, 1855 *Monmouthshire Beacon,* February 3, 1855
April 16–18 and 23–24	Broadmead Rooms, Bristol	*Bristol Mercury,* April 14 and 21, 1855
May 7–8	Town Hall, Weston-super-Mare, Somerset	*Weston-super-Mare Gazette and General Advertiser* May 5, 1855
May 30–June 1	Assembly Rooms, Taunton, Somerset	*Taunton Courier, and Western Advertiser,* May 30 and June 6, 1855 *Western Times,* June 2, 1855
June 14–15, 19–20, and 29	Royal Public Rooms, Exeter, Devon	*Exeter and Plymouth Gazette,* June 9 and 16, 1855
> July 7	Globe Hotel, Newton Abbot, Devon	*Exeter and Plymouth Gazette,* July 7, 1855
October 29–November 1	Union Hall, Princes Street, Penzance, Cornwall	*Cornish Telegraph,* October 31, 1855
November 28	Church of King Charles the Martyr, Falmouth, Cornwall Marriage to Jane Floyd	*Cornish Telegraph,* December 5, 1855 *Royal Cornwall Gazette,* December 7, 1855 Marriage certificate
December 10, 13, and 14	Royal Victoria Rooms, Southampton, Hampshire	*Hampshire Advertiser,* December 8, 1855

1856

Date	Event	Source
January 1–5	Mechanics Institution, Winchester, Hampshire	*Hampshire Chronicle,* December 29, 1855
January 30	Cornwall's Riding School, Gloucester Street, St. Helier, Jersey	*Chronique de Jersey,* January 30, 1856

Date	Event	Source
February 18 for a week	Assembly Rooms, Market Place, St. Peter Port, Guernsey	*Star,* February 16, 1856
March 31 for 1 week	Society's Hall, Kent Street, Portsea, Hampshire	*Hampshire Telegraph,* March 29, 1856
May 12–17	Town Hall, Ryde, Isle of Wight	*Isle of Wight Observer* May 10, 1856
May 26	Ryde Petty Sessions: one of HBB's employees charged with damage to a house	*Isle of Wight Observer,* May 31, 1856
May 28	No venue given Newport, Isle of Wight	*Isle of Wight Observer,* May 31, 1856
> June 7	Literary and Scientific Institution, Ventnor, Isle of Wight	*Isle of Wight Observer,* June 7, 1856 *Portsmouth Times and Naval Gazette,* June 7, 1856
July 7–11	Town Hall, Arundel, Sussex	*West Sussex Gazette,* July 3 and 10, 1856
July 29 for 6 nights	Town Hall, Brighton, Sussex	*Brighton Gazette,* July 24 and 31, 1856
August 18–22	Public Hall, Guildford, Surrey	*West Surrey Times,* August 16, 1856 *Sussex Advertiser,* August 26, 1856
August 25 and 26	Public Hall, Godalming, Surrey	*West Surrey Times,* August 23, 1856
September 22–24	Public Hall, Maidstone, Kent	*South Eastern Gazette,* September 16, 1856
October 20–24	Assembly Rooms, Faversham, Kent	*Faversham Gazette, and Whitstable, Sittingbourne, & Milton Journal,* October 18, 1856
November 3–13	Canterbury Hall, Canterbury, Kent	*Kentish Gazette,* October 28, November 4 and 11, 1856 *Canterbury Journal, Kentish Times and Farmers' Gazette,* November 15, 1856
December 15–18	Apollorian Hall, Dover, Kent	*Dover Telegraph and Cinque Ports General Advertiser,* December 13, 1856

Date	Event	Source
		1857
> February 7	Co-Operative Hall, Sheppey/Sheerness, Kent	*Maidstone Journal and Kentish Advertiser* Saturday 7 February 7, 1857
February 9–13	Lecture Hall, Nelson Street, Woolwich, South-East London	*Kentish Independent,* February 7 and 14, 1857
February 23–28?	Concert Room, Lecture Hall, Greenwich, South-East London	*Kentish Mercury,* February 21, 1857
> March 14	Blackheath Literary Association, Blackheath, South-East London	*Kentish Mercury,* March 14, 1857
March 16	No venue given Deptford, South-East London	*Kentish Mercury,* March 14, 1857
> June 13	Institution Hall Cheshunt, Hertfordshire	*Hertfordshire Guardian, Agricultural Journal, and General Advertiser,* June 13 and 16, 1857
June	Royal Hotel, Margate, Kent (rehearsing plays)	*Era,* June 28, 1857
July 31	Theatre Royal, Margate, Kent (performing three plays)	*South Eastern Gazette,* August 4, 1857
September 14	Margate County Court Action against Richard Thorne	*Kentish Gazette,* September 22, 1857 *South Eastern Gazette,* September 22, 1857
September 14	Music Hall, Ramsgate, Kent (play reading)	*Kentish Independent,* September 19, 1857
> October 4	Royal Park Theatre, Liverpool, Lancashire Acting in *The Nubian Captive*	*Era,* September 27 and October 4, 1857
November 2 and 3 November 14	Royal Pottery Theatre, Stafford, Staffordshire Acting in *Pocahontas* and *The Nubian Captive*	*Staffordshire Advertiser,* October 31 and November 7, 1857
		1858
< January 2	Mr. Luppino's Concert Room, Hertford, Hertfordshire	*Hertford Mercury and Reformer,* January 2, 1858

Date	Event	Source
> February 5	Corn Exchange, Braintree, Essex	*Chelmsford Chronicle,* February 5, 1858
March 15–19	Lecture Hall, Concert Room, Greenwich, South-East London	*Kentish Mercury,* March 13, 1858 *Jersey Independent and Daily Telegraph,* March 13, 1858
April 5 (Easter Monday)	Cornwall's Riding School, Gloucester Street, St. Helier, Jersey	*Jersey Independent and Daily Telegraph,* March 6, 1858, then further reports in paper until April 17, 1858
April 20	Royal Lodge (No. 722), St. Helier, Jersey Initiated as a Freemason	Library and Museum of Freemasonry
May 10, 11, and 12	Assembly Rooms, Market Place, St. Peter Port, Guernsey	*Star,* May 8, 1858
> June 12	Town Hall, Basingstoke, Hampshire	*Reading Mercury,* June 5, 1858 *Hampshire Chronicle,* June 12, 1858
July 6–17?	Lecture Hall, Nelson Street, Woolwich, South-East London	*Kentish Independent,* July 3 and 10, 1858
> October 5	Deal, Kent Action in court about bill posting	*Kentish Gazette,* October 5, 1858
November 11–13	Corn Exchange, Lewes, Sussex	*Sussex Advertiser,* November 16, 1858
> November 18	Town Hall, Gosport, Hampshire	*Hampshire Telegraph,* November 18, 1858
December 6–11	St. George's Hall, Portsea, Hampshire	*Hampshire Telegraph,* December 4, 1858
December 27–31	Town Hall, Ryde, Isle of Wight	*Isle of Wight Observer,* December 18, 1858, and January 1, 1859
1859		
January 31– February 2	No venue given Petersfield, Sussex	*West Sussex Gazette,* February 3, 1859
> February 5	Public Hall, Godalming, Surrey	*West Surrey Times,* February 5, 1859
February 17 and 18	No venue given Kingston-upon-Thames (?), Surrey	*Surrey Comet,* February 19, 1859

Date	Event	Source
February 21–24	No venue given Richmond, Surrey	*Surrey Comet,* February 19, 1859
March 2	Zetland Lodge (No. 752), Adam & Eve Tavern, Kensington, West London Passed in the Freemasons' hierarchy	Library and Museum of Freemasonry
March 8–10	Town Hall, Brentford, West London	*Windsor and Eton Express,* March 12, 1859 *West London Observer,* March 12, 1859
March 14–18	Temperance Hall, Black's Road, Hammersmith, West London	*West London Observer,* March 5, 12, and 19, 1859
March 16	Pack Horse Public House, Turnham Green, West London Spoke at the opening of Court Devonshire (No. 3154) of the Ancient Order of Foresters	*West London Observer,* March 19, 1859
> March 25	Town Hall, Uxbridge, Middlesex	*South Bucks Free Press, Wycombe and Maidenhead Journal,* March 25, 1859
March 28 for 1 week	Windsor Theatre, Windsor, Berkshire	*Windsor and Eton Express,* March 12 and 19, April 2, 1859
> April 15	Town Hall, Maidenhead, Berkshire	*South Bucks Free Press, Wycombe and Maidenhead Journal,* April 15, 1859
May 2, 3, 4	New Hall, London Street, Reading, Berkshire	*Reading Mercury,* April 30, 1859
May 7, 9, and 10	Corn Exchange, Wallingford, Oxfordshire	*Berkshire Chronicle,* May 7, 1859 *Reading Mercury,* May 14, 1859
> May 28	County Hall, Abingdon, Oxfordshire	*Oxford Chronicle and Reading Gazette,* May 28, 1859
June 2–4	Town Hall, Banbury, Oxfordshire	*Banbury Guardian,* June 2, 1859
June 14–18	Public Hall, Leamington Spa, Warwickshire	*Leamington Spa Courier,* Saturday June 11, 1859

Date	Event	Source
> June 27	Theatre Royal, Coventry, Warwickshire	*Coventry Herald,* June 24 and July 1, 1859
July 25	Corn Exchange, Hinckley, Leicestershire	*Leicester Guardian,* July 30, 1859
July 29	School room, Bulkington, Warwickshire	*Coventry Times,* August 3, 1859
September 5 and 6	St. Mary's Hall, Coventry, Warwickshire	*Coventry Herald,* September 2, 1859
September 21	Town Hall, Rugby, Warwickshire	*Leicestershire Mercury,* September 24, 1859 *Rugby Advertiser,* September 24, 1859
> September 30	Corn Exchange, Atherstone, Warwickshire	*Coventry Herald,* September 30 and October 1, 1859
October 17–21	No venue given Stafford, Staffordshire	*Staffordshire Advertiser,* October 15, 1859
October 25–27	No venue given Newport, Shropshire	*Shrewsbury Chronicle,* October 21, 1859
October 31–November 1	Town Hall, Wellington, Shropshire	*Wellington Journal,* October 29 and November 5, 1859 *Eddowes's Journal, and General Advertiser for Shropshire, and the Principality of Wales,* November 2, 1859
November 5, 7,8,9	National School Room, Dawley, Shropshire	*Shrewsbury Chronicle,* November 11, 1859 *Wellington Journal,* November 12, 1859
November 12, 14, 15, 16	Royal Oak Inn, Madeley, Shropshire	*Wellington Journal,* Saturday November 12, 1859
November 21–25	Assembly Rooms, Bridgnorth, Shropshire	*Wellington Journal,* Saturday November 12, 1859
December 12–17	Music Hall, Shrewsbury, Shropshire	*Eddowes's Journal, and General Advertiser for Shropshire, and the Principality of Wales,* December 7, 1859 *Shrewsbury Chronicle,* December 9, 1859 Poster in Shropshire Archives

Date	Event	Source
	1860	
January 17, 18, and 20	Theatre Royal, Newcastle-under-Lyme, Staffordshire	*Staffordshire Sentinel and Commercial & General Advertiser,* January 14, 1860
< January 27	No venue given Hanley, Staffordshire	*Staffordshire Sentinel and Commercial & General Advertiser,* January 21, 1860
> February 18	Town Hall, Burslem, Staffordshire	*Staffordshire Sentinel and Commercial & General Advertiser,* February 18, 1860
February 20–22	Theatre, Longton, Staffordshire	*Staffordshire Sentinel and Commercial & General Advertiser,* February 18, 1860
February 27–29	No venue given Newcastle-under-Lyme, Staffordshire	*Staffordshire Sentinel and Commercial & General Advertiser,* February 25 and March 3, 1860
March 13–17	Town Hall Assembly Room, Congleton, Cheshire	*Congleton & Macclesfield Mercury, and Cheshire General Advertiser,* March 17, 1860
No dates given	No venue given Leek, Cheshire	*Congleton & Macclesfield Mercury, and Cheshire General Advertiser,* March 17, 1860
No dates given	No venue given Macclesfield, Cheshire	*Congleton & Macclesfield Mercury, and Cheshire General Advertiser,* March 17, 1860
April 5	Lodge of Industry (no. 465), Norfolk Arms Hotel, Hyde, Cheshire Raised in the Freemasons' hierarchy	Library and Museum of Freemasonry
> April 7	Concert Room, Hyde, Cheshire	*Glossop Record,* April 7, 1860
May 14–20(?)	Theatre Royal, Bury, Lancashire	*Bury Times,* May 12 and 19, 1860
August 25	4 Cale Green, Stockport, Lancashire Birth of daughter Agnes Jane Floyd Brown	Birth certificate

Date	Event	Source
< November 11	Mechanics Institute, Manchester, Lancashire	*Era,* November 11, 1860
< December 17	Philosophical Hall, Huddersfield, Yorkshire	*Huddersfield Chronicle & West Yorkshire Advertiser,* December 15, 1860

1861

Date	Event	Source
April 7	North Street, Keighley, Yorkshire Census	Census
April 13–24	Lecture Hall, Church of England Institution, Burnley, Lancashire	*Burnley Advertiser,* April 13, 20, and 27, 1861 *Preston Chronicle,* May 4, 1861
> June 1	Mechanics Institution, Bacup, Lancashire	*Rochdale Observer,* June 1, 1861
June 18	In Stockport, Lancashire, but traveled to Bury to defend a civil court case in the County Court.	*Bury Times,* June 22, 1861
> November 3	No venue given Accrington, Lancashire	*Era,* November 3, 1861
December 3–26	Gallery of Illustration, Corporation Street, Manchester, Lancashire	*Manchester Courier and Lancashire General Advertiser,* November 30, 1861 *Manchester Guardian,* December 26, 1861 *Manchester Weekly Times and Examiner,* December 28, 1861

1862

Date	Event	Source
January 13–14	Town Hall, Leigh, Lancashire	*Leigh Chronicle and Weekly District Advertiser,* January 11, 1862
January 22–23	Public Hall, Atherton, Lancashire	*Leigh Chronicle and Weekly District Advertiser,* January 18, 1862
January 27–29	Concert Hall, Bolton, Lancashire	*Bolton Chronicle,* January 25, 1862
April 21–May 23	Cornwall's Riding School, Gloucester Street, St. Helier, Jersey	*Jersey Independent and Daily Telegraph,* April 19 to May 19, 1862

Date	Event	Source
July 28–August 1	Mechanics Institute, Plymouth, Devon	*Western Daily Mercury,* July 26, 1862
September 13–20	St. George's Hall, Stonehouse, Plymouth, Devon	*Western Daily Mercury,* September 15–20, 1862
> November 14	Assembly Room, St. Austell, Cornwall	*West Briton and Cornwall Advertiser,* November 14, 1862
> November 21	New Hall, Redruth, Cornwall	*West Briton and Cornwall Advertiser,* November 21, 1862 *Royal Cornwall Gazette,* November 21, 1862

1863

Date	Event	Source
January 3	New Hall, Redruth, Cornwall	*Lake's Falmouth Packet and Cornwall Advertiser,* January 10, 1863
January 15, 16, 19, 20, 21, 22	Polytechnic Hall, Falmouth, Cornwall	*Lake's Falmouth Packet and Cornwall Advertiser,* January 17, 1863 *Royal Cornwall Gazette,* January 23, 1863
February 2–7	Assembly Rooms, Truro, Cornwall	*Royal Cornwall Gazette,* January 30, 1863
< March 21	Assembly Rooms, Globe Hotel, Newton Abbot, Devon	*Western Times,* March 20, 1863
Easter week (Easter Sunday was April 5)	No venue given Torquay, Devon	*Western Times,* April 3, 1863
June 26 and 27	Beacon Assembly Rooms, Exmouth, Devon	*Western Times,* June 26 and July 3, 1863
July 13, 14, 17	Royal Public Rooms, Exeter, Devon	*Exeter Flying Post,* July 15, 1863 *Western Times,* July 17, 1863
< August 24	Assembly Rooms, Princes Street, Bristol	*Bristol Daily Post,* August 24, 1863
October 8–10	Assembly Rooms, Bath, Somerset	*Bath Chronicle and Weekly Gazette,* October 8, 1863
October 26(?)– November 16	Music Hall, Cardiff, Wales	*Cardiff and Merthyr Guardian, Glamorgan, Monmouth, and Brecon Gazette,* October 23 1863 *Cardiff Times,* November 13, 1863

Date	Event	Source
December 27 and 28	No venue given Aberdare, Mid-Glamorgan	*Merthyr Telegraph, and General Advertiser for the Iron Districts of South Wales,* January 2, 1864

1864

Date	Event	Source
February 15– < 7 March	Temperance Hall, Merthyr Tydfil, Mid-Glamorgan	*Western Daily Press,* February 22, 1864 *Cardiff Times,* March 11, 1864
> March 26	No venue given Pontypool, Monmouthshire	*Usk Observer, Raglan Herald, and Monmouthshire Central Advertiser,* March 26, 1864
March 28–April 8	Town Hall, Blaenarvon, Monmouthshire	*Hereford Times,* April 2, 1864 *Usk Observer, Raglan Herald, and Monmouthshire Central Advertiser,* April 2 and 9, 1864
April 16–14	Town Hall, Newport, Gwent	*Bristol Daily Post,* April 19, 1864
> August 5	Temperance Hall, Pontypridd, Mid-Glamorgan	*Cardiff Time,* August 5 and 12, 1864
October 25–29	Broadmead Rooms, Bristol	*Western Daily Press,* October 25, 26, and 27, 1864 *Bristol Times and Mirror,* October 29, 1864
October 28	25 Cumberland Street, Bristol Birth of son Edward Henry Brown	Birth certificate
November 14–17	Corn Exchange, Gloucester, Gloucestershire	*Gloucester Journal,* November 19, 1864 *Gloucester Chronicle,* November 12 and 19, 1864 *Stroud Journal,* November 19, 1864
November 19–26	Town Hall, Cheltenham, Gloucestershire	*Cheltenham Mercury,* November 12, 1864

1865

Date	Event	Source
January 5, 6, 7, 11, 12	Castle Hotel, Rhymney, Gwent	*Merthyr Telegraph, and General Advertiser for the Iron Districts of South Wales,* January 14, 1865

Date	Event	Source
> March 11	Assembly Rooms, Taunton, Somerset	*Western Gazette,* March 11, 1865
March 22, 23, 24	Royal Public Rooms, Exeter, Devon	*Exeter Flying Post,* March 22, 1865 *Taunton Courier, and Western Advertiser Wednesday,* March 15, 1865 *Sherborne Mercury,* March 14, 1865
June 20, 21, 22	Temperance Hall, Penryn, Cornwall	*Lake's Falmouth Packet and Cornwall Advertiser,* Saturday June 17, 1865

1866

> April 20	Neath, West Glamorgan Court case against the landlord of the Ystayfera Hotel.	*Cardiff Times,* April 20, 1866
> September 2 Returned around November 19	Theatre Royal, Newport, Gwent	*Era,* September 2, 1866

1867

> January 5	British Schoolroom, Treherbert, Mid-Glamorgan	*Cardiff Times,* January 5 and 12, 1867
January 17–19	National School, Dinas Powys (?), Mid-Glamorgan	*Cardiff Times,* January 26, 1867
< January 20(?)	National School, Cymmer, West Glamorgan	*Cardiff Times,* January 26, 1867
> May 5	Assembly Rooms, Weston-super-Mare, Somerset	*Era,* May 5, 1867
> August 10	Mechanics Institute, Swindon, Wiltshire	*Wiltshire and Gloucestershire Standard,* August 10, 1867
September 29, October 1 and 2	Corn Exchange, Faringdon, Oxfordshire	*Oxford Chronicle and Reading Gazette,* October 5, 1867 *Jackson's Oxford Journal,* October 5, 1867
October 3, 4, 5	County Hall, Abingdon, Oxfordshire	*Oxford Times,* October 12, 1867

Date	Event	Source
1868		
> March 14	Venues in South London, including Horns Assembly Room, Kennington, South London	*South London Chronicle,* March 14, 1868
< March 28(?)	Belmont Hall, Uxbridge, Middlesex	*Uxbridge & West Drayton Gazette,* April 4, 1868
June 9–11	Mechanics Institute, Braintree, Essex	*Essex Herald,* June 16, 1868 *Suffolk and Essex Free Press,* June 18, 1868 *Chelmsford Chronicle,* June 19, 1868
August 10–11	Athenaeum Lecture Hall, Bury St. Edmunds, Suffolk	*Bury Free Press,* August 8 and 15, 1868 *Cambridge Independent Press,* August 15, 1868
September 25, 26, 28, October 3 and 8–9	Lecture Hall, St. Andrews, Norwich, Norfolk	*Norfolk News,* September 26 and October 3, 1868 *Norfolk News,* October 3, 1868
October 20–29	Corn Hall, Great Yarmouth, Norfolk	*Yarmouth Independent,* October 24 and 31, 1868
November 23–27	Lecture Hall, Chatham, Kent	*Era,* November 29, 1868
1869		
February 1, 3, 5, 6, 9, 10, 12, 13	St. George's Hall, St. James's Hall, Ramsgate, Kent	*Thanet Advertiser,* January 30, February 6 and 13, 1869
< February 14	Assembly Rooms, Margate, Kent	*Thanet Advertiser,* February 20, 1869
March 5–6 March 12–13	Appollonian Hall, Wellington Hall, Dover, Kent	*Dover Express* Friday 5 and 12 March 1869
March 27 and 28	Town Hall, Folkestone, Kent	*Folkestone Express, Sandgate, Shorncliffe & Hythe Advertiser,* March 27, 1869
April 21–26	Corn Exchange, Maidstone, Kent	*Maidstone Telegraph,* Saturday 17 and 24 April 1869
July 12–15	Assembly Rooms, Bognor [now Bognor Regis], Sussex	*Horsham, Petworth, Midhurst and Steyning Express,* July 13, 1869
July 31, August 2–3	Circus Royal, Lake Road, Landpoint, Hampshire	*Hampshire Telegraph,* July 31, 1869

Date	Event	Source
September 8–11, 14	Portland Hall, Southsea, Hampshire	*Hampshire Telegraph,* September 4 and 11, 1869 *Portsmouth Times and Naval Gazette,* September 11, 1869
September 24, 25, 27 and 28	Victoria Rooms, Ryde, Isle of Wight	*Isle of Wight Observer,* September 25, 1869
October 2	No venue given Ventnor, Isle of Wight	*Isle of Wight Observer,* September 25, 1869 *Hampshire Telegraph,* October 9, 1869
October 13–16	Volunteer Drill Hall, Newport, Isle of Wight	*Hampshire Advertiser,* October 13 and 16, 1869
October 20–23	Foresters Hall, Cowes, Isle of Wight	*Hampshire Advertiser,* October 13, 1869 *Hampshire Telegraph,* October 30, 1869
December 6 for six nights	Town Hall, Hulme, Lancashire	*Manchester Courier and Lancashire General Advertiser,* December 4, 1869

1870

January 1589	Moreton Street, Manchester, Lancashire Birth of twin daughters, Annie Amelia Helena and Mary Emma Martha Brown	Birth certificates
January 15, 17, 18	Mechanics Hall, Heywood, Lancashire	*Rochdale Observer,* January 22, 1870
February 4 and 9	Rochdale Court, Rochdale, Lancashire Summonsed	*Rochdale Observer,* February 5 and 12, 1870
February 26, 29	Mechanics Institute, Burnley, Lancashire	*Burnley Advertiser,* February 26 and 5, March 1870
March 5, 7–11	Oddfellows Hall, Todmorden & Walsden, Yorkshire	*Rochdale Observer,* March 12, 1870
March 26–April 2	Temperance Hall, Bradford, Yorkshire	*Bradford Daily Telegraph,* March 24, 1870
April 18–28	Mechanics Institution, David Street, Manchester, Lancashire	*Manchester Evening News,* April 18–22, 1870 *Manchester Evening News,* April 27–28, 1870

Date	Event	Source
> May 29	Temperance Hall, Oldham, Lancashire	*Era,* May 29, 1870
June 13	89 Moreton Street, Manchester, Lancashire Death of Mary Emma Martha, aged 5 months	Death certificate
July 9, 11 and 12	Town Hall, Congleton, Staffordshire	*Staffordshire Sentinel and Commercial & General Advertiser,* July 16, 1870
> July 23	Temperance Hall, Leek, Staffordshire	*Staffordshire Advertiser,* July 23, 1870 *Staffordshire Sentinel and Commercial & General Advertiser,* July 23, 1870
August 6 and 8	Prince of Wales Theatre, Leigh, Lancashire	*Era,* August 14, 1870
> August 28	Masonic Rooms, Warrington, Cheshire	*Era,* August 28, 1870
August 29 and 30	Mechanics Institution, Hyde, Cheshire	*Ashton Weekly Reporter, and Stalybridge and Dukinfield Chronicle,* September 3, 1870
September 10, 12, 13	Town Hall, Ashton(?), Cheshire	*Ashton Weekly Reporter, and Stalybridge and Dukinfield Chronicle,* September 17, 1870
November 4, 5, 7, 8	Co-operative Hall, Bridge Street, Bolton, Lancashire	*Bolton Evening News,* November 3, 1870
1871		
> January 18	Educational Institute, Droylsden, Lancashire	*Ashton Weekly Reporter, and Stalybridge and Dukinfield Chronicle,* January 21, 1871
> March 18	Holly Mount School, Rawtenstall, Lancashire	*Preston Herald,* March 18, 1871
April 2	89 Moreton Street, Manchester, Lancashire	Census
August 5, 7, and 8	Town Hall, Glossop, Lancashire	*Ashton Weekly Reporter, and Stalybridge and Dukinfield Chronicle,* August 12, 1871
August 19 and 21	Prince of Wales Theatre, Leigh, Lancashire	*Leigh Chronicle and Weekly District Advertiser,* August 19, 1871

Date	Event	Source
September 2, 4, and 5	Public Hall, Hindley, Lancashire	*Wigan Observer and District Advertiser,* September 9, 1871
October 26	89 Moreton Street, Manchester, Lancashire Birth of son John Floyd Brown	Birth certificate
November 24 and 26	Public Hall, New Mills, Cheshire	*Hyde & Glossop Weekly News, and North Cheshire Herald,* December 2, 1871
November 28 and 29	St. Stephen's Schoolroom, Audenshaw, Lancashire	*Ashton Weekly Reporter, and Stalybridge and Dukinfield Chronicle,* December 2, 1871
> December 16	Educational Institute, Droylsden, Lancashire	*Ashton Weekly Reporter, and Stalybridge and Dukinfield Chronicle,* December 16, 1871

1872

Date	Event	Source
February 10, 12, and 13	Mechanics' Institution, Crewe, Cheshire	*Crewe Guardian,* February 10, 1872
February 20–March 2	Town Hall, Longton, Staffordshire	*Era,* March 3, 1872
> March 24	Mechanics' Institution, Hanley, Staffordshire	*Era,* March 24, 1872
April 29–May 11	Theatre Royal, Macclesfield, Cheshire	*Era,* May 5 and 12, 1872
June 1–15	Gymnasium Hall, Huddersfield, Yorkshire	*Era,* June 16, 1872
June 26	89 Moreton Street, Manchester, Lancashire Death of John Floyd, age 7 months	Death certificate
July 1–4	Mechanics' Institution, Heywood, Lancashire	*Heywood Advertiser,* July 5, 1872
> July 19	No venue given Todmorden, Lancashire	*Todmorden & District News,* July 19, 1872

1873

Date	Event	Source
May 8	Workhouse, Manchester, Lancashire	*Manchester Evening News,* May 9, 1873

Date	Event	Source
	1874	
17 February	Lanebottom Schoolroom, Walsden, Yorkshire	*Todmorden Advertiser & Hebden Bridge Newsletter,* February 20, 1874
> April 19	Lecture Hall, Newcastle-under-Lyne, Staffordshire	*Era,* April 19, 1874
> April 27	Theatre, Tunstall, Staffordshire	*Staffordshire Sentinel,* May 1, 1874
> May 18	Town Hall, Hanley, Staffordshire	*Staffordshire Sentinel,* May 25, 1874
	1875	
February 2, 4, and 5	Public Hall, Rochdale, Lancashire	*Era,* February 7, 1875
March 1–3	Odd Fellows Hall, Stockport, Lancashire	*Era,* March 7, 1875
July 3 (Saturday)	Departure of Henry, Jane, Edward and Annie Brown from Liverpool on the *Algeria*	Ship's passenger list
July 14	Arrived on the *Algeria,* New York	
	1876	
January 3 and 4	Town Hall, Boston, Massachusetts	*Boston Weekly Globe,* January 3, 1876
September 27 and 29	Central Hall, Newburyport, Essex County, Massachusetts	*Newbury Port Daily Herald,* September 27, 1876
	1877	
January 10	Mechanics Hall, Portland, Maine	*Portland Daily Press,* January 11, 1877
September	Montpelier, Washington County, Vermont	*Argus and Patriot,* September 5, 1877
September 19	Barron's Hall, Montpelier, Washington County, Vermont	*Argus and Patriot,* September 19, 1877
November 10, 14, and 17	Town Hall, Leominster, Worcester County, Massachusetts	*Fitchburg Sentinel,* December 14, 1877 *Leominster Enterprise,* January 9, 1878

Date	Event	Source
	1878	
May 9	Brookline, Norfolk County, Massachusetts	Handbill
May 30	Gothic Hall, Boston, Massachusetts	*Boston Globe*, May 31, 1878
	Bangor, Maine	*Bangor Daily Whig and Courier*, October 17, 1878
	1879	
November	Association Hall, Island Pond, Essex County, Vermont	*Essex County Herald*, December 5, 1879
December 15	Union Hall, Montpelier, Washington County, Vermont	*Argus and Patriot*, December 17, 1879
	1880	
March 15	School House Hall, Proctorsville, Windsor County, Vermont	*Rutland Weekly Herald and Globe*, March 15, 1880
	1881	
July	Tecumseh Park, London, Middlesex County, Ontario	*London Advertiser*, July 19, 1881
	1882	
February 24	Opera House, Cheybogan, Cheybogan County, Michigan	*Northern Tribune*, February 25, 1882
< March 11	Made a complaint against a nightwatchman in Cheybogan	*Northern Tribune*, March 11, 1882
March ?	St. Ignace, Mackinac County, Michigan	*Northern Tribune*, February 25, 1882
October 10	Markdale, Grey County, Ontario	*Markdale Standard*, September 28, 1882
> November 16	Town Hall, London, Middlesex County, Ontario	*London Daily Advertiser*, November 16, 1882
	1883	
> March 1	Town Hall, London, Middlesex County, Ontario	*London Daily Advertiser*, March 1, 1883
> August 16	Brockway Centre [now Yale], St. Clair County, Michigan Concert with the Jubilee Singers	*Weekly Expositor*, August 16, 1883

Date	Event	Source
November 23	Opera Hall, Cheybogan, Cheybogan County, Michigan	*Northern Tribune,* December 1, 1883

| | **1886** | |

| May? | City Hall, Kingston, Frontenac County, Ontario | *Daily British Whig,* May 4, 1886 |

| | **1889** | |

| February 26 | Brantford, Brant County, Ontario | *Brantford Evening Telegram,* February 2, 1889 |
| May 15 and 17, 1889 | Village Hall, Montpelier, Washington County, Vermont | *Argus and Patriot,* May 18, 1889 |

| | **1890** | |

| 1890 > | Living on Bright Street, Toronto | Assessment Roll for the Ward of St. David, City of Toronto |

| | **1892–3** | |

| | Sued Toronto General Hospital, but lost the case | *Toronto Daily Mail,* August 10 and 18, 1892 Martha Cutter's research |

| | **1897** | |

| 15 June 1897 | Toronto Died | Tombstone |
| 16 June 1897 | Toronto Necropolis Buried | Records of Toronto Necropolis |

Notes

Preface

1. Chater, K., *Untold Histories: Black People in England and Wales During the Period of the British Slave Trade c. 1660–1807* (Manchester: Manchester University Press, 2009); BASA *Newsletter* 37, September 2003, p. 33; "From Slavery to Show Business," *Ancestors*, December 2005, pp. 33–35. I have since revised the *Oxford Dictionary of National Biography* (ODNB) entry in the light of new research.

2. www.jeffreygreen.co.uk/147-henry-box-brown-escaped-slave-turned-show man.

3. Wood, M., *Blind Memory: Visual Representations of Slavery in England and America 1780–1865* (Manchester: Manchester University Press, 2000); Fisch, A.A., *American Slaves in Victorian England: Abolitionist Politics in Popular Literature and Culture* (Cambridge: Cambridge University Press, 2010), pp. 69–90; Rusert, B., "The Science of Freedom: Counterarchives of Racial Science on the Antebellum Stage," *African American Review* (45) no. 3, pp. 291–308; Spencer, S.S., "An International Fugitive: Henry Box Brown, Anti-Imperialism, Resistance & Slavery," *Social Identities* (12) no. 2, 2006, pp. 227–248; Brooks, D.A., *Bodies in Dissent: Spectacular Performances of Race and Freedom, 1850–1910* (Durham: Duke University Press, 2006), pp. 66–116.

4. I wrote the first books in Britain, possibly the world, about how to do research for television and radio programs: *The Television Researcher's Handbook* (London: BBC Books, 2nd ed., 1995) and *Research for Media Production* (Oxford: Focal Press, 2nd ed., 2002), which are now hopelessly out of date. More recently, I have written a number of books on genealogical research.

5. Ruggles, J., *The Unboxing of Henry Brown* (Richmond: Library of Virginia, 2003).

6. Chater, K., "From Slavery to Show Business," in which Jane Floyd's name and background were first revealed, was written at short notice. Dave Annal, an employee of TNA, had fast access to various records. I too would have realized her maiden name was Floyd if I'd gone through the longer, public route but I must credit him.

7. Wood, M., *Blind Memory: Visual Representations of Slavery in England and America 1780–1865* (Manchester: Manchester University Press, 2000), p. 107; Green, J., *Black Americans in Victorian Britain* (Barnsley, Yorkshire: Pen & Sword, 2018); Marsh, J. (ed.) *Pre-Raphaelite Sisters* (London: National Portrait Gallery, 2019), pp. 106-113. Fanny Eaton appears in the British censuses from 1861, when the family were living in London, TNA, HO RG9/105 f. 47, until 1901, when as a widow she was working as a cook on the Isle of Wight, TNA, RG13/1026 f.9. She died in Acton, West London, in 1924, aged 88, when she was living with a married daughter.

8. Wayne, M., *Imagining Black America* (New Haven: Yale University Press, 2014), pp. xii–xvii; Sarich, V., and Miele, F., *Race: The Reality of Human Differences* (Boulder: Westview Press, 2004); Malik, K., *Strange Fruit: Why Both Sides Are Wrong in the Race Debate* (Oxford: Oneworld Publications, 2008).

9. The most recent exploration of the issues, by Roderick Floud, appears in "The Changing Value of Money," *History Today* (69), no. 3, March 2019, pp. 42–45.

Prologue

1. Chappelear, George Warren, *Families of Virginia (Vol. III) Barret* (Harrisonburg, VA: The Cavalier Press, 1934), pp. 16, 21. Henry Box Brown is not mentioned in the book. See https://archive.org/details/barret 00chap/page/20, accessed July 31, 2017. There are two family trees online: the first at www. werelate.org/wiki/Family:Charles_Barrett_ and_Mary_Chiswell_(1) and another in Ridgeley, J.M., *The Virginia Magazine of History and Biography* (20), no. 2, April 1912, pp. 208–209, at www.jstor.org/stable/424 3197?seq=1#metadata_info_tab_contents, but the second only deals with the descent of three of Charles senior's sons, the Rev. Robert, James Winston, and William Barret, not the eldest son, Charles, junior, and is probably less reliable since much more information has become available since 1912. See also Gwathmey, J.H., *Twelve Virginia Counties: Where the Western Migration Began* (Baltimore, 1979), pp. 242, 247, at https:// archive.org/details/twelvevirginiaco00gwat, all accessed August 1, 2017.

2. United States Census, 1820, database, FamilySearch, at https://familysearch.org/ ark:/61903/1:1:XHLZ-GDM, accessed July 31, 2017.

3. Trollope, A., *North America* (1862, repub. London: Granville Publishing, 1986), p. 76. Also at http://www.gutenberg.org/ files/1866/1866-h/1866-h.htm.

4. Douglass, F., *Narrative of the Life of Frederick Douglass Critical Edition*, edited by McKivigan, J.R., Hinks, P.P., and Kaufman, H.L. (New Haven: Yale University Press, 2016), p. 33. A list of Ryland's works is at http://www.worldcat.org/identities/lccn-n93040608/ accessed April 18, 2017; *Baptist Missionary Magazine* (15), 1835, p. 347; *Particulars of the dreadful tragedy in Richmond, on the morning of the 19th July, 1852 ... the murderess and murderer, Jane and John Williams, their sentence, confessions and execution upon the gallows* (Richmond, 1852).

5. NA, *Richmond Enquirer*, April 11, 1848. In 1849 Henry told James Miller McKim he had been married for 14 years: McKim papers, March 28, 1849, Rare and Manuscripts Collection, Carl A. Kroch Library, Cornell University, in Grover, K., *The Fugitive's Gibraltar: Escaping Slaves and Abolitionism in New Bedford* (Amherst: University of Massachusetts Press, 2009), p. 320, n. 89. NA, *Richmond Enquirer*, 6 February 1849.

6. Brown, H.B., *Narrative of the Life of Henry Box Brown, Written by Himself* (Manchester, 1851) edited by John Ernest, pp. 102–103.

7. Ruggles, *Unboxing*, pp. 32–36. Hollis Robbins says the dates were March 29–30 (which the Wikipedia article accepts) but he shows no evidence for this revision: Robbins, H., "Fugitive Mail: The Deliverance of Henry 'Box' Brown and Antebellum Postal Politics," *American Studies* (50), no. 1/2, Spring/Summer 2009, pp. 5–25, at www. jstor.org/stable/41057153, accessed October 9, 2018. Ruggles's references are impeccable, and a letter dated March 26, 1849 (see note 9 below), shows Henry was in Philadelphia by this date. On May 29 he was speaking in Boston; see note 16 below.

8. Marcus Wood explores how white abolitionists appropriated and altered both Henry's psalm and the images of his emergence from the box to their purposes, diminishing Henry's role: Wood, M., *Blind Memory: Visual Representations of Slavery in England and America 1780–1865* (Manchester: Manchester University Press, 2000), p. 108ff.

9. Lucretia Mott to Joseph and Ruth Dugdale, March 26, 1849, in Palmer, B.W. (ed.), *Selected Letters of Lucretia Coffin Mott* (Champaign: University of Illinois Press, 2002), p. 179; Still, W., *The Underground Railroad: A Selection of Authentic Narratives* (Philadelphia, 1872, reprinted London: Arcturus Publishing, 2017), p. 84, also at https:// archive.org/details/undergroundrailr00 stil.

10. *The Liberator*, January 21, 1842.

11. Gliddon's racial theories appear in Nott, J.C., and Gliddon, G., *Types of Mankind, or Ethnological Researches Based upon the Ancient Monuments, Paintings, Sculptures, and Crania of Races* (Philadelphia: Lippincott, Grambo & Company, 1854); Lewis, Robert Benjamin, *Light and Truth*, p. 115, at https:// archive.org/stream/lighttruth 00lewi/light-

truth00lewi_djvu.txt, accessed August 30, 2017.

12. *Leamington Spa Courier*, July 31, 1852, p. 4; letter, Joseph Ricketson to Debra Weston, April 29, 1849, Weston Papers; Charles Morgan, *Diary*, April 4, 1849, in Grover, K., *The Fugitive's Gibraltar: Escaping Slaves and Abolitionism in New Bedford, Massachusetts* (Amherst: University of Massachusetts Press, 2001), p. 203.

13. April 12, 1849, reported in *The Liberator*, April 20, 1849; Still, W., *Underground Railroad*, pp. 281–284. Still gives no date for this, but advertisements for Green's capture were placed in *The Baltimore Sun* on May 28 and June 1, 1857. Lear married William McAdam and they settled in Elmira, but she died only three years after her escape.

14. *The Liberator*, April 20, 1849.

15. *The Liberator*, June 8, 1849.

16. Bibb, H., *Narrative of the Life and Adventures of Henry Bibb, an American Slave, Written by Himself* (New York, 1849); Jackson, J.A., *The Experience of a Slave in South Carolina* (London, 1862); Blight, D.W., "The Slave Narratives: A History and a Source," *History Now*, at www.gilderlehrman.org/history-by-era/literature-and-language-arts/essays/slave-narratives-genre-and-source, accessed July 31, 2017.

17. Olney, J., "'I Was Born': Slave Narratives, Their Status as Autobiography and as Literature," *Callaloo*, no. 20, pp. 46–73, at www.jstor.org/stable/2930678, accessed July 31, 2017.

18. Ostrowski, C., "Slavery, Labor Reform, and Intertextuality in Antebellum Print Culture: The Slave Narrative and the City-Mysteries Novel," *African American Review* (40), no. 3, Fall 2006, pp. 493–506, accessed October 9, 2018.

19. Brown, *Narrative* (1849), p. 13.

20. *The Liberator*, September 14, October 12, October 26, and November 2, 1849; *The Liberator*, September 7, 1849; Letter from the Rev. Daniel S. Whitney in *Practical Christian*, November 10, 1849. There was some unease among the Methodists in the audience, as there had been a funeral in the church that same day, but this was probably because of the applause; their minister praised Henry: "His narrative is certainly a swift witness against what passes for Christianity in this land."

21. Ruggles, *Unboxing*, pp. 79–80.

22. Platt, V.B., "The East India Company and the Madagascar Slave Trade," *William and Mary Quarterly* (26), no. 4, October 1969, pp. 548–577.

23. New York *Evening Post*, December 28, 1840; Dresser, A., *The Narrative of Amos Dresser, etc.* (New York, 1836).

24. *The Liberator*, April 26 and May 31, 1850. There is a Clarkson Street in Worcester today. The Wikipedia entry on Roberts seems to be well documented: https://en.wikipedia.org/wiki/Benjamin_F._Roberts.

25. *The Liberator*, May 31, 1850. The Boston episode is described by Wolfe, S.J., "Bringing Egypt to America: George Gliddon and the Panorama of the Nile," *Journal of Ancient Egyptian Interconnections* (8), 2016, pp. 1–20, at www.academia.edu/32246666/Journal_of_Ancient_Egyptian_Interconnections_BRINGING_EGYPT_TO_AMERICA_GEORGE_GLIDDON_AND_THE_PANORAMA_OF_THE_NILE, accessed August 30, 2017.

26. Brown, W.W., *A Description of William Wells Brown's original panoramic views of the scenes in the life of an American slave: from his birth in slavery to his … to his first home of freedom on British soil* (1849), Preface, at https://digital.library.cornell.edu/catalog/ss:18167969, accessed October 13, 2018. Wells Brown's text is reprinted in Ripley, C.P., Rossbach, J.S. Finkenbine, R. E., Spiers, F., and Susie, D. (eds.), *Black Abolitionist Papers*, Vol. 1, 1830–1865 (Chapel Hill: University of North Carolina Press, 2015), p. 191ff.

27. Brown, H.B., *Narrative* (1851), pp. 60–61.

28. *Boston Post*, September 5, 1850, and other journals. *The Liberator*, September 6, 1850, reported the fine and that Kelton appealed but stated that Henry would not be in the city at the next court sitting, so Kelton probably got away with it.

Act 1: Scene 1

1. *Chelmsford Chronicle*, October 19, 1849.

2. *Gore's Liverpool General Advertiser*, November 7, 1850; *Westmorland Gazette*, November 9, 1850; Broadbent, R.J., *Annals of the Liverpool Stage* (Liverpool, 1908), p. 336; *Census of Great Britain, 1851; Religious*

Worship—Abridgement of the Official Report of Horace Mann, Esq., to the Registrar General of Births, Marriages and Deaths, showing the Number of Places of Worship, and of Sittings, and Attendants, etc. (London, 1854).

3. *Liverpool Mercury*, November 5, 8, 12, and 15, 1850; *Liverpool Mail*, November 16, 1851.

4. The 1772 Mansfield Judgement in the case of *Somerset v. Stewart* ruled that slavery, "involuntary servitude," had never existed in England and Wales since the establishment of common law in medieval times, so while in this country people were free. While researching *Untold Histories*, I found or was sent the baptism and burial records of some 100 black Americans in the city between 1700 and 1812, and many more in the hinterland. Color and/or ethnicity are almost never mentioned in marriage records both before and after the introduction of printed registers in 1753, so it is impossible to know how many settled in and around the city. *Liverpool Mercury*, March 20, 1855; *Liverpool Mail*, March 24, 1855. I searched more than five years after 1850, more than 100 reports of black people in newspapers from all over the country, before I found this example of blatant racial prejudice.

5. *Bell's New Weekly Messenger*, September 14, 1851.

6. *Era*, December 22, 1850, Old Bailey Online, www.olbaileyonline.org, case no. T18501021-1800, accessed December 11, 2018. McKenna, N., *Fanny and Stella: The Young Men Who Shocked Victorian England* (London: Faber & Faber, 2013), p. 106, mentions the case and describes the transgender world in which Scott lived. The name may have been an alias: A ship called the *Eliza Scott* is often listed in the mercantile press in the 1840s and 1850s.

7. Douglass, Frederick, *My Bondage and My Freedom* (1855), p. 371, at http://docsouth.unc.edu/neh/douglass55/douglass55.html, accessed July 30, 2017.

8. Sweeney, F., *Frederick Douglass and the Atlantic World* (Liverpool: Liverpool University Press, 2007); Kramer, L.S., "David Dorr's Journey Towards Selfhood in Europe," in Lindsay, L.A., and Sweet, J.W., *Biography and the Black Atlantic* (Philadelphia: University of Pennsylvania Press, 2013), pp. 150–171.

9. Brown, W.W., *Three Years in Europe; or, Places I Have Seen and People I Have Met* (London, 1852, reprinted Wokingham, Berkshire: Dodo Press, 2008), pp. 4 and 211. David Dorr also visited the Crystal Palace and, like Wells Brown, was not impressed by the American stand. Dorr, D.F., *A Colored Man Around the World* (1858; Ann Arbor: University of Michigan Press, 1999), ed. M.J. Schueller, pp. 19–20.

10. Letter to Samuel May, General Agent of the American Anti-Slavery Society, April 27, 1854, Anti-Slavery collection of Boston Public Library, in Sterling, D. (ed.), *We Are Your Sisters: Black Women in the Nineteenth Century* (New York: W.W. Norton, 1997), pp. 146–147.

11. Jacobs, H., *Incidents in the Life of a Slave Girl. Written by Herself*, ed. Lydia Child (Boston, MA, 1861), p. 275.

12. Jacobs, H., *Incidents in the Life of a Slave Girl: Written by Herself, with "A True Tale of Slavery" by John S. Jacobs*, ed. Jean Fagan Yellin (Cambridge: Harvard University Press, 2009). *A True Tale of Slavery* is at https://docsouth.unc.edu/neh/jjacobs/jjacobs.htm, accessed December 11, 2018.

13. Cannadine, D., *The Rise and Fall of Class in Britain* (1998, London: Penguin, 2nd ed., 2000); Cannadine, D., *Ornamentalism: How the British Saw Their Empire* (2001, London: Penguin, 2nd ed., 2002).

14. I found some 300 official documents in which they appear, but only in the following newspapers was color mentioned: the *Era*, March 1 and May 24, 1884; *Huddersfield Chronicle*, March 6, 1886; *Hackney and Kingsland Gazette*, April 18, 1883; *London Evening Standard*, March 6, 1895; NA, *London & Brighton*, July 20, 1887. When Cyril entered a lunatic asylum his complexion was described as "light brown" and his birthplace was (erroneously) given as St Vincent: Wiltshire and Swindon History Centre, Records of Fisherton House, J7/190/70, p. 68. Nowhere in the accounts of his treatment was his ethnicity mentioned as a possible contributory factor.

15. It appears, however, that Cooke just described Liverpool as "a place accursed of heaven and abhorrent to nature—their wealth is the price of human misery; and there is not a brick in their houses that is not cemented with human blood." Dunlap,

W., *Memoirs of the Life of George Frederick Cooke*, volume 2 (1813), p. 399. By the 1850s, however, the anecdote developed from this may have become accepted as fact. *Liverpool Mail,* March 18, 1843; Watkins, J., *Struggles for Freedom; or The Life of James Watkins, Formerly a Slave in Maryland US* (Manchester, UK, 1860), pp. 42–43.

16. *Morning Advertiser,* November 17, 1826; *Bell's Life in London and Sporting Chronicle,* July 9, 1843; *Era,* January 1, 1846; *North Star,* October 27, 1848, and June 29, 1849.

17. Pickering, M., "The Blackface Clown," in *Black Victorians, Black Victoriana,* ed. Gretchen Gerzina (New Brunswick: Rutgers University Press, 2003), pp. 161–174; Meer, S., *Uncle Tom Mania: Slavery, Minstrelsy, and Transatlantic Culture in the 1850s* (Athens: University of Georgia Press, 2005). Maybe I was tragically unaware, but as a child in West London I did not equate *The Black & White Minstrel Show,* which was a popular program on television for twenty years from 1958 to 1978, with the people I saw in the street. The way the male minstrels were made up and dressed was just something that went with the style of song they sang. The women were not made up in blackface, and both sexes were elegantly dressed in Edwardian style. It seemed then old-fashioned, a show parents and grandparents enjoyed, and I don't remember my friends and me imitating it. Nor did I link the show with black American performers on radio or on disc, or with the black British performers who were often featured in variety shows on television, like the singers Shirley Bassey (born 1937 in Cardiff, Wales), Kenny Lynch (born 1938 in London, d. 2019), Cleo Laine (born 1927 in Uxbridge, Middlesex), Adelaide Hall (born 1901 in the United States but from 1938 in Britain, d. 1993), Cy Grant (born 1919 in Guyana, d. 2010), the pianist Winifred Atwell (born 1946 in Trinidad, d. 1983), and numerous others.

18. *Northern Whig,* March 16, 1850; *Leicester Journal,* June 30, 1854, gives the first reference so far found to the song; *Liverpool Mercury,* November 26, 1850.

19. PQ, *Manchester Guardian,* December 18, 1850.

20. *Blackburn Standard* April 9, 1851; *Preston Chronicle* January 25 and February 8, 1851.

21. *Burnley Express,* September 12, 1925; TNA, HO 107/2251/f.469.

22. TNA, HO107/2036 f. 731; HO107/1812 f. 115; HO107/1499 f. 106; HO107/1545 f. 11; HO 107/1505 f. 614; HO 107/ 2321 f. 550.

23. Brown, W.W., *Three Years in Europe,* p. 92.

24. The actual lecture was not reported in the press, but Henry carried the letters with him, and they were produced when he appeared in Nottingham three years later and published in the *Nottinghamshire Guardian,* May 11, 1854.

25. Letter from Richard Webb to the *National Anti-Slavery Standard* in New York, quoted in Ruggles, *Unboxing,* p. 126.

26. *Christian Hymns for Public and Private Worship,* a collection compiled by the Cheshire Pastoral Association of Connecticut. Later this book went into numerous editions, spreading the popularity of the previously neglected hymn. Only the first verse of Merrick's hymn and the last verse of Watts's, slightly modified, appear in the *Narrative,* p. 14:

Oh may his conduct, all divine, [the
    Narrative says Christ's conduct]
To us a model prove
Like his, O God, our hearts incline
Our enemies to love.

27. Swain, C., *English Melodies* (London, 1827), pp. 5–6; *Oxford Dictionary of National Biography* at www.oxforddnb.com, accessed January 12, 2019.

28. Brown, *Narrative* (1849), p. 55.

29. Brown, *Narrative* (1851), pp. 46–47.

30. An advertisement for five nights of lectures appeared in the *Bradford Observer,* April 24, 1851, and reports in the issues of May 3 and 8 show the two were very successful here. *Leeds Times,* May 17 and 24, 1851; *Dorset County Chronicle,* May 24, 1851. Ruggles, *Unboxing,* p. 128. This event is also cited in Sweeney, F., and Rice, A., "Liberating Sojourns? African Americans and Transatlantic Abolition 1845–1865," in *Slavery & Abolition* (33), no. 2, June 2012, pp. 181–182: the restaging in October 2009 was considerably more successful than the event it memorialized. Daphne Brooks gives the event as an example of a shrewd publicity stunt, which it would have been had it attracted a larger paying audience; Brooks, D., *Bodies*

in Dissent, pp. 66–67. Audrey Fisch mentions the event but her emphasis is on the content of the panorama, not the restaging, *American Slaves in Victorian Britain*, p. 73f.

31. *Era*, March 13, 1842, February 13, 1848; *Northern Star and Leeds General Advertiser*, April 19, 1851. The Wikipedia biography seems well researched and documented.

32. *Daily Missouri Republican*, June 20, 1851; *Richmond Enquirer*, June 20, 1851; *Buffalo Courier*, June 21, 1851; *Portage Sentinel*, July 7, 1851; *Weekly Raleigh Register*, June 25, 1851; AAS, *Oshkosh Democrat*, June 27, 1851. *Leeds Mercury*, May 24, 1851.

33. Letter James Buchanan to William Learned Marcy, November 11, 1853, quoted in Wilson, F., *Crusader in Crinoline* (Philadelphia: J. B. Lippincott Company, 1941), p. 231.

34. J.C.A. Smith to Lloyd Garrison, July 12 and August 6, 1851, in Boston Public Library, Anti-Slavery Collection, MS A.1.2 v.20, p. 66, and MS A.1.2 v.20, p. 88, quoted in Ruggles, *Unboxing*, p. 132ff. Smith sent a similar letter to Gerrit Smith on August 6, 1851, in Ripley et al., *Black Abolitionist Papers*, vol. 1, pp. 293–297.

35. Olmsted wrote a series of articles about the southern United States in 1852–1857 for the *New York Daily Times*, and these were later collected and published in three volumes. In 1861 they were condensed as *Journeys and Explorations in the Cotton Kingdom* and published in London. His observations about the limitations of the local inhabitants are too many to list. Franklin, J., *From Slavery to Freedom: A History of Negro Americans* (New York: Knopf, 5th ed., 1980), p. 143; Fox-Genovese, E., and Genovese, E.D., "The Southern Slaveholders Against the Modern World," in Perman, M. (ed.), *The Coming of the American Civil War* (Lexington, MA: D.C. Heath & Co., 3rd ed., 1993), pp. 131–142.

36. Fought, L., *Women in the Life of Frederick Douglass* (Oxford: Oxford University Press, 2017), p. 131ff, p. 147 ff, and p. 265.

37. Farrison, W., *William Wells Brown Author and Reformer* (Chicago: University of Chicago Press, 1969), pp. 107–108 and 169–171 ; Sterling, D. (ed.), *We Are Your Sisters*, pp. 144–146, which includes a letter she wrote in an effort to learn the whereabouts

of her daughters, in which she also complains about her husband's failure to support her. In Ezra Greenspan's *William Wells Brown: An African American Life* (New York: W.W. Norton, 2014), Elizabeth appears only in footnotes on pp. 82 and 100.

38. Watkins does not appear in the 1871 or the 1881 British censuses. In the 1861 census he claimed to be 30, but was more likely 40. TNA RG9/2948 f. 74. *Illustrated Berwick Journal*, June 2, 1865, p. 4. Although it is claimed that in 1880 Watkins appears in the census in Baltimore, I have been unable to find him there either as James Watkins or Sam Berry (his real name), http://revealinghistories.org.uk/who-resisted-and-campaigned-for-abolition/people/james-watkins-abolitionist.html, accessed January 5, 2019; https://familysearch.org/ark:/61903/1:1:MN31-WRX, accessed January 5, 2019.

39. I have been unable to find out what was in the drink named after the Swedish soprano Jenny Lind, although a reference to it being drunk in gentlemen's clubs suggests it was an alcoholic drink: *Punch or the London Charivari*, vol. XII, January–June 1847, p. 220. Thanks to Simon Fowler for the Biblical reference. Spruce beer is rich in vitamin C, so was brewed on board ships, although no one realized the reason for its health benefits at the time. See http://zythophile.co.uk/2016/04/20/a-short-history-of-spruce-beer-part-one-the-danzig-connection, accessed February 20, 2019.

40. Ruggles, *Unboxing*, p. 150. Smith does not appear in the 1861 census. *Huddersfield Chronicle*, June 21, July 5, and August 16, 1851.

41. *Liverpool Mail*, November 16, 1850; *Leeds Intelligencer*, May 3, 1851; *North & South Shields Gazette and Northumberland and Durham Advertiser*, October 8, 1852; *Nottinghamshire Guardian*, June 1, 1854; *Brighton Gazette*, July 31, 1856; *Birmingham Journal*, July 31, 1852.

42. *Kentish Mercury*, February 28, 1857; *Hertfordshire Guardian, Agricultural Journal, and General Advertiser*, June 16, 1857; *Portsmouth Times and Naval Gazette*, June 7, 1856.

43. *Manchester Times*, October 8, 1851; Calman, A.L., *The Life and Labours of John Ashworth* (Manchester, 1875), at https://archive.org/details/lifeandlaboursj00calm

goog/page/n7, accessed January 27, 2018. The essay is reproduced at pp. 292–293.

44. AAS, *Morning Star,* November 26, 1851.

45. PQ, *Manchester Guardian* January 7, 1852; *Manchester Times* January 7, 1852. Leucy was committed to trial in Knutsford in Cheshire, but I have been unable to find any report of any trial there. *The Anti-Slavery Harp* is at http://utc.iath.virginia.edu/abolitn/absowwbahp.html, accessed January 27, 2018.

Act 1: Scene 2

1. *Bolton Chronicle,* December 21, 1851. The next year *The Narrative of the Life of James Watkins, formerly a "chattel" in Maryland US,* was published in Bolton, now part of Greater Manchester. At the end of this publication, Watkins listed the 38 anti-slavery meetings at which he had spoken in the Manchester area, along with the "names of gentlemen who presided over them" (p. 48). Most were ministers. There was a further edition published in 1860 in Oldham, also now part of Greater Manchester, and the list of meetings now occupies 12 pages. Most are in the Midlands and North, but there were engagements in Wales and Ireland. At http://docsouth.unc.edu/neh/watkins/watkins.html, accessed October 2, 2017.

2. *Frederick Douglass's Paper,* July 31, 1851, in *The Life and Writings of Frederick Douglass, Vol. 5 (Supplementary Volume), 1844–1860,* ed. Philip S. Foner (New York, 1975), p. 199. There is no reference at all to Henry in the entire volume.

3. *Wolverhampton Chronicle,* March 1852, reproduced at www.wolverhamptonhistory.org.uk/people/migration/slavery2/brown, accessed August 2, 2016. Kossuth returned to London after his U.S. tour but fell out with some of his own supporters and by 1854 was no longer headline news. Henry never repeated this parallel with Kossuth, but this variety of approaches showed him testing his market.

4. *Liverpool Mail,* November 16, 1850; *Leeds Intelligencer,* May 3, 1851; *North & South Shields Gazette and Northumberland and Durham Advertiser,* October 15, 1852; *Hertfordshire Guardian, Agricultural Jour-* *nal, and General Advertiser,* June 13, 1857; *Westmorland Gazette,* November 9, 1850; *Monmouthshire Merlin,* February 2, 1855; *Maidstone Journal and Kentish Advertiser,* February 7, 1857; *Kentish Independent,* February 14, 1857.

5. *Herald,* March 24, 1852. I have been unable to find the word *ludicious* in any dictionary. It is most likely a misprint for ludicrous but it may be a word Brindley himself coined from the Latin *ludo* = I play, to imply that Henry was playing games and not to be taken seriously.

6. Kenneth Macaulay of the Inner Temple (d. 1867), *Alumni Oxoniensis (1715–1886),* vol. 3, p. 889. Serjeant Miller (d. 1876) of the Middle Temple later became a judge on the Midlands circuit; *Pall Mall Gazette,* August 9, 1876. Only surnames were given for the juniors and I have been unable to identify them further.

7. The *Leamington Spa Courier,* July 31, 1852, carried a full account of Henry's evidence, including some details not published elsewhere. It was presented in the style used in court documents, so the reporter either took down what was said in shorthand or persuaded the clerk to allow him access to a transcript of the recorded evidence, which was common practice. It appears to be the closest representation of how Henry conducted himself. Although it is not verbatim, it does record what was said that was pertinent to the matter. Unfortunately, the court records of the Midlands circuit were destroyed in the late 19th century, so this newspaper report cannot be compared to the official account.

8. *London Gazette,* August 1, 1851, p. 1986.

9. *Morning Chronicle,* July 30, 1852; *Birmingham Journal,* July 31, 1852; *Leamington Spa Courier,* July 31, 1852; *Aris's Birmingham Gazette,* August 2, 1852. The *Morning Chronicle* piece was copied in the London *Evening Standard,* the *Coventry Standard,* and the London *Evening Mail* on 30 July 1852, and in the *Staffordshire Advertiser* and the London *Daily News* on July 31, 1852.

10. *Wolverhampton Herald,* August 4, 1852; NA, London *Express,* July 31, 1852.

11. *Wolverhampton Herald,* August 4, 1852; *Morning Chronicle,* July 30, 1852; *Birmingham Journal,* July 31, 1852; *Aris's Birmingham Gazette,* August 2, 1852. The London

Evening Standard, the *Coventry Standard*, and the London *Evening Mail* reproduced most of the *Morning Chronicle* piece on July 30, 1852, and the *London Daily News*, the *Leamington Spa Courier*, and the *Staffordshire Advertiser* did the same on July 31, 1852. The London *Express* of July 31, 1852, covered broadly the same ground but added some details not found in the others. *Birmingham Journal*, July 3, 1852; *Aris's Birmingham Gazette*, August 2, 1852; *Wolverhampton and Staffordshire Herald*, August 4, 1852. The judge was Sir Edward Hall Alderson; he was a Baron of the Exchequer so had the honorary title of Baron Alderson.

12. *Staffordshire Advertiser*, April 23, 1853. Brindley issued a notice that he, editor and manager of the newspaper, had given up the post: *Aris's Birmingham Gazette*, April 25, 1853, and *Wolverhampton Chronicle and Staffordshire Advertiser*, April 27, 1853. The first issue of the *Wolverhampton Journal* to survive in the British Library's collection is that of September 3, 1853; BL, shelfmark 1853–1858 NEWS6790 NPL. *London Gazette*, June 2, 1854. There is a family history of Brindley at http://www.stsepulchres.org.uk/burials/brindley_thomas.html, accessed December 3, 2018.

13. PQ, *Critic*, September 1, 1852; the *Despatch* piece was reprinted in the *Dover Telegraph and Cinque Ports Advertiser*, August 14, 1852, *Wiltshire and Gloucestershire Standard*, August 14, 1852, and *Sligo Champion*, August 16, 1852. The *British Army Despatch* is not yet on line: BL, BLL01013 918383.

14. *Frederick Douglass's Paper*, August 27, 1852, reproduced in Brown, *Narrative*, edited by John Ernest, p. 158. The name Pekel seems to be of Dutch origin. NA, *New England Farmer*, August 14, 1852; see also *Burlington Courier*, August 19, 1852; *Louisville Daily Courier*, August 18, 1852; *Vermont Christian Messenger*, August 18, 1852 (all NA).

15. NA, *Dixon Telegraph of Illinois*, August 28, 1852.

16. NA, *Boston Post*, August 14 and 19, 1852.

17. Franklin Pierce was elected President of the United States in 1853. He is regarded by many as the worst president, but this is a contested title.

18. Harvard University, Houghton Library, Wendell Phillips Papers, September 1, 1852, at http://pds.lib.harvard.edu/pds/view/47900027?n=33&printThumbnails=no&oldpds, accessed August 1, 2016. AAS, *Independent*, June 19, 1862.

19. Brown, W.W., *Three Years*, p. 53ff.

20. Hayes, L. M., *Reminiscences of Manchester and Its Surrounding Areas from 1840* (1905, new edition, Manchester: Empire Publications, 2005), p. 360.

21. In 1792 Olaudah Equiano was told he might sue for libel two newspapers that published a claim that he was not born in Africa but on the Danish island of Santa Cruz in the West Indies. He refuted this in the sixth edition of his *Interesting Narrative* (1792), rather than take legal action; Shyllon, F., *Black People in Britain 1555–1833* (Oxford: Oxford University Press, 1977), pp. 266 and 263. In 1833 Mary Prince, a slave born in Bermuda, gave evidence in a case of libel, when her former employer John Woods of Antigua sued Thomas Pringle, saying he had not properly verified Prince's claims, published in *The History of Mary Prince, A West Indian Slave, Related by Herself* (1831). Woods won. The hearing was on February 21, 1833, in the Court of Common Pleas in London and was covered in a number of newspapers.

22. The *Wolverhampton Herald* is currently not digitized and seems to be accessible only in the British Library (UIN BLL0 1013901267), but there was (and still is) a copying service, and for those unable to travel it would have been possible to hire someone to go to Colindale in northwest London, where the Newspaper Library was located until 2011, to copy the advertisements, texts, and other newspapers' reports in order to produce a full and accurate picture.

23. Brooks, D.A., *Bodies in Dissent* (Durham: Duke University Press, 2006), pp. 95–110.

24. Ernest, J., *Narrative*, pp. 176–177.

25. Wood, M., *Blind Memory*, pp. 103–107, and "'All Right!': The Narrative of Henry Box Brown as a Test Case for the Racial Prescription of Rhetorics and Semiotics," *American Antiquarian Society* (107), no. 1, January 1, 1997, p. 65; Rusert, B., "The Science of Freedom: Counterarchives of Racial Science

on the Antebellum Stage," *African American Review* (45), no. 3, Fall 2012, pp. 291–308.

26. Fisch, A.A., "'Negrophilism' and British Nationalism: The spectacle of the black American abolitionist," *Victorian Review* (19), no. 2, Winter 1993, pp. 20–47. This was later republished as chapter 4 in *American Slaves in Victorian England; Abolitionist Politics in Popular Literature and Culture* (Cambridge: Cambridge University Press, 2000).

27. *The Times*, January 12, 1858; *Era*, August 14, 1859.

28. Brine, G.A., *The King of the Beggars: the Life and Adventures of George Atkins Brine* (London, 1883), p. 34ff. Although Brine gives no date for this episode, by internal evidence it seems to have been in the early 1850s.

29. *Durham County Advertiser*, December 3, 1852; *Stirling Observer*, January 27, 1853. Jeffrey Green's website has a fuller account of his and others' many false pretences: http://www.jeffreygreen.co.uk/111-the-false-pretences-of-alfred-wood-1852-1853, accessed soon after Green posted it in 2013. It is worth noting that even today many viewers of soap operas seem to confuse fiction with reality.

30. Fisch, A. A., *American Slaves in Victorian England*, pp. 91–100.

31. See Draper, N., *The Price of Emancipation: Slave-ownership, Compensation and British Society at the End of Slavery* (Cambridge: Cambridge University Press, 2010) and the website Legacies of British Slave-ownership at www.ucl.ac.uk/lbs. The £20 million debt (£17 billion in contemporary terms) the UK government incurred was not finally paid off until 2015. In 1862 Abraham Lincoln was considering a similar scheme but it was never implemented. Letter, Abraham Lincoln to James A. McDougal, March 4, 1862, Rare Books and Special Collections, University of Rochester Library, at https://rbscp.lib.rochester.edu/lincoln/letter-info?Print=400, accessed May 26, 2019.

Act 1: Scene 3

1. Brown, *Narrative*, p. 8. I used the World Health Organization's definition of clinically obese, but by other organizations' classifications he was overweight.

2. Wells Brown, *Three Years,* pp. 45–46. The repetition of "Sir" cannot have failed to please him either, and he may have exaggerated this for his audience in America; Hayes, *Reminiscences*, p. 157.

3. *Bristol Daily Post*, April 19, 1864.

4. *Brighton Gazette*, July 31, 1856; *Nottinghamshire Guardian*, June 1, 1854; *Kentish Gazette*, November 4, 1856; *Isle of Wight Observer*, January 1, 1859.

5. *Fife Herald*, August 19, 1852; Edinburgh *Evening Courant*, September 7, 1852; *Caledonian Mercury*, September 23, 1852; *Greenock Advertiser*, September 7, 1852.

6. *North & South Shields Gazette and Northumberland and Durham Advertiser*, November 5, 1852.

7. The *Sunderland News and North of England Advertiser*, founded in 1851 by businessman John Candlish, later Member of Parliament for the town, was Liberal in politics. It failed to build an advertisement base and was discontinued in 1855; the last issue in the British Library and in the local studies library in Sunderland is May 1855; and it looks as if following issues are no longer extant. It is not yet available online, but Henry's letter was reproduced in the *Bolton Chronicle*, November 27, 1852, and numerous other newspapers.

8. Letter, Mott to Dugdales, March 26, 1849, in Palmer (ed.), *Selected Letters of Lucretia Coffin Mott*, p. 179.

9. Grandy, *Narrative*, p. 24ff.

10. *Reynolds Newspaper* September 12, 1852; *Era*, September 19, 1852; *London Daily News*, September 21, 1852.

11. *Glasgow Constitutional*, April 2, 1853; *The Life of Josiah Henson, Formerly a Slave, Now an Inhabitant of Canada, as Narrated by Himself* (Boston, 1849). Unlike Henry, Henson had managed to escape with his wife, and with two of their 12 children.

12. *Preston Chronicle*, February 26 and March 5, 1853.

13. Jackson, J., *The History of the Scottish Stage* (Edinburgh, 1793), p. 349ff. Who she was or what else she did in her career are as yet unknown. Lindfors, B., *Ira Aldridge: Performing Shakespeare in Europe 1852–55* (New York: University of Rochester Press, 2013). Wilson, H.J., *The Challenge of Nineteenth Century Theatre in Sheffield*, Ph.D. thesis (University of Sheffield, 2014), pp. 95–96, at

https://etheses.whiterose.ac.uk/7501, accessed August 21, 2017.

14. At https://archive.org/details/road-tostageconta00rede/page/n4, pp. 77–78, accessed January 27, 2018.

15. *Sheffield Independent,* July 30, 1853, and September 17, 1853.

16. *Manchester Times,* October 22, 1853; *Huddersfield Chronicle,* November 5, 1853; *Saunders's News-Letter,* July 26, 1853, passim; *Cumberland Pacquet and Ware's Whitehaven Advertiser,* November 7, 1854; PQ, *Manchester Weekly Times and Examiner,* December 17, 1865.

17. Rice, C., *Tavern Singing in Early Victorian London: the Diaries of Charles Rice for 1840 and 1850,* ed. Lawrence Senelick (Society for Theatre Research, UK, 1997), p. 71ff. *Bell's Life in London and Sporting Chronicle,* 29 May 1836; 9 and 16 June 1839.

18. *Sheffield Independent,* December 3, 1853; *Lancaster Gazette,* December 3 and 17, 1853; *Chelmsford Chronicle,* December 9, 1853; *Silurian, Cardiff, Merthyr, and Brecon Mercury, and South Wales General Advertiser,* December 3, 1853; *Hereford Journal,* December 7, 1853; *Staffordshire Advertiser,* December 10, 1853; *Portsmouth Times and Naval Gazette,* December 24, 1853; *Connaught Watchman,* December 14, 1853; *Dorset County Chronicle,* December 8, 1853; *Bell's Life in London and Sporting Chronicle,* December 11, 1853; *Era, December 25, 1853; Bristol Mercury,* December 31, 1853; *Hereford Times,* December 10 and 17, 1853.

19. Brown, W.W., *Three Years,* pp. 59–60.

20. *Staffordshire Sentinel and Commercial & General Advertiser,* January 21 and 28, 1854; *Clotel, or the President's Daughter* was published in London in 1853; *Oxford Chronicle and Reading Gazette,* June 11, 1853; *Hereford Times,* December 17, 1853.

21. *Aris's Birmingham Gazette,* March 20 and April 17, 1854.

22. *Derby Mercury,* April 26, 1854; TNA, HO/107 2319 f. 274.

23. *Staffordshire Sentinel and Commercial & General Advertiser,* January 21 and 28, 1854. TNA, RG9/435 f.33. *Nottinghamshire Guardian,* June 1, May 11, 1854; *Leicester Journal,* June 30 and July 7 1854; *Oxford Journal,* September 16, 1854.

24. *North Wales Chronicle,* December 17,

1854; *Monmouthshire Merlin,* February 2, 1855.

25. Henry had been in the country for four years, which gives a figure of half a million people annually. He had appeared in 48 venues, so approximately 4,500 in each place. Although he appeared for up to a week in large cities it was only for a couple of days in small towns and villages and he did not attract a full audience in all of them. Even allowing for periods when his appearances may not have been reported in the press, this probably an exaggerated figure. *Taunton Courier, and Western Advertiser,* June 6, 1855.

Act 2: Scene 4

1. Registers of St Hilary, Cornwall, at https://familysearch.org/ark:/61903/1:1:NGM5-7VQ, accessed some time in autumn 2005.

2. TNA, HO 107/142 f. 38. Jane was actually seven; in this census ages were rounded down. There are two possible women who might be Jane's mother: Ann Roberts was married on August 20, 1827, and Ann Hodge was married on May 20, 1828, both in St. Hilary, both to men named John Floyd, events also on FamilySearch.

3. TNA, HO 107/1918 f. 43.

4. *Cornish Telegraph,* March 3, 1852, January 12, 1853, April 26, 1854.

5. McGrady, R., *Music and Musicians in Early Nineteenth-Century Cornwall: The World of Joseph Emidy 'Slave, Violinist and Composer'* (Exeter: Exeter University Press, 1991). A descendant, Marjorie Emidy, has detailed the family's subsequent history in *The Emidy Family* (self-published in the United States, 2000). *West Briton,* May 1, 1835; *Royal Cornwall Gazette,* May 16 and October 23, 1835.

6. At the 1851 census he was in Liskeard in Cornwall, staying in a coffee house; TNA, HO107/1902/300 f.203. His autobiography is at https://docsouth.unc.edu/nch/jbrown.

7. *Cornish Telegraph,* January 12, 1853; *Royal Cornwall Gazette,* February 18, 1853; TNA, HO RG9/1351 f. 74; *Western Gazette,* June 23, 1865, May 8, 1868; *Sherborne Mercury,* October 30, 1866 and January 22 and 29, 1867. His advertisements stated he was a black man, the "celebrated American herb-

alist," offering treatments for the stomach, liver, coughs, and eyes. In 1859 he was living in Trowbridge, where his advertisements included testimonials from grateful patients: James Johnson thanked him for restoring his hair; J. Eyeres for restoring his sight; Sarah Stocker's leg had been cured; and William Roynton's scrofulous tumors had been healed; *Wiltshire Times and Trowbridge Advertiser*, December, 25, 1858, and January 1, 1859. Brown seems to have died in London in 1876; *New Georgia Encyclopedia*. It is hard to reconstruct his life since his name is so common.

8. *Exeter and Plymouth Gazette*, June 9 and 16, 1855; *Western Times*, June 16, 1855.

9. Martineau, H., *Retrospect of Western Travel* (1838), vol. 1, p. 228, at http://oll.libertyfund.org/titles/martineau-retrospect-of-western-travel-3-vols, accessed October 7, 2017; Douglass, F., *Narrative*, ed. E.W. Blyden, p. 32.

10. Lorimer, D.A., *Colour, Class and the Victorians: English Attitudes to the Negro in the Mid-Nineteenth Century* (Leicester: Leicester University Press, 1978), pp. 19–20; 63–66. The copy in the library of University College London has been well read. During the 40-odd years since its publication, passages indicating racial discrimination and prejudice have been heavily underlined by generations of students (and possibly tutors), but the passages with more nuanced reports are unmarked, like pp. 34–40, where Lorimer recounts incidents involving black people treated sympathetically.

11. Green, J., *Black Americans in Victorian Britain*, pp. 1–2, 26, 142–143. Essex Record Office, T/Z 151/41. There is an image of Freeman's gravestone on the Find A Grave website, www.findagrave.com/memorial/5085 8108/joseph-freeman, accessed March 3, 2018. The family appears in the 1871 census, but there is no American-born Joseph Freeman in the 1861 census; either he had not yet arrived in Britain or he was then using another surname; FreeBMD, December Quarter 1863, Chelmsford, vol. 4a, p. 277; TNA, RG10/1662 f.177.

12. *The Times*, January 12, 1858. Williams had been arrested before and was sentenced to 14 days with hard labor; London *Evening Standard*, February 10, 1859. Pieza withdrew the charge. Green, J., *Black Americans in Vic-*

torian England, pp. 88 and 146. Elaw, Z., *Memoirs of the Life, Religious Experience, Ministerial Travels and Labours, of Mrs. Zilpha Elaw, an American Female of Colour. Together with Some Account of the Great Religious Revivals in America* (London, 1846); FreeBMD, December Quarter 1850, Poplar, vol. 2, p. 381; TNA, HO 44/46/26; PROB 11/2198/110.

13. *Cornish Telegraph*, October 31, 1855.

14. Truro Register Office, marriage certificate. I obtained this from the local register office, as it provides a facsimile of the original register.

15. Seven years later he said it was his second visit to Redruth; *West Briton and Cornwall Advertiser*, November 21, 1862.

16. *Essex Standard,* February 1, 1865. He implied his parents had bought their freedom; Brown, *Narrative*, pp. 16 and 27.

17. Brown, *Narrative*, p. xxvii.

18. *Cornish Telegraph*, December 5, 1855; *Royal Cornwall Gazette*, December 7, 1855.

19. *Hampshire Advertiser*, December 8, 1855; *Hampshire Chronicle*, December 22, 1855.

20. *Oxford Dictionary of National Biography*, at http://www.oxforddnb.com/abstract/10.1093/ref:odnb/9780198614128.001.0001/odnb-9780198614128-e-98525?rskey=vePBF7&result=21; *La Chronique de Jersey*, October 4, 1817. Jea's autobiography, *The Life, History, and Unparalleled Sufferings of John Jea, the African Preacher. Compiled and Written by Himself* (Portsea, England, 1811), is at https://docsouth.unc.edu/neh/jeajohn/menu.html; *Worcestershire Chronicle*, September 24, 1851. Anna Baghiani, archivist of the Société Jersiaise, drew my attention to the website https://members.societe-jersiaise.org/history/niers.html (accessed October 24, 2017), which contains reports of these and other black people in Jersey, up to the mid–1940s.

21. At www.jerseyoperahouse.co.uk/about-us/history-heritage, accessed October 24, 2017.

22. *Chronique de Jersey*, January 30, 1856, scan sent by Anna Baghiani.

23. LMA, CLC/B/002/10/01/005, p. 94. This has been preserved in the Chubb collection of newspaper cuttings, annotated "Jersey paper," but the exact name of the publication and the date are missing.

24. Legacy of British Slave Ownership database at www.ucl.ac.uk/lbs/search, accessed September 23, 2017. There was also one unsuccessful applicant. The majority have English surnames.

25. Few newspapers from Guernsey have survived from before 1869, but the Guernsey *Star*, January 26, 1856, reported that he was on the island and reprinted from the *Liverpool Mercury* an account of his escape. He also advertised a week of forthcoming appearances in the issue of February 16, 1856. Thanks to Sarah Ferbrache of the Prilaux Library for these references. *Isle of Wight Observer*, May 10 and June 7, 1856; *Portsmouth Times and Naval Gazette*, June 7, 1856; *Hampshire Advertiser*, May 31, 1856; PQ, *Musical Gazette*, August 2, 1856.

26. *West Sussex Gazette*, July 3, 1856; *West Surrey Times*, August 23, 1856. There is no indication of when the visit to Sompting happened. Anglican ministers supported conservative values; he does not advocate antislavery sentiments, but that the young should count their blessings to be at liberty in Britain.

27. *South Eastern Gazette*, September 16, 1856; *Faversham Gazette*, and *Whitstable, Sittingbourne, & Milton Journal*, October 18, 1856; *Kentish Gazette*, October 28, 1856; *Dover Telegraph and Cinque Ports General Advertiser*, December 13, 1856; *Maidstone Journal and Kentish Advertiser*, February 7, 1857; *Kentish Independent*, February 7 and 14, 1857; *Kentish Mercury*, February 21, 1857; March 14, 1857; *Hertfordshire Guardian, Agricultural Journal, and General Advertiser*, June 13 and 16, 1857.

Act 2: Scene 5

1. www.margatelocalhistory.co.uk, accessed March 21, 2019. TNA, HO 107/1629 f.224; RG 9/535 f.89.

2. BL, Add. Ms 59266 W (*The Nubian Captive*); Add. Ms 59266 X (*Pocahontas*) and Add. Ms 59266 Y (*The Fugitive Free*); Add. MS 43025 (*Warrior Boy*). *Era*, July 20 and 27, 1851. *Morning Advertiser*, October 16, 1851. *Bells' Weekly Messenger*, October 18, 1851. *Era*, November 16, 1851, March 21 1852. Sarah Thorne was the daughter of Richard Thorne, the manager of both the Pavilion Theatre in East London and the Theatre

Royal in Margate. At her first appearance on stage she was 14 years old. BL, Add. MS 43028, *Morning Advertiser*, June 29, 1853. BL, Add. MS 43030; Add. MS 43034. The latter may have had an alternative title, *Achmet Prince of Abyssinia*. The World Catalogue website lists many playbills from the Pavilion Theatre on which Burton's name appears. Some of the plays he wrote are not in the Lord Chamberlain's archives so nothing is known more about them. At http://worldcat.org/identities/lccn-no95054815, accessed June 11, 2019.

3. *Era*, June 28, 1857; *South Eastern Gazette*, August 4, 1857.

4. *Kentish Gazette* and *South Eastern Gazette*, September 22, 1857.

5. *Era*, September 27 and October 4, 1857.

6. Postance, H., *The Struggles of a Parish in the South End* (1883), quoted in Wilcox, Alastair, *Living in Liverpool: A Collection of Sources for Family, Local and Social Historians* (Newcastle-upon-Tyne, 2011), p. 224.

7. *Wigan Observer and District Advertiser*, October 16, 1857; *Staffordshire Advertiser* October 31 and November 7, 1857; *Era*, October 4, 1857.

8. *The Wreck of the Northern Belle* (Ramsgate, 1857); *A Hand Book and Companion to Ramsgate Margate Broadstairs Kingsgate Minister etc* (Ramsgate, 1859); BL, Add. MS 53018 D; *Morning Advertiser*, January 15, 1863.

9. Hill, E. S., "'Morgan Smith: Successor to Ira Aldridge," *Black American Literature Forum* (16), no. 4, Winter, 1982, pp. 132–135; Norris, W., "Additional Light on S. Morgan Smith," *African American Review* (20), no. 1–2, Spring/Summer 1986, pp. 75–79. Lindfors, B., *The Theatrical Career of Samuel Morgan Smith* (Trenton, NJ: Africa World Press, 2018) is a full-length biography.

10. *Era*, August 3, 1879. He does not appear in either the English or the Scottish censuses for 1881. The death of a George Dunbar, aged 60, is registered in Luton in the March quarter of 1891 (FreeBMD), but others of the name, with less likely years of birth, are also registered in other places.

11. TNA, RG11/0515 f.111. *Era*, 3 February 1883. Much more information about his time in Britain is in a letter he wrote to Frederick Douglass: Library of Congress, Douglass

Papers, General Correspondence 136, letter Paul Molyneaux to Frederick Douglass, 3 November 1886, on www.loc.gov, accessed 19/02/2020. *Western Daily Press*, 1, 2, 3, 7 April 1886; *Reading Mercury*, 3, 10 July 1886. The tour can be tracked through the British Newspaper Archive. He was buried in the Old Burying Ground, Cambridge, Middlesex County, Massachusetts, USA, on 27 June 1891, www.findagrave.com,accessed 19/02/ 2020.

12. TNA, RG10/0539 f. 75; *Era*, August 20, 1871. There is no marriage for a George Gross between 1868 and 1871 in the GRO indices or on FreeBMD.

13. *Era*, July 1, 1866, and August 4, 1867. The name is very close to that of William Gustavus Allen (c. 1826–1888), an American university lecturer in New York who had one black grandparent. He married a white pupil in 1853 and the couple was forced to leave America. For a while he ran a school in Islington in North London and attributed his failure there to prejudice, but his other ventures were equally unsuccessful. He is missing from the 1861 and 1871 censuses, but by 1881 he had become a professor of music. TNA, RG 11/41 f.117. Or is the similarity of the names just a coincidence?

14. There is an extensive literature on Victorian sermons. Francis, K. A., Gibson, W. Morgan-Guy, J., Tennant, B., and Ellison, R.H. (eds.), *The Oxford Handbook of the British Sermon 1689–1901* (Oxford University Press, Oxford, 2012) includes a useful chapter, "Parish Preaching in the Victorian Era: The Village Sermon," by Frances Knight.

15. *Hertford Mercury and Reformer*, January 2, 1858; Ziter, E., *The Orient on the Victorian Stage*, p. 134; *Spectator*, May 10, 1851.

16. In a rare error, Jeffrey Ruggles misread a report of one of Henry's appearances, concluding that the Holy Land became a new, final segment in the American Slavery presentation. Probably following him, John Ernest said he had incorporated it, but they were always kept separate. Ruggles, J., *Unboxing*, p. 152; Ernest, John (ed.), *Narrative*, pp. 175–176. *Chelmsford Chronicle*, February 5, 1858.

17. https://artuk.org/discover/artists/ mills-edward-active-18821918, accessed December 12, 2018.

18. Hall had joined the Royal Navy in 1852 and was part of a brigade sent to quell the uprising. Although the local paper where the ship returning him and his division landed in Britain and others who copied the story did mention his color, the official notice of his award in the *London Gazette* did not mention his ethnicity; he was just Captain of the Foretop on HMS (Her Majesty's Ship) *Shannon*. *Morning Advertiser*, January 7, 1859, reproduced a piece from the *West Sussex Gazette*, but I have been unable to trace the original; it may have been inserted in a later, slip edition not now online; *London Gazette*, February 1, 1859. Hall survived to retire to Canada, where he died in 1904. See www.vconline.org.uk/william-e-hall-vc/ 4586877103, accessed December 12, 2018.

19. www.thegazette.co.uk/London/issue/ 22050/page/3402/data.pd, accessed August 26, 2016.

20. "The Evidence of the Lucknow Story," *Spectator*, September 6, 1890, summarizes the evidence for and against.

21. *Jersey Independent and Daily Telegraph*, March 6, April 7, 10, and 14, 1858.

22. Library and Museum of Freemasonry, Annual Returns to the Grand Lodge of the Royal Sussex Lodge No. 722, 1858–1863, Box f19. During the German occupation of the Channel Islands in World War II many records were destroyed to protect the population, so further details are not extant.

23. Susan Snell and John Ellis are currently researching black Freemasons in 18th-century Britain; Révauger, C., *Black Freemasonry: From Prince Hall to the Giants of Jazz* (Rochester, VT: Inner Traditions/ Bear & Co., 2016).

24. Guernsey *Star*, May 8, 1858. Fielden, Samuel, *Autobiography of Samuel Fielden* (United States, 1887), at http://dwardmac. pitzer.edu/Anarchist_Archives/haymarket/ Fielden.html, accessed August 1, 2016. Thanks to Audrey Dewjee for drawing my attention to this reference.

25. *Kentish Gazette*, October 5, 1858.

26. *Glasgow Herald*, October 4, 1858; *Belfast Morning News*, October 4, 1858; *Staffordshire Advertiser*, October 23, 1858; *Nottinghamshire Guardian*, October 7, 1858; *Leicester Journal*, October 15, 1858; *Hampshire Chronicle*, October 9, 1858; *Brighton Gazette*, October 21, 1858; *Era*, October 10 1858.

27. *Sussex Advertiser*, November 16, 1858;

Hampshire Telegraph, November 18, 1858; *Isle of Wight Observer*, January 1, 1859.

28. *West Sussex Gazette*, February 3, 1859.

29. Information about his birthplace from Alan Beechey, a descendant. *West London Observer*, March 12, 1859. Chadwick also wrote poetry, promoted temperance, and was involved in spiritualism; he briefly edited *The Spirit World*.

30. Brooks, D.A., *Bodies in Dissent*, p. 123f. The advertisement in the *West London Observer* of March 12, 1859, which appears in the same issue as the review Brooks references, makes it clear that they were separate presentations on separate days and that Jane would be presenting the Holy Land.

31. *Chelmsford Chronicle*, December 9, 1853.

32. Unfortunately, the records of this Lodge held in the Library and Museum of Freemasonry (Box D14) are incomplete: There is no record of the meeting where he took this step to becoming a full Freemason.

33. *West London Observer*, March 19, 1859. The Windsor Castle in King Street is now a shop, but the Old Pack Horse is still in business; www.oldpackhorsechiswick.co.uk. Thanks to Peter Nixon for searching the archives of the Ancient Order of Foresters— alas, no further information about Henry's membership or any of his activities in the Society has been found as yet.

34. *Windsor and Eton Express*, March 12 and 19, 1859; *Reading Mercury*, April 23 and May 14, 1859; *Oxford Chronicle* and *Reading Gazette*, May 28, 1859.

35. *Coventry Herald*, July 1, 1859; *Manchester Courier and Lancashire General Advertiser*, March 24, 1855; *Bradford Observer*, March 29, 1855; *Era*, July 8, 1860, January 19, 1862. The last reference to Arr Hee in the *Era* was on June 1, 1873.

36. Frost, Thomas, *Circus Life and Circus Celebrities* (London, 1881), at www.circushistory.org/Frost/Frost5.htm, p.p 136–138. The Wikipedia article seems well referenced: https://en.wikipedia.org/wiki/Chung_Ling_Soo. Both accessed August 1, 2016.

37. *Rugby Advertiser* and *Leicestershire Mercury*, September 24, 1859; *Rugby Advertiser*, September 24, 1859; *Coventry Herald*, September 30, 1859; *Staffordshire Advertiser*, October 15, 1859; *Shrewsbury Chronicle*, October 21, 1859.

38. *Shrewsbury Chronicle*, November 4, 1859; *Eddowes's Journal, and General Advertiser for Shropshire, and the Principality of Wales*, November 2, 1859; *Wellington Journal*, November 5, 1859; *Shrewsbury Chronicle*, November 11, 1859; *Wellington Journal*, November 12, 1859; *Eddowes's Journal, and General Advertiser for Shropshire, and the Principality of Wales*, December 7, 1859.

39. Shropshire Archives, 655/4/367; *Windsor and Eton Express*, March 12 and 19, 1859. I am grateful to the current secretary of the Freemasons' Windsor Lodge for checking the local records. *Windsor & Eton Express*, April 2, 1859.

40. *Staffordshire Sentinel and Commercial & General Advertiser*, January 14, 21, and February 18, 1860.

41. *Congleton & Macclesfield Mercury, and Cheshire General Advertiser*, March 17, 1860.

42. *Staffordshire Sentinel and Commercial & General Advertiser*, February 18 and April 7, 1860. It was agreed that in future the charge would be reduced to £2 2s.

43. *Staffordshire Sentinel and Commercial & General Advertiser*, February 18 and March 3, 1860; *Congleton & Macclesfield Mercury, and Cheshire General Advertiser*, March 17, 1860; *Glossop Record*, April 7, 1860; *Bury Times*, May 12 and 19, 1860. Unfortunately, the documents from the Hyde Lodge held in the Library and Museum of Freemasonry are incomplete, so there is no further information about his contact with the Freemasons there.

44. The Shatwell family appears in the 1861 census a few months later, TNA, RG9/2568 f.116; GRO, birth certificate, March Quarter 1860, Manchester, vol. 8d, p. 179. Cheshire Record Office, Registers of St Mary Stockport on FamilySearch and MP; *Era*, November 11, 1860; *Huddersfield Chronicle*, December 15 and 29, 1860.

45. TNA, RG9/3226 f. 5.

46. *Burnley Advertiser*, April 20, 1861.

47. *Rochdale Observer*, June 1, 1861; *Bury Times*, June 22, 1861; *Era*, November 3, 1861.

48. *Manchester Courier and Lancashire General Advertiser*, November 30, 1861; *Leigh Chronicle and Weekly District Advertiser*, January 11 and 18, 1862. *Freedom's Song* is probably the psalm he sang on being released from the box. I have been unable to

trace the Nubian Family song; it may be another he adapted from an existing minstrelsy song to give it new meaning. *Bolton Chronicle,* January 25, 1862.

49. *Wigan Observer and District Advertiser,* March 15, 1862.

50. *Jersey Independent and Daily Telegraph,* April 19, 21, 24, 25, 28, May 12 and 24, 1862. Gabeldu was recaptured.

51. *West Briton and Cornwall Advertiser,* November 14 and 21, 1862; *Royal Cornwall Gazette,* November 21, 1862 (although when the previous visit took place is not known); *Lake's Falmouth Packet and Cornwall Advertiser,* January 10, 1863; *Royal Cornwall Gazette,* January 30, 1863; *Western Times,* March 20, April 3, June 26, July 3, 1863; *Exeter Flying Post,* July 15, 1863; *Bath Chronicle and Weekly Gazette,* October 8, 1863; *Cardiff and Merthyr Guardian, Glamorgan, Monmouth, and Brecon Gazette,* October 23, 1863; *Cardiff Times,* November 13, 1863.

Act 3: Scene 6

1. *Cardiff Times,* November 13, 1863.

2. Jackson, L., *Palaces of Pleasure: From Music Halls to the Seaside to Football, How the Victorians Invented Mass Entertainment* (New Haven: Yale University Press, 2019), particularly the section on the growth of the early music hall, pp. 56–76. Henry never seems to have performed in a music hall and the content of his entertainments was more respectable than what was offered there, but this shows the increasing appetite for pure amusement among the working classes.

3. Martineau, H., *Letters on Mesmerism* (London, 1845) p. 1ff; Moore, W., *The Mesmerist: The Society Doctor Who Held Victorian London Spellbound* (London: Weidenfeld & Nicolson, 2017), details the career of John Elliotson (1791–1868) and the controversy his practice of mesmerism aroused in the medical world.

4. *Liverpool Mail,* April 13, 1850. At his first appearance in Liverpool, H.E. Lewis included mesmerism at a distance and also phrenology. When the mesmerism at a distance experiment was repeated under scientific conditions in the Medical School of the University of Aberdeen it failed; Wakefield, R., *Hidden Depths: The Story of Hypnosis* (Hove, Sussex: Psychology Press, 2003),

p. 208. Lewis's career was cut short in 1857 when he died following a fall from his horse. Had he lived, he might have become a more significant figure. A fuller biography appears on Jeffrey Green's website, http://www.jeffreygreen.co.uk/141-h-e-lewis-the-negro-mesmerist-1851-1855, accessed August 31, 2016. *Liverpool Mercury,* November 15, 1850.

5. *Chester Chronicle,* August 10, 1850; *Liverpool Mercury,* November 15, 1850; *Manchester Courier,* November 30, 1850, and others; *Isle of Wight Observer,* April 10, 1858.

6. *Era,* November 4 and February 5, 1860, July 21, 1861.

7. *Era,* December 23 1860; February 10 and March 10 and 24, 1861; March 24, 1861; *Nottingham Evening Post* and *London and Provincial Entr'acte,* October 11, 1879. To be an American was an advantage in his professional field, but he never claimed this so I presume he was British.

8. Cutter, M.J., "Will the Real Henry 'Box' Brown Please Stand Up?," *Commonplace* (16), 1, Fall 2015, at http://commonplace.org/book/will-the-real-henry-box-brown-please-stand-up, accessed November 12, 2016. Rusert, B., "The Science of Freedom: Counterarchives of Racial Science on the Antebellum Stage," p. 300.

9. *Era,* November 27, 1859.

10. *Era,* May 27, 1860, and May 10 and November 22, 1868.

11. *Dumfries and Galloway Standard,* March 3, 1852; *Fife Herald,* November 20, 1851. The Free Church of Scotland was and is Presbyterian and evangelical. Before his visit to Scotland, H.E. Lewis went to Ireland, where he had considerable success. He also toured England, where there are no reports of him being connected with the devil. Elsewhere in Scotland he received a warm welcome and bought a house in Banffshire, where he offered to treat patients, *Elgin Courant and Morayshire Advertiser,* October 22, 1852.

12. *Merthyr Telegraph, and General Advertiser for the Iron Districts of South Wales,* January 2, 1864; *Western Daily Press,* February 22, 1864.

13. *Cardiff Times,* March 11, 1864.

14. *Aberdare Times,* January 2, 1864; *Usk Observer, Raglan Herald, and Monmouthshire Central Advertiser,* March 26, April 2 and 9, 1864; *Monmouthshire Merlin,* April 9

and 16, 1864; *Cardiff Times*, August 5 and 12, 1864; *Bristol Daily Post*, April 19, 1864.

15. *Merthyr Telegraph, and General Advertiser for the Iron Districts of South Wales*, August 20 and September 10, 1864.

16. GRO, birth certificate, December Quarter 1864, Bristol, vol. 6a, p. 31.

17. *Bristol Daily Post*, October 26, 1864; *Western Daily Press*, October 27, 1864; *Bristol Times and Mirror*, October 29, 1864; *Cheltenham Mercury*, November 12, 1864.

18. *Glasgow Saturday Post, and Paisley and Renfrewshire Reformer*, May 21, 1864, reported their American act.

19. Fawkes, R., *Dion Boucicault* (London: Quartet Books, 1979) pp. 152–154; London *Evening Standard*, October 3, 1864; *Brighton Guardian*, April, 24 1867; *Canterbury Journal, Kentish Times and Farmers' Gazette*, November 27, 1869; *Cheltenham Chronicle*, August 22, 1865.

20. Magus, J., *Magical Heroes: The Lives and Legends of Great African American Magicians* (Marietta, Georgia: Magus Enterprises, 1995), pp. 1–30. There is a biography by John A. Hodgeson, *Richard Potter: America's First Black Celebrity* (Charlottesville: University of Virginia Press, 2015), which I have not yet read. A number of websites also offer different variants on elements of Potter's biography.

21. *Scots Magazine*, May 1, 1800.

22. Magus, *Magical Heroes*, pp. 51 and 31. He tells Henry's story in fictionalized form. Also correspondence with Mr Magus, who is revising his publication for a second edition.

23. The claim that Africans invented many innovations that were "stolen" by white people has a long history. Interviewed in February 1937, Fannie Berry of Petersburg, Virginia, stated that "My master tole us dat de niggers started the railroad, an' dat a nigger lookin' at a boilin' coffee pot on a stove one day got the idea dat he could cause it to run by putting wheels on it ... the idea was stole from him an' dey built de steamengine." Rawick, George P. (ed.), *The American Slave: A Composite Autobiography*, vol. 17 (Westport, CT: Greenwood Press, 1941), p. 1f. This seems to be an appropriation of a British invention, made by the Scot James Watt around 1774. Cultures that feel themselves to have been marginalized make similar claims. While teaching a course on research for the media in the mid 1990s, I was amused to hear from one of the participants, a well-educated Russian woman, that railways, television, and radio had all been invented in Russia but the West would not admit this. *Gloucester Journal*, November 19, 1864.

24. *Gloucester Journal*, December 17, 1864; *Cheltenham Chronicle*, December 20, 1864; baptism registers of St. James, Bristol, on FamilySearch and FMP, accessed August 31, 2017.

25. *Merthyr Telegraph and General Advertiser for the Iron Districts of South Wales*, January 14, 1865; *Monmouthshire Merlin*, September 15, 1866.

26. *Western Gazette*, March 11, 1865; *Exeter Flying Post*, March 22, 1865.

27. *Taunton Courier and Western Advertiser*, March 15, 1865; *Sherborne Mercury*, March 14 and 28, 1865; *Dorset County Chronicle*, March 23, 1865. The reference to his white feet suggests John Brown had vitiligo, uneven skin pigmentation. The riot had taken place on November 5, 1864, resulting from the annual Guy Fawkes Day celebrations; no mention is made of John Brown in the newspaper accounts: *Dorset County Chronicle*, November 10, 16, and 23, 1864.

28. *Lake's Falmouth Packet and Cornwall Advertiser*, June 17, 1865.

29. Hannah Watts's work for the Box Browns emerged when in 1868 she gave evidence in a trial, unconnected with her previous employers: *Cardiff and Merthyr Guardian, Glamorgan, Monmouth, and Brecon Gazette*, March 14, 1868; *Cardiff and Merthyr Guardian, Glamorgan, Monmouth, and Brecon Gazette*, February 16, 1866; *Baner ac Amserau Cymru (Banner and Times of Wales)*, February 21 and 28, 1866.

30. *Cardiff Times*, April 20, 1866.

31. *Baner ac Amserau Cymru*, February 21 and 28, 1866; *Cardiff Times*, April 20, 1866; *Era*, September 2, 1866; *Monmouthshire Merlin*, October 6 and December 15, 1866; *Western Daily Press*, December 10 and 14, 1866; *Cardiff Times* and *Usk Observer, Raglan Herald, and Monmouthshire Central Advertiser*, December 15, 1866.

32. *Cardiff Times*, January 5 and 12, 1867.

33. *Monmouthshire Beacon* and *Hereford Times*, April 6, 1867. The murder remains unsolved.

34. *Era*, May 5, 1867; *Oxford Chronicle and Reading Gazette*, October 5, 1867.

35. *Oxford Times*, October 12, 1867.

36. *Freemasons Magazine and Masonic Mirror*, November 2 and 9, 1867, December 21, 1867, January 4 and 18, 1868, February 15, 1868, at www.masonicperiodicals.org, accessed October 2, 2018.

37. Rusert, B., "The Science of Freedom: Counterarchives of Racial Science on the Antebellum Stage," pp. 291–308.

38. Cutter, M.J., "Will the Real Henry Brown Please Stand Up"; Fisch, A.A., *American Slaves in Victorian England*, p. 82; Rusert, B., "The Science of Freedom."

39. Moore, W., *The Mesmerist: The Society Doctor Who Held Victorian London Spellbound* (London: Weidenfeld & Nicholson, 2017), p. 137ff.

40. *South London Chronicle*, March 14, 1868.

41. *Uxbridge & West Drayton Gazette*, April 4, 1868

42. *Essex Herald*, June 16, 1868; *Suffolk and Essex Free Press*, June 18, 1868; *Chelmsford Chronicle*, June 19, 1868.

43. *Cambridge Independent Press*, August 15, 1868; *Bury Free Press*, August 8 and 15, 1868; *Norfolk News*, September 28 and October 3, 1868; *Bury and Norwich Post*, October 27, 1868; *Yarmouth Independent*, October 24 and 31, 1868.

44. *Thanet Advertiser*, January 30, February 6 and 13, 1869.

45. *Thanet Advertiser*, February 20, 1869.

46. At this time, libel and slander were not synonyms, but they were covered by different acts of legislation; libel was written and slander was spoken.

47. *Dover Express*, March 5 and 12, 1869; *New Zealand Herald*, October 16, 1865; *Kilmore Free Press*, September 18, 1873, at https://trove.nla.gov.au/newspaper/article/70057726, accessed December 22, 2018. Joseph Jacobs (1813–1870) was apparently the first professional magician to visit Australia.

48. *Folkestone Express, Sandgate, Shorncliffe & Hythe Advertiser*, March 27, 1869; *Maidstone Telegraph*, April 17 and 24, 1869. Quoted in Winter, A., *Mesmerized: Powers of Mind in Victorian Britain* (Chicago: University of Chicago Press, 1998), p. 112.

49. *Maidstone Telegraph*, April 17 and 24, 1869.

50. *Bristol Daily Post*, August 24, 1863. John Henry Pepper published *The True History of the Ghost: All about Metempsychosis* in London in 1890 and also *The Boy's Playbook of Science* in 1866, showing how amusing effects could be produced.

51. *Portsmouth Times and Naval Gazette*, September 11, 1869; *Isle of Wight Observer*, September 25, 1869; *Hampshire Telegraph*, October 9, 13, 16, and 30, 1869.

Act 3: Scene 7

1. *Soulby's Ulverston Advertiser and General Intelligencer*, November 26, 1863.

2. Tocqueville, A. de, *Journeys to England and Ireland* (1835, republished New Haven: Yale University Press, 1958), pp. 104–107.

3. Trollope, *North America*, vol. 2, p. 76; Wells Brown, *Three Years in Europe*, p. 49.

4. Jacobs, *Incidents*, pp. 276–277.

5. Hayes, *Reminiscences*, p. 113. It was not until 1956 that a Clean Air Act was passed in the United Kingdom, followed by initiatives to clean public buildings of centuries of pollution.

6. *Manchester Guardian*, December 31, 1862.

7. Hayes, *Reminiscences*, p. 290.

8. *Manchester Courier and Lancashire General Advertiser*, December 4, 1869; *Rochdale Observer*, January 22 and February 12, 1870.

9. *Burnley Advertiser*, February 26, 1870.

10. GRO, birth certificates, March Quarter 1870, Manchester, vol. 8d, p. 380. *Rochdale Observer*, March 12, 1870; *Bradford Daily Telegraph*, March 24, 1870; *Manchester Evening News*, April 18–22 and 27–28, 1870; *Era*, May 29, 1870.

11. Manchester Cathedral Archives, Mancath/2/2/3, baptism registers of Manchester Cathedral on Ancestry, accessed September 8, 2016.

12. GRO, death certificate, June Quarter 1870, Manchester, vol. 8d, p. 252.

13. *Staffordshire Sentinel and Commercial & General Advertiser*, July 16 and 23, 1870; *Staffordshire Advertiser*, July 23, 1870; *Era*, August 14 and 28, 1870; *Ashton Weekly Reporter, and Stalybridge and Dukinfield Chronicle*, September 3 and 17, 1870, and January 21, 1871.

14. *Ashton Weekly Reporter, and Stalybridge and Dukinfield Chronicle*, September 17, 1870; *Bolton Evening News*, November 3, 1870; *Ashton Weekly Reporter, and Stalybridge and Dukinfield Chronicle*, January 21, 1871; *Preston Herald*, March 18, 1871.

15. TNA, RG 10/406 f. 42.

16. *Leeds Intelligencer*, June 26 and September 4, 1852; *Ipswich Journal*, April 2 and 23, 1859; *Monmouthshire Merlin*, September 6, 1862.

17. *Ashton Weekly Reporter, and Stalybridge and Dukinfield Chronicle*, August 12, 1871; *Leigh Chronicle and Weekly District Advertiser*, August 19, 1871. GRO, birth certificate, December Quarter 1871, Manchester, vol. 8d, p. 348. Manchester Cathedral Archives, Mancath/2/2/3, baptism registers of Manchester Cathedral on Ancestry, accessed September 8, 2016.

18. GRO, death certificate, June Quarter 1872, Manchester, vol. 8d, p. 255. *Hyde & Glossop Weekly News, and North Cheshire Herald,* December 2, 1871; *Ashton Weekly Reporter, and Stalybridge and Dukinfield Chronicle*, December 2, 1871. Records of Ardwick Cemetery on FMP, accessed September 8, 2016. As the surname Brown is so common and the mother's surname does not appear in the indices until 1911, it is impossible to know without considerable time and expense whether they had any other children up until 1875.

19. *Heywood Advertiser*, July 5, 1872.

20. *Manchester Evening News*, May 9, 1873; *Staffordshire Sentinel*, May 25, 1874.

21. GRO, death certificate, December Quarter 1874, Prestwich, vol. 8d, p. 308; TNA, RG 37/94, records of Ardwick Cemetery on FMP, accessed September 8, 2016. I have not found a record of Mary Emma Martha's burial, but she too was probably interred here.

22. Manchester Archives, ratebooks on FMP, accessed September 8, 2016.

23. *Era*, February 7 and March 7, 1875; "New York Passenger Lists, 1820–1891," on *FamilySearch*, https://www.familysearch.org/ark:/61903/3:1:939V-R792-J2?i=280&cc=1849782, accessed March 10, 2018. Henry gives his age as 50 (actually he was 60) and his occupation as Professor. Thanks to Martha Cutter for this reference.

Epilogue

1. See, for example, Theroux, P., *Deep South: Four Seasons on Back Roads* (New York: Eamon Dolan/Houghton Mifflin Harcourt, 2015). When I started to read this, I thought his journeys had been undertaken in the 1970s; then a reference to Bill Clinton made me look at the date of publication. More recently, the events in Charlottesville, Virginia, and the rise in right-wing separatism show this is a continuing problem.

2. Detailed in Fought, *Women in the World of Frederick Douglass*, pp. 251–254.

3. *Boston Globe*, January 3, 1876; *Portland Daily Press,* January 11, 1877; at www.newspapers.com, both accessed April 14, 2019.

4. *Argus and Patriot*, September 5 and 19, 1877. Thanks to Jim Magus for this reference. *Argus and Patriot*, May 27, 1875, at www.newspapers.com, accessed April 14, 2019.

5. *Boston Globe*, May 31, 1878, at www.newspapers.com, accessed April 14, 2019.

6. Advertised for sale on an online auction site, www.liveauctioneers.com, in August 2014. Accessed January 10, 2019.

7. Haskins, J., and Bennett, K., *Conjure Times: Black Magicians in America* (New York: Walker & Co., 2001), pp. 30–33, reproduces these and other stories from Magus, *Magical Heroes.*

8. Found by David Price and reproduced in his *Magic: A Pictorial History of Conjurers in the Theater* (New York: Cornwall Books, 1985), p. 58.

9. *Essex County Herald*, December 5, 1879, at www.newspapers.com, accessed April 14, 2019.

10. *Argus and Patriot*, December 17, 1879; *Rutland Weekly Herald and Globe*, March 15, 1880; *Argus and Patriot*, May 18 and 26, 1880 all at www.newspapers.com, accessed April 14, 2019.

11. Riddell, W.R., "The Slave in Canada," *Journal of Negro History* (5), no. 3, July 1920, pp. 316–333, at www.jstor.org/stable/2713625, accessed April 28, 2019.

12. *Voice of the Fugitive*, May 21, 1851; Frost, K.S., Walls, B., Neary, H.B., and Armstrong, F.H. (eds.), *Ontario's African Canadian Heritage: Collected Writing by Fred Landon, 1918–1967* (Toronto: Dundurn, 2009),

p. 245; Silverman, J., Bellavance, M., and Rudin, R., "'We shall Be Heard!' The Development of the Fugitive Slave Press in Canada," *Canadian Historical Review* (65), no. 1, March 1984, pp. 54–72, at https://muse.jhu.edu/article/571837, accessed January 28, 2019. Census returns for Ontario, Canada, 1851–1891, at www.bac-lac.gc.ca/eng/census/Pages/census.aspx.

13. Winks, R.W., "Negro School Segregation in Ontario and Nova Scotia," *Canadian Historical Review* (50), no. 2, June 1969, pp. 164–191, at https://muse.jhu.edu/article/568470, accessed January 28, 2019; Frost et al., *Ontario's African Canadian Heritage*, pp. 173–176.

14. Population figures at www150.statcan.gc.ca/n1/pub/75-001-x/1991002/88-eng.pdf, accessed December 1, 2018. French-speaking Montreal was then the most populous city in Canada, with a population of 140,747.

15. *London Advertiser*, July 19, 1881, at www.news.google.com, accessed January 28, 2019.

16. *Northern Tribune*, February 25 and March 11, 1882, at www.newspapers.com, accessed April 14, 2019.

17. *London Advertiser*, November 16, 1882, and March 1, 1883, at www.news.google.com/newspapers, accessed January 28, 2019.

18. *Northern Tribune*, December 1, 1883, at www.newspapers.com, accessed April 14, 2019.

19. *Daily British Whig*, May 4, 1886, at news.ourontario.ca/2800630/page/3?n=2, accessed January 16, 2019.

20. Toronto City Directory at www.torontopubliclibrary.ca/history-genealogy/lh-digital-city-directories.jsp, where the family were living at 40, Bright Street. Toronto Public Library, Assessment Roll for the Ward of St. David, City of Toronto, which lists Henry as a professor of Animal Magnetism (1888), professor (1889, 1894, 1985, 1896), concert conductor (1890 and 1891), and with no occupation filled in (1892, 1893). Thanks to Martha Cutter for these references.

21. *Brantford Evening Telegram*, February 2, 1889, at www.newspapers.com, accessed April 14, 2019.

22. "Michigan Marriages, 1868–1925," database with images, at FamilySearch, https://familysearch.org/ark:/61903/1:1:NQWS-X2X, accessed January 16, 2018.

23. United States Census, 1900, at Family Search, https://familysearch.org/ark:/61903/1:1:M3Q6-DJY, accessed August 1, 2016.

24. Toronto Public Library; thanks to Martha Cutter for this. The records of the Necropolis are digitized at www.familysearch.org/ark:/61903/3:1:S3HT-XCMW-TZN?i=117&cc=1627831, accessed March 17, 2019.

25. "United States Census, 1910," database with images, *FamilySearch*, http://FamilySearch.org: 14 June 2016. Citing NARA microfilm publication T624. Washington, DC: National Archives and Records Administration, n.d. Directory at https://archive.org/stream/kanedirectory1910wood/kanedirectory1910wood_djvu.txt. Both accessed August 1, 2016.

26. NA, *Kane Republican*, August 1, 1916.

27. U.S. World War I Draft Registration cards at FamilySearch, www.familysearch.org/ark:/61903/1:1:K6VN-1XX, accessed August 1, 2016.

28. "United States Census, 1920," database with images at FamilySearch, http://familysearch.org, accessed June 14, 2016. Citing NARA microfilm publication T625. Washington, DC: National Archives and Records Administration, n.d., accessed August 1, 2016.

29. Pennsylvania Death Certificates, 1906–1963, Record Group 11, subgroup: Bureau of Health Statistics and Research; Death Certificates (Series #11.90), found by Jeffrey Ruggles, referenced in Cutter, "Will the Real Henry Box Brown...?," no pagination. "Pennsylvania, County Marriages, 1885–1950," at FamilySearch, https://familysearch.org/ark:/61903/1:1:VFQ5-ZQ4, accessed August 1, 2016. NA, *Kane Republican,* September 16, 1963.

30. "Pennsylvania, County Marriages, 1885–1950," database with images, at Family Search, https://familysearch.org/ark:/61903/1:1:VF7M-Z4B: 11 March 2018, accessed September 1, 2018.

31. U.S. World War II Draft Registration Cards, 1942, at FamilySearch, https://familysearch.org/ark:/61903/1:1:VQFR-RRD, accessed August 1, 2016.

32. "Vermont Vital Records, 1760–1954," at FamilySearch,https://familysearch.org/ark:/61903/ 1:1:VNRW-ZCL, accessed August 1, 2016.

33. NA, *Kane Republican*, September 26, 1953.

34. Manley Jefferson's grave is at www.findagrave.com/memorial/14939051, accessed August 1, 2016. NA, *Kane Republican*, April 20, 1965.

35. NA, *Kane Republican*, April 13, 1971.

Bibliography

Not all these works are cited in the text, but they contributed to my understanding of the societies and milieus in which Henry Box Brown lived. I have inserted the U.S. states and British counties outside major cities and where there might be confusion, to distinguish between American and British publications.

Ball, Edward, *Slaves in the Family* (New York: Viking, 1998).

Blackett, R.J.M., *Building an Anti-Slavery Wall: Black Americans in the Atlantic Abolitionist Movement, 1830–1860* (Baton Rouge: Louisiana State University Press, 1983).

Broadbent, R.J., *Annals of the Liverpool Stage* (Liverpool, 1908).

Brooks, Daphne A., *Bodies in Dissent: Spectacular Performances of Race and Freedom, 1850–1910* (Durham: Duke University Press, 2006).

Brown, Derren, *Confessions of a Conjuror* (London: Transworld, 2010).

Brown, Henry Box, *Narrative of the Life of Henry Box Brown, Written by Himself* (1851), ed. John Ernest (Chapel Hill: University of North Carolina Press, 2008).

Brown, Henry Box, *Narrative of the Life of Henry Box Brown, Written by Himself* (1851), introduction by Richard Newman, ed. Henry Louis Gates (Oxford: Oxford University Press, 2002).

Brown, William Wells, *Three Years in Europe; or, Places I Have Seen and People I Have Met* (London, 1852, reprinted Wokingham, Berkshire: Dodo Press, 2008). Also at https://docsouth.unc.edu/neh/brown52/menu.html.

Cannadine, David, *Ornamentalism: How the British Saw Their Empire* (2001; 2nd ed., Penguin, London, 2002).

Cannadine, David, *The Rise and Fall of Class in Britain* (1998; 2nd ed., Penguin, London, 2000).

Cutter, Martha J., *The Illustrated Slave: Empathy, Graphic Narrative, and the Visual Culture of the Transatlantic Abolition Movement 1800–1852* (Athens: University of Georgia Press, 2017).

Delbanco, Andrew, *The War Before the War: Fugitive Slaves and the Struggle for America's Soul from the Revolution to the Civil War* (New York: Penguin Press, 2018).

Douglass, Frederick, *Narrative of the Life of Frederick Douglass Critical Edition*, ed. John R. McKivigan, Peter P. Hinks, and Heather L. Kaufman (New Haven: Yale University Press, 2016).

Farrison, William Edward, *William Wells Brown Author and Reformer* (Chicago: University of Chicago Press, 1969).

Fisch, Audrey A., *American Slaves in Victorian England: Abolitionist Politics in Popular Literature and Culture* (Cambridge: Cambridge University Press, 2010).

Fought, Leigh, *Women in the World of Frederick Douglass* (Oxford: Oxford University Press, 2017).

Franklin, John Hope, *From Slavery to Freedom: a History of Negro Americans* (New York: A.A. Knopf, 1947). My edition is the fifth, published 1980.

Frost, Thomas, *Circus Life and Circus Celebrities* (London, 1881), at www.circushistory.org/Frost/Frost5.htm.

Gerzina, Gretchen (ed.), *Black Victorians, Black Victoriana* (New Brunswick: Rutgers University Press, 2003).

Gilmore, Paul, *The Genuine Article: Race, Mass Culture, and American Literary Manhood* (Durham,: Duke University Press, 2001).

Gilroy, Paul, *The Black Atlantic: Modernity and Double Consciousness* (Cambridge: Harvard University Press, 1993).

Green, Jeffrey, *Black Americans in Victorian Britain* (Barnsley, Yorkshire: Pen & Sword, 2018).

Harris, J. William, *Society and Culture in the Slave South* (London: Routledge, 1992).

Haskins, Jim, and Benson, Kathleen, *Conjure Times: Black Magicians in America* (New York: Walker & Co., 2001).

Hayes, Louis M., *Reminiscences of Manchester and Its Surrounding Areas from 1840* (1905; new edition, Manchester: Empire Publications, 2005).

Heartfield, James, *The British and Foreign Anti-Slavery Society: A History, 1838–1956* (London: Hurst, 2016).

Honour, Hugh, *The Image of the Black in Western Art, Vol. 4, From the American Revolution to the First World War, Part 2: Black Models and White Myths* (Cambridge: Harvard University Press, 1990).

Isenberg, Nancy, *White Trash: The 400-Year Untold History of Class in America* (New York: Viking, 2016).

Jackson, Lee, *Palaces of Pleasure: From Music Halls to the Seaside to Football, How the Victorians Invented Mass Entertainment* (New Haven, CT, and London: Yale University Press, 2019).

Kift, Dagmar, *The Victorian Music Hall: Culture, Class, and Conflict* (Cambridge: Cambridge University Press, 1996).

Kolchin, Peter, *American Slavery 1619–1877* (New York: Hill & Wang, 1993).

Lasch-Quinn, Elizabeth, *Race Experts: How Racial Etiquette, Sensitivity Training, and New Age Therapy Hijacked the Civil Rights Revolution* (New York: W.W. Norton and Co., 2001).

Levine, Robert S., *The Lives of Frederick Douglass* (Cambridge: Harvard University Press, 2016).

Lindfors, Bernth, *Early African Entertainments Abroad* (Madison: University of Wisconsin Press, 2014).

Lindfors, Bernth, *Ira Aldridge*, 4-volume biography (Rochester: University of Rochester Press, 2011–2015).

Lindfors, Bernth, *The Theatrical Career of Samuel Morgan Smith* (Trenton, NJ: Africa World Press, 2017).

Lindsay, Lisa. A., and Sweet, John Wood, *Biography and the Black Atlantic* (Philadelphia: University of Pennsylvania Press, 2014).

Lorimer, Douglas A., *Colour, Class and the Victorians: English Attitudes to the Negro in the Mid-Nineteenth Century* (Leicester: Leicester University Press, 1978).

Lotz, Rainer, and Pegg, Ian, *Under the Imperial Carpet: Essays in Black History 1780–1950* (Crawley, Surrey: Rabbit Press, 1986).

Madera, Judith, *Black Atlas: Geography and Flow in Nineteenth-Century African American Literature* (Durham: Duke University Press, 2015).

Magus, Jim, *Magical Heroes: The Lives and Legends of Great African American Magicians* (Marrietta, GA: Magus Enterprises, 1995).

Marsh, Jan (ed.), *Black Victorians: Black People in British Art 1800–1900.* (Aldershot, Surrey: Lund Humphries, 2005).

Mavor, Elizabeth (ed.), *Fanny Kemble: The American Journals* (London: Weidenfeld & Nicholson, 1990).

McGrady, Richard, *Music and Musicians in Early Nineteenth-Century Cornwall: The World of Joseph Emidy "Slave, Violinist and Composer"* (Exeter: University of Exeter Press, 1991).

Meer, Sarah, *Uncle Tom Mania: Slavery, Minstrelsy, and Transatlantic Culture in the 1850s* (Athens: University of Georgia Press, 2005).

Moore, Wendy, *The Mesmerist: The Society Doctor Who Held Victorian London Spellbound* (London: Weidenfeld & Nicholson, 2017).

Morley, Henry, *The Journal of a London Playgoer* (2nd ed. 1891; reprinted Leicester: Leicester University Press, 1974).

Olmsted, Frederick Law, *Journey to the Seaboard Slaves States* (New York, 1856); *Journey Through Texas* (New York, 1857); and *Journey in the Back Country in the Winter of 1853-4* (New York, 1860), all at https://archive.org.

Pease, Jane H., and Pease, William H., *They Who Would Be Free: Blacks' Search for Freedom 1830-1861* (New York: Atheneum, 1974).

Perman, Michael (ed.), *The Coming of the American Civil War* (Lexington, MA: D.C. Heath & Co., 3rd ed., 1993).

Pickering, Michael, *Blackface Minstrelsy in Britain* (Farnham, Surrey: Ashgate, 2008).

Preston, Ann, *Cousin Ann's Stories for Children* (Philadelphia,1849), at http://online books.library.upenn.edu/webbin/book/lookupid?key=olbp63958.

Price, David, *Magic: A Pictorial History of Conjurers in the Theater* (New York: Cornwall Books, 1985).

Quarles, B., *Black Abolitionists* (New York: Oxford University Press, 1969).

Rede, Leman Thomas, *The Road to the Stage* (1827; 2nd rev. ed., 1835) at https://archive.org/details/roadtostageconta00rede.

Rice, Alan J., and Crawford, Martin (eds.), *Liberating Sojourn: Frederick Douglass and Transatlantic Reform* (Athens: University of Georgia Press, 1999).

Rice, Charles, *Tavern Singing in Early Victorian London: the Diaries of Charles Rice for 1840 and 1850,* ed. Lawrence Senelick (London, UK: Society for Theatre Research, 1997).

Ripley, C. Peter (ed.), *The Black Abolitionist Papers,* Vol. I, *Britain 1830-1865*; Vol. 5, *The United States, 1859-1865* (Chapel Hill: University of North Carolina Press, 2015).

Ruggles, Jeffrey, *The Unboxing of Henry Brown* (Richmond: Library of Virginia, 2003).

Sterling, Dorothy (ed.), *We Are Your Sisters: Black Women in the Nineteenth Century* (New York: W.W. Norton & Co., 1984).

Stone, Alex, *Fooling Houdini* (London: Heinemann, 2012).

Stowe, Harriet Beecher, *Uncle Tom's Cabin* (*Boston: John P. Jewitt,* 1852).

Sweeney, Fionnghuala, *Frederick Douglass and the Atlantic World* (Liverpool: Liverpool University Press, 2007).

Temperley, Howard, *British Antislavery 1833-1870* (London: Longman, 1972).

Trollope, Anthony, *North America* (London, 1862).

Trollope, Fanny, *Domestic Manners of the Americans* (London, 1832).

University of London, *Staging Magic: The Story Behind the Illusion* (exhibition catalogue, 2019).

Wakefield, Robin, *Hidden Depths: the Story of Hypnosis* (Hove, Sussex: Psychology Press, 2003).

Wayne, Michael, *Imagining Black America* (New Haven: Yale University Press, 2014).

Wilcox, Alastair, *Living in Liverpool: A Collection of Sources for Family, Local and Social Historians* (Newcastle-upon-Tyne: Cambridge Scholars Publishing, 2011).

Williams, Donald E., Jr., *Prudence Crandall's Legacy: the Fight for Equality in the 1830s, Dred Scott, and* Brown v. Board of Education (Middletown, CT: Wesleyan University Press, 2014).

Wood, Marcus, *Blind Memory: Visual Representations of Slavery in England and America 1780-1865* (Manchester: Manchester University Press, 2000).

Articles Accessed Through JSTOR at www.jstor.org

Blackett, R.J.M., "Fugitive Slaves in Britain: The Odyssey of William and Ellen Craft," *Journal of American Studies* (12) no. 1, pp. 41–62.

Ernest, John, "Outside the Box: Henry Box Brown and the Politics of Antislavery Agency," *Arizona Quarterly* (63) no. 4, Winter 2007, pp. 1–24.

Ernest, John, "Traumatic Theology in the 'Narrative of the Life of Henry Box Brown, Written by Himself,'" *African American Review* (41) no. 1, pp. 19–31.

Gara, Larry, "The Professional Fugitive in the Abolition Movement," *Wisconsin Magazine of History* (48) no. 3, pp. 196–204.

Jones, Douglas A., "Black Politics but Not Black People: Rethinking the Social and 'Racial' History of Early Minstrelsy," *TDR/The Drama Review* (57), no. 2, Routes of Blackface: Special Issue (Summer 2013), pp. 21–37.

Robins, Hollis, "Fugitive Mail: The Deliverance of Henry 'Box' Brown and Antebellum Postal Politics," *American Studies* (50) no. 1/2, pp. 5–25.

Rusert, Britt, "The Science of Freedom: Counterarchives of Racial Science on the Antebellum Stage," *African American Review* (45) no. 3, Special Issue: On Black Performance, pp. 291–308.

Spencer, Suzette S., "An International Fugitive: Henry Box Brown, Anti-Imperialism, Resistance & Slavery" in *Social Identities* (12) no. 2, 2006, pp. 227–248.

Sweeney, Fionnghuala, and Rice, Alan, "Liberating Sojourns? African Americans and Transatlantic Abolition 1845–1865," *Slavery & Abolition* (33) no. 2, June 2012, pp. 181–189.

Wolff, Cynthia Griffin, "Passing beyond the Middle Passage: Henry 'Box' Brown's Translations of Slavery," *Massachusetts Review* (37) no. 1, pp. 23–46.

Articles on Project Muse, at https://muse.jhu.edu

Buescher, John Benedict, "Cornering the Market on Fraud: Stage Magicians versus Spirit Mediums," *Magic, Ritual, and Witchcraft* (9) no. 2, 2014, pp. 210–223.

Silverman, Jason, Bellavance, Marcel, and Rudin, Ronald, "'We Shall be Heard!' The Development of the Fugitive Slave Press in Canada," *Canadian Historical Review* (65), no. 1, March 1984, pp. 54–72.

Winks, Robin W., "Negro School Segregation in Ontario and Nova Scotia," *Canadian Historical Review* (50), no. 2, June 1969, pp. 164–191.

Other Articles and Sources

Cutter, Martha, J., "Will the Real Henry 'Box' Brown Please Stand Up?," at commonplace.org/book/will-the-real-henry-box-brown-please-stand-up.

Fielden, Samuel, *Autobiography of Samuel Fielden* (United States, 1887), at http://dwardmac.pitzer.edu/Anarchist_Archives/haymarket/Fielden.html.

Floud, Roderick, "Pricing the Past," *History Today* (69), no. 3, March 2019, pp 40–44.

Fukuyama, Francis, "Against Identity Politics: The New Tribalism and the Crisis of Democracy" in *Foreign Affairs*, September/October 2018, at www.foreignaffairs.com/articles/americas/2018-08-14/against-identity-politics-tribalism-francis-fukuyama. This thesis is now available as a full-length book: *Identity: the Demand for Dignity and the Politics of Resentment* (New York: Farrar, Strauss & Giroux, 2018).

Green, Jeffrey, website of biographies of black people in Victorian & Edwardian England, www.jeffreygreen.co.uk.

Odd Fellows Historical Archive, www.odd-fellows.co.uk.

Plunkett, J., "Moving Panoramas c. 1800 to 1840: The Spaces of Nineteenth-Century Picture-Going," *Interdisciplinary Studies in the Long Nineteenth Century* (2013), at www.19.bbk.ac.uk/articles/10.16995/ntn.674, accessed 26/08/2016.

Riddell, William Renwick, "The Slave in Canada," *Journal of Negro History* (5) no. 3, July 1920, at https://archive.org/details/slaveincanada00ridd/page/n6.

Rosenberg, Cory, "Ole Zip Coon Is a Mighty Learned Scholar: Blackface Minstrelsy as Reflection and Foundation of American Popular Culture," *Gettysburg College Journal of the Civil War Era* (3) 1/6, 2013, pp. 55–81, at https://cupola.gettysburg.edu/cgi/viewcontent.cgi?article=1004&context=gcjcwe.

Staging Magic, exhibition catalogue from Senate House Library, University of London (January–June 2019), at https://www.senatehouselibrary.ac.uk/exhibitions-and-events/exhibitions/staging-magic/resources.

Slave Narratives at http://docsouth.unc.edu and Other Sites

Aga, Selim, *Incidents Connected with the Life of Selim Aga, a Native of Central Africa* (Aberdeen, 1846).

Brown, Henry Box, *Narrative of the Life of Henry Box Brown, Written by Himself* (Manchester, 1851).

Brown, Henry Box & Stearns, Charles, *Narrative of Henry Box Brown, Who Escaped from Slavery, Enclosed in a Box 3 Feet Long and 2 Wide. Written from a Statement of Facts Made by Himself. With Remarks Upon the Remedy for Slavery* (Philadelphia, 1849).

Brown, John, *Slave Life in Georgia: A Narrative of the Life, Sufferings, and Escape of*

John Brown, A Fugitive Slave, Now In England (London, 1855).

Brown, William Wells, *Narrative of William W. Brown, a Fugitive Slave. Written by Himself* (Boston, 1847).

Craft, William, *Running a Thousand Miles for Freedom; or, The Escape of William and Ellen Craft from Slavery* (London, 1860).

Douglass, Frederick, *Narrative of the Life of Frederick Douglass, an American Slave* (Boston, 1845); *My Bondage and My Freedom* (New York, 1855).

Fedric, Francis, *Slave Life in Virginia and Kentucky; or, Fifty Years of Slavery in the Southern States of America*, ed. the Rev. Charles Lee (London, 1863).

Grandy, Moses, *Narrative of the Life of Moses Grandy, Late a Slave in the United States of America* (Boston, 1844).

Henson, Josiah, *Truth Is Stranger Than Fiction. Father Henson's Story of His Own Life*, ed. Samuel A. Eliot (Boston, 1858).

Jackson, John Andrew, *The Experience of a Slave in South Carolina* (London, 1862).

Jacobs, Harriet Ann, *Incidents in the Life of a Slave Girl. Written by Herself*, ed. Lydia Maria Child (Boston, 1861).

Jea, John, *The Life, History, and Unparalleled Sufferings of John Jea, the African Preacher. Compiled and Written by Himself* (Portsea, 1811).

Pennington, J.W.C., *The Fugitive Blacksmith* (London, 1849); *A Narrative of Events of the Life of J. H. Banks, an Escaped Slave, from the Cotton State, Alabama, in America* (Liverpool, 1861).

Roper, Moses, *Narrative of the Adventures and Escape of Moses Roper, from American Slavery. With an Appendix, Containing a List of Places Visited by the Author in Great Britain and Ireland and the British Isles, and Other Matter* (Berwick-on-Tweed, 1848).

Ward, Samuel Ringgold, *Autobiography of a Fugitive Negro: His Anti-slavery Labours in the United States, Canada and England* (London, 1855).

Watkins, James, *Narrative of the Life of James Watkins, Formerly a "Chattel" in Maryland, U. S.; Containing an Account of His Escape from Slavery, Together with an Appeal on Behalf of Three Millions of Such "Pieces of Property," Still Held Under the Standard of the Eagle* (Bolton, 1852); *Struggles for Freedom: Or the Life of James Watkins, Formerly a Slave in Maryland, U. S.; in which is Detailed a Graphic Account of His Extraordinary Escape from Slavery, Notices of the Fugitive Slave Law, the Sentiments of American Divines on the Subject of Slavery, etc., etc.* (Manchester, 1860).

Index

Numbers in **bold italics** indicate pages with illustrations